THE CRUSADES THROUGH ARAB EYES

AMIN MAALOUF

The Crusades Through Arab Eyes

Translated by
JON ROTHSCHILD

Introduced by
MALISE RUTHVEN

LONDON
THE FOLIO SOCIETY
MMXII

The Crusades Through Arab Eyes was first published in
France as *Les Croisades vues par les Arabes* by J.-C. Lattès, Paris, 1983.
The first English edition was published by Saqi Books in 1984.
This edition follows the text of the 2006 Saqi Books edition,
with minor emendations.

This edition published by
The Folio Society Ltd,
44 Eagle Street, London WC1R 4FS.
www.foliosociety.com

Published by arrangement with Saqi Books and with Schocken Books,
an imprint of The Knopf Doubleday Publishing Group,
a division of Random House, Inc.

Frontispiece: Kilij Arslan's light cavalry were effective archers,
but their arrows proved to be futile against the heavily armoured Franj forces

Typeset at The Folio Society in Arno Pro.
Printed on Abbey Wove paper at Martins the Printers Ltd,
Berwick-upon-Tweed, and bound by Hunter & Foulis, Edinburgh,
in buckram, blocked with a design by Joe McLaren

CONTENTS

ILLUSTRATIONS

Mounted archer. Fragment of a moulded pottery flask, Aleppo, Syria, Ayyubid, thirteenth century.
(© *The Trustees of the British Museum*) *frontis*

C686, fo. 81a. (*The Institute of Oriental Manuscripts, Russian Academy of Sciences, St Petersburg*)

Preaching in a mosque. Illumination by al-Wasiti, from the *Maqamat* of al-Hariri, Baghdad, Iraq, 1237. Bibliothèque nationale de France, MS Arabe 5847, fo. 84v. (*Bibliothèque nationale de France*)

BETWEEN PAGES 130 AND 131

Poet with musicians and singers. Illumination from Abū al-Faraj al-Iṣbahānī, *Kitāb al-Aghānī* ('Book of Songs'), Mosul, Iraq, 1219. (*Egyptian National Library, Cairo, Egypt/Giraudon/The Bridgeman Art Library*)

Bazaar at the camp of the Banu Shayba. Illumination by ʿAbd al Muʾmin al-Khuwayyī, from Urwa b. Huzam al-ʿUdhri, *Varqa va Gulshah* ('The Romance of Varqa and Gulshah'), Konya, Turkey, Seljuk, 1250. Topkapi Saray Museum MS Hazine 841, fo. 3v. (*Topkapi Saray Museum, Istanbul/Werner Forman Archive*)

Two foot soldiers in Crusader-style military dress. Bas relief from Konya, Turkey, Seljuk, thirteenth century. (*Turkish and Islamic Art Museum Istanbul/Collection Dagli Orti/The Art Archive*)

Umayyad mosque, Damascus. Illumination by Ustad Osman, from Muḥammad Ibn Amir Hasan al-Suʿudi, *Mataliʾ al-saadet* ('The Book of Felicity'), Turkey, 1582. Bibliothèque nationale de France, MS Suppl Turc 242, fo. 77. (*Bibliothèque nationale de France*)

Assassination of Niẓām al-Mulk. Illumination from Rashīd al-Dīn Hamādanī, *Jāmiʿ al-Tawārīkh*, Ilkhanid, Iran, 1314. Topkapi Saray Museum, MS H 1653, fo. 360b (© *Topkapi Saray Museum, Istanbul*)

Mangonel. Illumination from Murda Ibn ʿAli al-Tarsusi, *Tabṣirah fī al-hurūb* ('Treatise on Armoury'), Syria, 1150–1200. Bodleian Library MS Huntington 264, fo. 134v–135r. (*Bodleian Library, Oxford*)

Marinus, Andromachus and Andromachus the Younger. Illumination from Muḥammad Ibn Abi al-Fath, *Kitāb al-Diryāq* ('Book of Antidotes'), Jazīrah, Northern Iraq, 1199. Bibliothèque nationale de France, MS Arabe 2964, fo. 34. (*Bibliothèque nationale de France*)

BETWEEN PAGES 194 AND 195

Horseman. Hammered brass with gold, silver and niello inlay (detail) by Muḥammad Ibn al-Zain from the Baptistère de St Louis, Syria or Egypt, late thirteenth to early fourteenth century. (© *Musée du Louvre/Franck Raux/RMN-GP*)

Sultan dispensing justice. Illumination from ʿAbdullāh Ibn al-Muqaffaʿ, *Kalīla wa Dimna*, Egypt, 1385–95. Egyptian National Library MS Adab Farsi 61, fo. 100. (*Egyptian National Library, Cairo/Giraudon/The Bridgeman Art Library*)

Officers conducting a prisoner. Miniature gouache painting, Baghdad, Iraq, 1275–1325. (© *Musée du Louvre/Hervé Lewandowski/RMN-GP*)

Battle beneath the walls of a town. Opaque watercolour on paper, Ayyubid, Egypt, twelfth century. (© *The Trustees of the British Museum*)

Copper dirham struck in the name of Saladin, probably minted at Māyyāfariqīn, Turkey, 1190. Inv. no. C 315. (© *The David Collection, Copenhagen, Photo Pernille Klemp*)

Crossbow. Illumination from Murda Ibn ʿAli al-Tarsusi, *Tabṣirah fī al-hurūb* ('Treatise on Armoury'), Syria, 1150–1200. Bodleian Library MS Hunt 264, fo. 102b. (*Bodleian Library, Oxford*)

The ascension of the Prophet Muḥammad on Buraq. Illumination from Mir Haydar, *Miraj-nama* ('Book of Ascension'), Timurid, Iran, 1436. Bibliothèque nationale de France, MS Suppl Turc 190, fo. 17 (*Bibliothèque nationale de France*)

Christians in procession. Bronze pyxis with copper and silver inlay, Syria, *c.*1250. (© *V&A Images*)

The Mongols under Hülegü conquer Baghdad. Illumination from a Persian manuscript, fourteenth century. Staatsbibliothek zu Berlin MS Saray-Alben (Diez-Alben), fo. 70, image 7. (*SBB/Ruth Schacht/bpk*)

INTRODUCTION

The historian Marc Bloch, who died a martyr's death when shot by the Nazis, observed that 'once an emotional chord has been struck, the limit between past and present is no longer regulated by a mathematically measurable chronology'. Although we are not far off from the millennium of the First Crusade launched by Pope Urban II in 1095, the language and symbols of this archetypical conflict between Western Europe and the Islamic world live on. Immediately after the terrorist attacks on New York and Washington on 11 September 2001 President George W. Bush announced 'This crusade . . . this war on terror is going to take a while.' His favourite pastor, Franklin Graham – son of Billy Graham whose 'Crusades for Christ' had made him the world's best-known evangelical superstar – stated, with all the fervour of a medieval Crusader: 'The God of Islam is not the same God [as ours]. He's not the son of God of the Christian or Judaeo-Christian faith. It is a different God, and I believe it is a very evil and wicked religion.'

Although the US president toned down his language under pressure from outraged Muslim allies, reducing his crusade to a much simpler 'war on terror', the C-word had been uttered, and could not be unsaid. His comment was a propaganda gift to the dissident Saudi revolutionary Osama bin Laden – leader of the al-Qaeda Islamist movement responsible for 9/11 – who for years had been talking about Jewish-Crusader attacks on Islam. When America and its allies attacked his protectors – the Taliban regime in Afghanistan – bin Laden quickly responded, citing the 'original crusade' that brought 'Richard from Britain [sic], Louis from France, Barbarossa from Germany. Today the crusading countries rushed [to arms] as soon as Bush raised the cross. They accepted the rule of the cross.'

Despite the 'loss' of the Latin states collectively known by the Europeans as Outremer ('over the sea'), with the fall of Acre, the last Crusader stronghold, in 1291, the concept of the crusade and its symbols retain their potency. With English national identity now in the ascendant, St George's Cross, emblem of the English Crusader knights, is an increasingly visible presence on vehicles, clothing and at sporting events, upstaging the union flag. Moral activists, not necessarily Christian, proclaim 'crusades' against perceived social evils, from drugs to pornography. So when born-again Christian George W. Bush needed words to respond to the most devastating attack on the US mainland since the American Civil War, his use of the word was instinctive.

In the world after 9/11, when there has been much discussion of a 'clash of civilisations' between Islamic and Western worlds, it is good to be reminded how the original Crusader enterprise appeared to the peoples of the Levant – Christian and Jewish, as well as Muslim – whose lands became the objects of ambitions that were anything but moral.

As Amin Maalouf clearly shows in his book, the Muslim chroniclers were more clear-eyed than their Christian counterparts: they saw the Crusades, not as a holy war by Christians against Islam, but as a land grab by people from Western Europe of territories that had been ruled by Muslims since the seventh century. Carol Hillenbrand, the scholarly author of *The Crusades: Islamic Perspectives* (Edinburgh, 1999), notes that 'the concept of Crusade is a Western one. It has no particular resonance for Islamic ears, and the Muslim historians are not concerned with it. For them, these are simply wars with an enemy.' Indeed the Arabic term for the Crusades, *al-hurub al-salabiyya* ('the wars of the cross'), did not appear until the anti-colonial struggles of the nineteenth century. The Crusaders' Muslim contemporaries employed much less emotive, secular terms: 'the wars of the Franks' (Arabic *Faranj* or *Ifranj*, or in Maalouf's preferred colloquial usage, the Franj).

The barbaric and predatory nature of the invasion emerges from the Muslim accounts rendered by Maalouf, but so too does the civilising influence of the Orient on the invading Europeans. As a Levantine Catholic, he takes a less polemical view than some of his Arab contemporaries, who see the conflict through the prism of nationalism or the distorting lens of the current Islamist revival.

*

Maalouf began his career as a journalist in his native Lebanon, before settling in France where he now lives. As a reporter with the *An-Nahar*, Lebanon's leading Arabic-language daily, he travelled widely, interviewing world leaders and witnessing dramatic events. He was in Addis Ababa for the Marxist coup in 1974 and covered the American defeat in Saigon the following year. When the Lebanese civil war broke out in 1975 he decided to migrate with his wife and young children to Paris. Although he came from a family with deep roots in the Levant – his ancestors had been Christians long before the coming of Islam – he was shocked by the religious polarisation that occurred in Beirut and was loath to retreat to a separatist Christian ghetto. As he explained in his book *On Identity* (1998), 'The fact of simultaneously being Christian and having as my mother tongue Arabic, the holy language of Islam, is one of the basic paradoxes that have shaped my identity.'

In Paris he switched, without apparent difficulty, to writing in French, in which language he achieved both mastery and recognition. He joined the magazine *Jeune Afrique*, rising to become its editor-in-chief before devoting himself to writing fiction and non-fiction books, including the present volume. His novel *Le Rocher de Tanios* (*The Rock of Tanios*, 1993), set in Lebanon at the beginning of the nineteenth century, when imperial Britain and France were meddling in the region's politics, won the Prix Goncourt, France's premier literary award. In 2011 he was elected to the Académie française, joining the ranks of France's literary 'immortals'.

True to his skills as a journalist and novelist, Maalouf's account of the Crusades through Muslim eyes has a powerful narrative thrust. He uses his sources deftly, teasing out details, whether blood-curdling or morally inspiring, that bring this complex and often confusing story alive. Hillenbrand has welcomed his book as a 'breath of fresh air' that is 'lively and always popular with students'. Ever the careful scholar, however, she sees its approach is 'unashamedly general', being neither 'comprehensive nor academic'. Readers whose appetites are whetted by Maalouf may be inspired to explore Hillenbrand's more detailed account of the Muslim response to the Crusades, which is impressively comprehensive and readable.

The complexity of the Muslim response was partly due to divisions within Muslim societies, including their variegated religious character. Unlike the Catholic Church, which imposed rigid theological conformity on believers and systematically persecuted heretics, Islam allowed space for the 'Peoples of the Book' – adherents of the Jewish and Christian scriptural traditions that preceded Islam – provided these 'protected' peoples – known as the *ahl al-dhimma* – acknowledged the supremacy of Islamic rule. This did not mean, however, that Muslims put adherents of other faiths on an equal footing. As God's final revelation to humankind Islam was assumed to have superseded Judaism and Christianity: Jews and Christians were in error, because their scriptures (the Torah and the Gospel) had become 'corrupted'. Christians, moreover, were sometimes referred to as polytheists, since it was thought that the Holy Trinity, conceived as a triple deity rather than a theological formula devised to represent the divine–human axis, was the object of Christian worship. Polytheism – the 'association' of any beings thought to detract from God's unity – was the theological error against which the Koran inveighed most vehemently. Local Christians, however, were tolerated despite their presumed religious errors, and in any case the theological divisions between the Seljuk Turks who were strictly observant Sunnis, and the Fatimid Ismāʿīli Shiʿis – adherents of an Islamic doctrine that was both more rationalist and hierarchical than Sunnism – were as great as, if not greater than, those dividing Muslims from Christians and Jews. The length of time it took the Muslims to regroup their forces under Turkish and Kurdish leaders, with frequent instances of collaboration between Christian and Muslim warlords, largely accounted for the Crusaders' initial success in establishing fortified kingdoms and principalities crowned by magnificent hilltop castles in the lands lying between Antioch and Jerusalem.

In a medieval society the religious freedoms enjoyed by the numerous non-Muslim sects amounted to a level of limited political autonomy, since the religious leaders (bishops, patriarchs and rabbis) were also secular heads of their communities. Yet unlike the local Christians and Jews, the Franj were seen as unambiguously alien. The writer al-Masʿudi, who died in 956, more than a century before the first Crusader invasion (and is therefore not represented in Maalouf's account), expressed views about the Franj that would have been widely shared in the region.

> The power of the sun is weak among them because of their distance from it; cold and damp prevail in their regions, and snow and ice follow one another in endless succession. The warm humour is lacking among them; their bodies are large, their natures gross, their understanding dull, their tongues heavy. Their colour is so excessively white that it passes from white to blue; their skin is thin and their flesh thick. Their eyes are also blue, matching the character of their colouring; their hair is lank and reddish because of the prevalence of damp mists. Their religious beliefs lack solidity, and this is because of the nature of cold and the lack of warmth.

The aristocratic chronicler Usāmah Ibn Munqidh (1095–1188), who fought against the Crusaders and whose memoirs, written in his ninetieth year, feature prominently in Maalouf's narrative, was explicit in his condemnation of the Crusaders' lack of personal hygiene as well as their sexual laxity. He also described with horror their primitive system of trial by combat, which he witnessed in Nablus, contrasting it with the much more rational Muslim legal process based on the Koran. Interestingly, his memoir also contains a detailed account of torture by immersion in water as practised by the Franj. It is chilling to recall that an almost identical technique was used more than eight centuries later by CIA interrogators investigating Khalid Shaikh Muhammad, the Muslim jihadist widely assumed to have masterminded the attacks on the World Trade Center and Pentagon.

Muslim perceptions of the Franj, however, were far from being uniformly negative. Usāmah, who was a diplomat as well as a soldier, came to believe that the barbarian mores of knights, such as the brutal and thuggish Reynald of Châtillon, could be refined by their long sojourn in the much more civilised Orient. 'Among the Franj,' Usāmah explains 'we find some people who have come to settle among us and who have cultivated the society of the Muslims. They are far superior to those who have freshly joined them in the territories they now occupy.' The Spanish-born traveller Ibn Jubayr (1145–1217), whose celebrated travelogue features prominently in Maalouf's book, left an impressive description of the peaceful landscape of farms and villages in the vicinity of Tyre. The land was efficiently cultivated with Muslim peasants living in comfort and security under Frankish overlords. As a pious Muslim, Ibn Jubayr's honest recognition of this fact makes him uncomfortable, for after noting a reality that seems to contradict his religious allegiance he adds, 'May God preserve us from temptation!'

> All the regions controlled by the Franj in Syria are subject to this same system: the landed domains, villages and farms have remained in the hands of the Muslims. Now, doubt invests the hearts of a great number of these men when they compare their lot to that of their brothers living in Muslim territory. Indeed, the latter suffer from the injustice of their coreligionists, whereas the Franj act with equity.

Although the Crusades ended in defeat in the Levant, the outcome was balanced in the broader geopolitical context by the victory of Christendom in Iberia, where the Crusaders of the 'reconquista' faced less formidable logistical obstacles than their coreligionists in Outremer. Moreover, the Muslim triumph in the Levant was only temporary. Indeed, despite the recovery of the Franj-occupied lands it marked the beginning of the long Islamic decline. Maalouf addresses this paradox in his Epilogue. 'At the time of the Crusades,' he writes, 'the Arab world, from Spain to Iraq, was still the intellectual and material repository of the planet's most advanced civilisation. Afterwards, the centre of world history shifted decisively to the West.' As a Lebanese Arab, he takes a somewhat Arabist line in partly attributing Muslim decline to a vacuum in Arab leadership, pointing out that the great Muslim heroes in the struggle against the Franj – Zangī, Nūr al-Dīn, Saladin and Baybars – were either Turks or Kurds. But he also notes other, more significant, reasons.

The relationship between Muslim decline and the rise of the West has long been the subject of debate among historians. One important aspect concerns the role of external factors such as the effects of the Mongol invasions, culminating in the destruction of Baghdad in 1258, contrasted with the discovery and conquest of the Americas, which vastly increased the wealth of Europe vis-à-vis the Middle East. But internal factors also played their part, with scholars contrasting the relative autonomy of European cities and corporations with their absence in the lands of Islam. As an entity that exceeded the sum of its parts the Western city corporation transcended individual mortality, facilitating the accumulation of wealth and its reinvestment. Islamic law, by contrast, mandated the distribution of wealth through rules of inheritance that impeded capital accumulation. Maalouf does not enter fully into this debate, but has significant insights to offer. Thus he takes Ibn Jubayr to task for suggesting that the equity and sound administration he honestly records in the Franj-controlled areas of Syria could constitute a mortal danger to the Muslims who might be persuaded to turn their backs on their coreligionists, even abandon their religion, if they experienced better conditions in a Frankish-ruled society. As Maalouf concludes:

> The notion of the 'citizen' did not yet exist, of course, but the feudal landowners, the knights, the clergy, the university, the bourgeoisie and even the 'infidel' peasants all had well-established rights. In the Arab East, the judicial procedures were more rational, but the arbitrary power of the prince was unbounded. The development of merchant towns, like the evolution of ideas, could only be retarded as a result.

Currently there are struggles being waged between protesting citizens and their government on lands once occupied by the Franj, and between the indigenous population and groups of settlers from Europe and America who are encroaching on these lands. Despite the appearance of modernity, the conflicts affecting today's Levant are strikingly similar to those that afflicted the region almost a millennium ago. The indigenous people lack political and civil rights, and still suffer from the unbounded power of their rulers, power that, when challenged, responds with the brutal exercise of military force.

The incomers who arrived in search of a solution to what was essentially Europe's problem – its failure to accommodate a vigorous and talented minority holding a different set of religious beliefs – now enjoy full civil rights and a system of accountable government which, fearing loss of their religious identity, they are unable, or unwilling, to extend outside their fortified garrison state. Nourished from afar, the Crusader states proved unsustainable once the impulse for settlement had abated. Today's Outremer, sustained by its American patron, seems militarily all-powerful, like its medieval predecessors during their heyday. But in an environment of growing hostility and turbulence there is no guarantee that it will retain this pre-eminence indefinitely.

MALISE RUTHVEN

TRANSLATOR'S NOTE

Arabic words and names in this book have been transliterated according to a system that allows those who know the Arabic alphabet to reconstruct the original spelling. Readers curious about the pronunciation of these names and words can refer to the 'Note on Pronunciation'. Others will not miss much if they simply ignore the dots and bars of the transliteration and pronounce the words as if they were English. Where a name or word has a standard English form (like Saladin), it has been used. The glossary gives brief definitions of all the Arabic words that occur in the book, whether they have been Anglicised or not. The intent of the glossary is not to provide scholarly descriptions of the terms, but to help in achieving one of the author's main goals: to make his book intelligible to those who have no specialist knowledge of Arab history.

A NOTE ON PRONUNCIATION

As Amin Maalouf has said, he intends his work to be accessible to readers with no expert knowledge of the Middle East or the Arab world. At the same time, there seems little doubt that *The Crusades Through Arab Eyes* will be of special value to the growing number of people whose interest in Arab history and culture is more than merely casual. For this reason, it has been decided to transliterate the Arabic names and words that appear in the text. The standard system of transliteration adopted will be immediately comprehensible to those who know the Arabic alphabet. For those who do not, what follows is a rough guide to pronunciation.

The Arabic letters designated by ṣ, ḍ, ẓ and ṭ are known as 'emphatic', or 'velarised', consonants. Their pronunciation is similar to the equivalent letters without the dots, except that the back of the tongue is raised slightly (towards the velum) and they are articulated more strongly, giving them a somewhat 'dark' sound. The ḥ is a very strongly aspirated sound originating in the back of the throat; although it has no equivalent in any European language, its sound is not unlike that of an emphatically articulated *h*. The symbol ʾ represents a glottal stop, the sound that begins each syllable of the English expression 'uh-oh' or the Cockney *t*. The symbol ʿ represents another sound with no European equivalent; phonetically, it is a voiced guttural stop produced in the very back of the throat, by constricting the larynx.

The combination *dh* represents the sound of the *th* in the English word *then*; *kh* is similar to the *ch* in the German *ach* or the Scottish *loch*, but is somewhat more guttural; *gh* represents a sound similar to the Parisian *r*, more or less the sound made when gargling.

Bars over the vowels (ā, ī, ū) indicate that they are to be pronounced long. Classical written Arabic, though rich in consonants, has only six pure vowels, three long and three short. The short ones are similar to the vowels in *cat*, *did* and *put*; their long equivalents are, roughly, f*a*ther, s*ee*n and f*oo*d. The diphthong *ay* is pronounced like the *i* in *bite*, *aw* like the *ow* in *down*.

All the other letters, including combinations of letters (*th* as in *think*, *sh* as in *share*), are similar to their English equivalents. The *q* is pronounced further back in the throat than the *k*.

In general, if the last syllable of a word has a long vowel or a diphthong, that syllable is accented. If the word has no long vowel or diphthong, it is accented on the third syllable from the end. Otherwise, the accent tends to fall on the penultimate syllable.

The hyphen does not stand for a sound, but simply indicates that the two components of a word are closely linked grammatically (for example *al-*, meaning 'the', which is prefixed to the word which follows). It can be ignored in pronunciation.

To Andrée

FOREWORD

The basic idea of this book is simple: to tell the story of the Crusades as they were seen, lived and recorded on 'the other side' – in other words, in the Arab camp. Its content is based almost exclusively on the testimony of contemporary Arab historians and chroniclers.

These latter spoke not of Crusades, but of Frankish wars, or 'the Frankish invasions'. The word designating the Franks was transcribed in many ways, according to region, author and period. In the various chronicles, we find Faranj, Faranjat, Ifranj, Ifranjat and other variants. For the sake of consistency, I have chosen to use the briefest form, *Franj*, a word which is used in colloquial Arabic even today to designate Westerners, and the French in particular.

I was concerned not to burden my narrative with the many bibliographical, historical or other notes that are necessary in a work of this kind, and I have therefore grouped them all together at the back of the book, where they are arranged by chapter. Those who want to know more can usefully read them, but they are by no means indispensable to an understanding of the story, which is meant to be accessible to all. Rather than offer yet another history book, I have sought to write, from a hitherto neglected point of view, what might be called the 'true-life novel' of the Crusades, of those two centuries of turmoil that shaped the West and the Arab world alike, and that affect relations between them even today.

CHRONOLOGY

BEFORE THE INVASION

622 The emigration – or *hijra* – of the Prophet Muḥammad from Mecca to Medina. Beginning of the Muslim calendar.

638 The caliph ʿUmar takes Jerusalem.

C.7/8 The Arabs build an enormous empire, from the Indus river in the east to the Pyrenees in the west.

809 Death of the caliph Hārūn al-Rashīd: the Arab empire at its apogee.

C.10 Although their civilisation is still flourishing, political decline among the Arabs begins. The caliphs lose their power to Turkish and Persian military officers.

1055 The Seljuk Turks are rulers of Baghdad.

1071 The Seljuks crush the Byzantines at Malazgerd and seize Asia Minor. They soon control the entire Muslim East except for Egypt.

INVASION

1096 Kilij Arslan, sultan of Nicaea, crushes a Frankish invasion army led by Peter the Hermit.

1097 First great Frankish expedition. Nicaea is taken; Kilij Arslan is defeated at Dorylaeum.

1098 The Franj take Edessa and then Antioch, and triumph over a Muslim rescue army commanded by Karbūqa, ruler of Mosul. The incident of cannibalism in Maʿarra.

1099 Fall of Jerusalem, followed by massacres and plunder. Debacle of the Egyptian rescue army. The *qāḍī* of Damascus, al-Ḥarawi, leads a delegation of refugees to Baghdad to denounce the lack of action by Muslim leaders in face of the invasion.

OCCUPATION

1100 Baldwin, count of Edessa, escapes an ambush near Beirut and proclaims himself king of Jerusalem.

1104 Muslim victory at Ḥarrān, which checks the Frankish eastward advance.

1108 Curious battle near Tel Bāshir: two Islamo-Frankish coalitions confront one another.

1109 Fall of Tripoli after a 2,000-day siege.

1110 Fall of Beirut and Saida.

1111 Ibn al-Khashāb, the *qāḍī* of Aleppo, organises a riot against the caliph of Baghdad to demand intervention against the Frankish occupation.

1112 Victorious resistance at Tyre.

1115 Alliance of Muslim and Frankish princes of Syria against an army despatched by the sultan.

1119 Ilghazi, ruler of Aleppo, crushes the Franj at Sarmada.

1124 The Franj take Tyre: they now occupy the entire coast, except for Ascalon.

1125 Ibn al-Khashāb is murdered by the Assassins sect.

RIPOSTE

1128 Failure of a Franj thrust at Damascus. Zangī the ruler of Aleppo.

1135 Zangī tries, unsuccessfully, to take Damascus.

1137 Zangī captures Fulk, king of Jerusalem, then releases him.

1140 Alliance of Damascus and Jerusalem against Zangī.

1144 Zangī takes Edessa, destroying the first of the four Frankish states of the Orient.

1146 Murder of Zangī. His son Nūr al-Dīn replaces him in Aleppo.

VICTORY

1148 Debacle at Damascus for a new Frankish expedition led by Conrad, emperor of Germany, and Louis VII, king of France.

1154 Nūr al-Dīn takes control of Damascus, unifying Muslim Syria under his authority.

1163–9 The struggle for Egypt. Shīrkūh, lieutenant of Nūr al-Dīn, finally wins. Proclaimed vizier, he dies two months later. He is succeeded by his nephew Saladin.

1171 Saladin proclaims the overthrow of the Fatimid caliphate. Sole master of Egypt, he finds himself in conflict with Nūr al-Dīn.

1174 Death of Nūr al-Dīn. Saladin takes Damascus.

1183 Saladin takes Aleppo. Egypt and Syria now reunited under his aegis.

1187 The year of victory. Saladin crushes the Frankish armies at Ḥiṭṭīn, near Lake Tiberias. He reconquers Jerusalem and the greater part of the Frankish territories. The occupiers now hold only Tyre, Tripoli and Antioch.

REPRIEVE

1190–2 Setback for Saladin at Acre. Intervention of Richard the Lionheart, king of England, enables the Franj to recover several cities from the sultan, but not Jerusalem.

1193 Saladin dies in Damascus at the age of fifty-five. After several years of civil war, his empire is reunited under the authority of his brother al-ʿĀdil.

1204 The Franj take Constantinople. Sack of the city.

1218–21 Invasion of Egypt by the Franj. They take Damietta and head for Cairo, but the sultan al-Kāmil, son of al-ʿĀdil, finally repels them.

1229 Al-Kāmil delivers Jerusalem to the emperor Frederick II of Hohenstaufen, arousing a storm of indignation in the Arab world.

EXPULSION

1244 The Franj lose Jerusalem for the last time.

1248–50 Invasion of Egypt by Louis IX, king of France, who is defeated and captured. Fall of the Ayyubid dynasty; replaced by the rule of the Mamluks.

1258 The Mongol chief Hülegü, grandson of Genghis Khan, sacks Baghdad, massacring the population and killing the last ʿAbbasid caliph.

1260 The Mongol army, after occupying first Aleppo and then Damascus, is defeated at the battle of ʿAyn Jālūt in Palestine. Baybars at the head of the Mamluk sultanate.

1268 Baybars takes Antioch, which had been allied with the Mongols.

1270 Louis IX dies near Tunis in the course of a failed invasion.

1289 The Mamluk sultan Qalāwūn takes Tripoli.

1291 The sultan Khalīl, son of Qalāwūn, takes Acre, putting an end to two centuries of Frankish presence in the Orient.

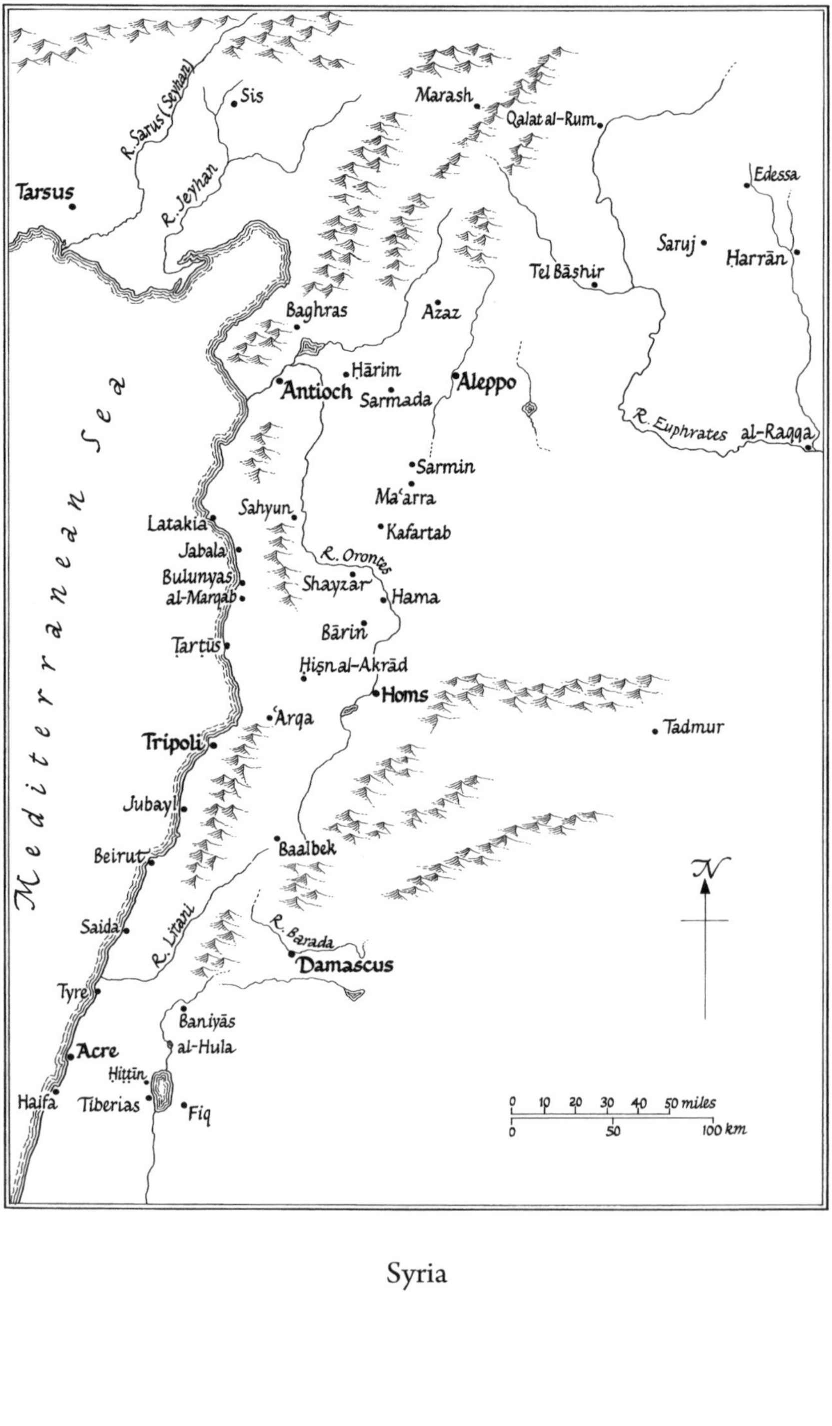
Sis
R. Sarus (Seyhan)
Tarsus
R. Jeyhan
Marash
Qalat al-Rum
Edessa
Saruj
Ḥarrān
Tel Bāshir
Baghras
Azaz
Ḥārim
Antioch
Sarmada
Aleppo
R. Euphrates
al-Raqqa
Mediterranean Sea
Sarmin
Maʿarra
Kafartab
Sahyun
Latakia
Jabala
Bulunyas
al-Marqab
R. Orontes
Shayzar
Hama
Bārin
Ṭarṭūs
Ḥiṣn al-Akrād
Homs
ʿArqa
Tadmur
Tripoli
Jubayl
Baalbek
Beirut
N
Saida
R. Litani
R. Barada
Damascus
Tyre
Baniyās
al-Hula
Acre
Ḥiṭṭīn
Haifa
Tiberias
Fiq
0 10 20 30 40 50 miles
0 50 100 km

Syria

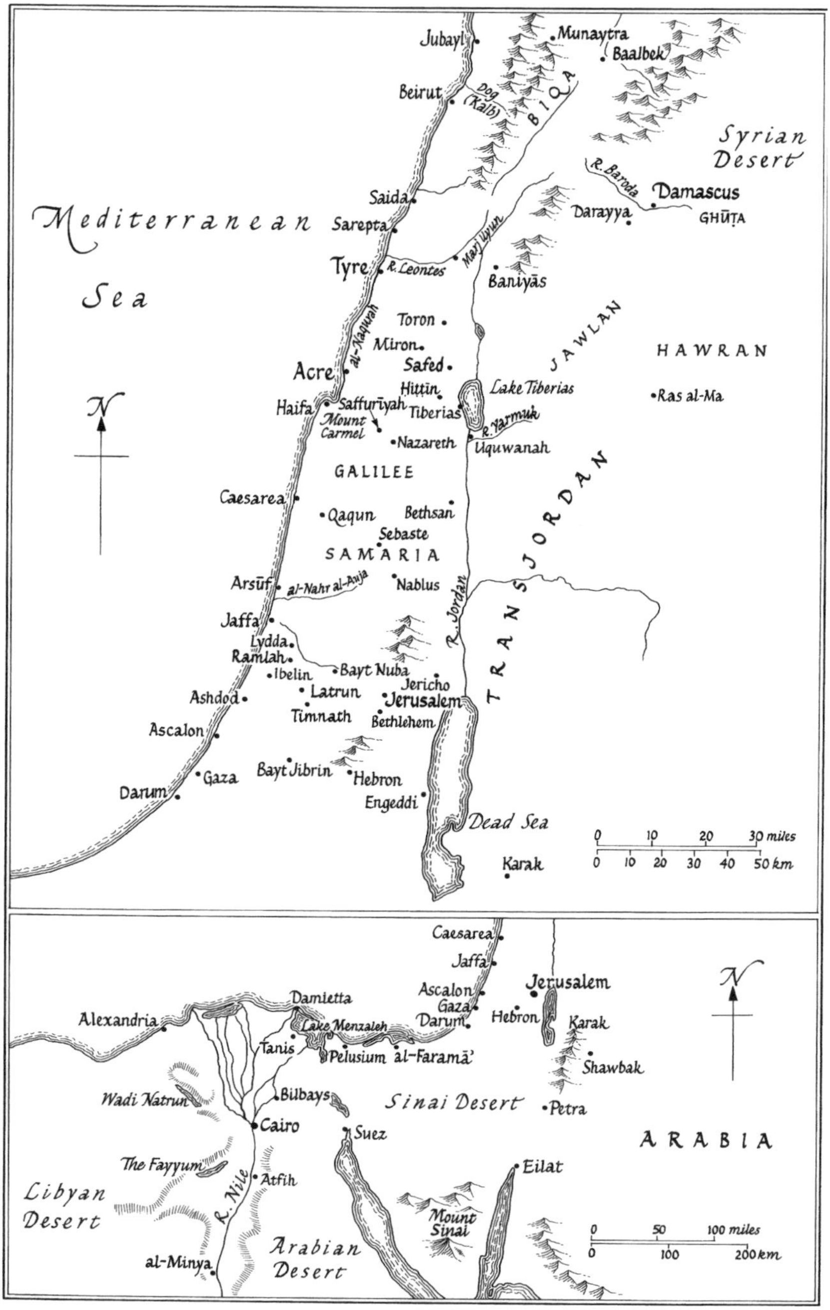

Palestine and Egypt

THE CRUSADES THROUGH ARAB EYES

PROLOGUE

Baghdad, August 1099

Wearing no turban, his head shaved as a sign of mourning, the venerable *qāḍī* Abū Ṣaʿad al-Ḥarawi burst with a loud cry into the spacious *dīwān* of the caliph al-Mustaẓhir Billāh, a throng of companions, young and old, trailing in his wake. Noisily assenting to his every word, they, like him, offered the chilling spectacle of long beards and shaven skulls. A few of the court dignitaries tried to calm him, but al-Ḥarawi swept them aside with brusque disdain, strode resolutely to the centre of the hall, and then, with the searing eloquence of a seasoned preacher declaiming from his pulpit, proceeded to lecture all those present, without regard to rank.

'How dare you slumber in the shade of complacent safety,' he began, 'leading lives as frivolous as garden flowers, while your brothers in Syria have no dwelling place save the saddles of camels and the bellies of vultures? Blood has been spilled! Beautiful young girls have been shamed, and must now hide their sweet faces in their hands! Shall the valorous Arabs resign themselves to insult, and the valiant Persians accept dishonour?'

'It was a speech that brought tears to many an eye and moved men's hearts,' the Arab chroniclers would later write. The entire audience broke out in wails and lamentations. But al-Ḥarawi had not come to elicit sobs.

'Man's meanest weapon', he shouted, 'is to shed tears when rapiers stir the coals of war.'

If he had made this arduous trip from Damascus to Baghdad, three long summer weeks under the merciless sun of the Syrian desert, it was not to plead for pity but to alert Islam's highest authorities to the calamity that had just befallen the faithful, and to implore them to intervene without delay to halt the carnage. 'Never have the Muslims been so humiliated,' al-Ḥarawi repeated, 'never have their lands been so savagely devastated.' All the people travelling with him had fled from towns sacked by the invaders; among them were some of the few survivors of Jerusalem. He had brought them along so that they could relate, in their own words, the tragedy they had suffered just one month earlier.

The Franj had taken the holy city on Friday, the twenty-second day of the month of Shaʿbān, in the year of the Hegira 492, or 15 July 1099, after a forty-day siege. The exiles still trembled when they spoke of the fall of the city: they stared into space as though they could still see the fair-haired and heavily armoured warriors spilling through the streets, swords in hand, slaughtering men, women and children, plundering houses, sacking mosques.

Two days later, when the killing stopped, not a single Muslim was left alive within the city walls. Some had taken advantage of the chaos to slip away, escaping through gates battered down by the attackers. Thousands of others lay in pools of blood on the doorsteps of their homes or alongside the mosques. Among them were many *imāms*, *ʿulamāʾ* and Sufi ascetics who had forsaken their countries of origin for a life of pious retreat in these holy places. The last survivors were forced to perform the worst tasks: to heave the bodies of their own relatives, to dump them in vacant, unmarked lots, and then to set them alight, before being themselves massacred or sold into slavery.

The fate of the Jews of Jerusalem was no less atrocious. During the first hours of battle, some participated in the defence of their quarter, situated on the northern edge of the city. But when that part of the city walls overhanging their homes collapsed and the blond knights began to pour through the streets, the Jews panicked. Re-enacting an immemorial rite, the entire community gathered in the main synagogue to pray. The Franj barricaded all the exits and stacked all the bundles of wood they could find in a ring around the building. The temple was then put to the torch. Those who managed to escape were massacred in the neighbouring alleyways. The rest were burned alive.

A few days after the tragedy, the first refugees from Palestine arrived in Damascus, carrying with them, with infinite care, the Koran of ʿUthmān, one of the oldest existing copies of the holy book. Soon afterwards the survivors of Jerusalem duly approached the Syrian capital. When they glimpsed the distant outlines of the three minarets of the Umayyad mosque looming up from its square courtyard, they unrolled their prayer rugs and bowed to give thanks to the Almighty for having thus prolonged their lives, which they had thought were over. Abū Ṣaʿad al-Ḥarawi, grand *qāḍī* of Damascus, welcomed the refugees with kindness. This magistrate, of Afghan origin, was the city's most respected personality, and he offered the Palestinians both advice and comfort. He told them that a Muslim need not be ashamed of being forced to flee from his home. Was not Islam's first refugee the Prophet Muḥammad himself, who had to leave Mecca, his native city, whose population was hostile to him, to seek refuge in Medina, where the new religion had been more warmly received? And was it not from his place of exile that he launched the holy war, the *jihād*, to free his country of idolatry? The refugees must therefore consider themselves *mujāhidīn*, soldiers of the holy war, so highly honoured in Islam that the *hijra*, the Prophet's 'emigration', was chosen as the starting point of the Muslim calendar.

Indeed, for many believers, exile is a duty in the event of occupation. The great traveller Ibn Jubayr, an Arab of Spain who visited Palestine nearly a century after the beginning of the Frankish invasion, was to be shocked when he found that some Muslims, 'slaves to their love for their native land', were willing to accept life in occupied territory.

'There is no excuse before God', he would say, 'for a Muslim to remain in a city of unbelief, unless he be merely passing through. In the land of Islam he finds shelter from the discomforts and evils to which he is subjected in the countries of the Christians, as, for example, when he hears disgusting words spoken about the Prophet, particularly by the most besotted, or finds it impossible to cleanse himself properly, or has to live among pigs and so many other illicit things. Beware! Beware of entering their lands! You must seek God's pardon and mercy for such an error. One of the horrors that strikes any inhabitant of the Christian countries is the spectacle of Muslim prisoners tottering in irons, condemned to hard labour and treated as slaves, as well as the sight of Muslim captives bearing iron chains round their legs. Hearts break at the sight of them, but they have no use for pity.'

Although excessive from a doctrinal standpoint, Ibn Jubayr's words nevertheless accurately reflect the attitude of the thousands of refugees from Palestine and northern Syria who gathered in Damascus in that July of 1099. While they were sick at heart at having been forced to abandon their homes, they were determined never to return until the occupiers had departed for ever, and they resolved to awaken the consciences of their brothers in all the lands of Islam.

Why else would they have followed al-Ḥarawi to Baghdad? Was it not to the caliph, the Prophet's successor, that Muslims must turn in their hour of need? Was it not to the prince of the faithful that they should address their complaints and their tales of woe?

In Baghdad, however, the refugees' disappointment was to be as great as their hopes had been high. The caliph al-Mustaẓhir Billāh began by expressing his profound sympathy and compassion. Then he ordered seven exalted dignitaries to conduct an inquiry into these troublesome events. It is perhaps superfluous to add that nothing was ever heard from that committee of wise men.

The sack of Jerusalem, starting point of a millennial hostility between Islam and the West, aroused no immediate sensation. It would be nearly half a century before the Arab East would mobilise against the invader, before the call to *jihād* issued by the *qāḍī* of Damascus in the caliph's *dīwān* would be celebrated in commemoration of the first solemn act of resistance.

At the start of the invasion, few Arabs were as perspicacious as al-Ḥarawi in weighing the scope of the threat from the West. Some adapted all too rapidly to the new situation. Most, bitter but resigned, sought merely to survive. Some observed more or less lucidly, trying to understand these events, as unexpected as they were novel. The most touching of these was the Damascene chronicler Ibn al-Qalānisi, a young scholar born of a family of notables. A witness to the story from the outset, he was twenty-three when the Franj arrived in the East in 1096, and he assiduously and regularly recorded all the events of which he had some knowledge. His chronicle faithfully recounts, in a fairly detached manner, the advance of the invaders as seen from his native city.

For him it all began during those anxious days when the first rumours drifted into Damascus.

Part One

INVASION (1096–1100)

Regard the Franj! Behold with what obstinacy they fight for their religion, while we, the Muslims, show no enthusiasm for waging holy war.

SALADIN

I

The Franj Arrive

'In that year, news began to trickle in about the appearance of Franj troops, coming down from the Sea of Marmara in an innumerable multitude. People took fright. This information was confirmed by King Kilij Arslan, whose territory was closest to these Franj.'

The king, Kilij Arslan, whom Ibn al-Qalānisi mentions here was not yet seventeen when the invaders arrived. The first Muslim leader to be informed of their approach, this young Turkish sultan with the slightly slanting eyes would be the first to inflict a defeat upon them – but also the first to be routed by the formidable knights.

In July 1096 Kilij Arslan learned that an enormous throng of Franj was en route to Constantinople. He immediately feared the worst. Naturally, he had no idea as to the real aims of these people, but in his view nothing good could come of their arrival in the Orient.

The sultanate under his rule covered much of Asia Minor, a territory the Turks had only recently taken from the Greeks. Kilij Arslan's father, Süleymān, was the first Turk to secure possession of this land, which many centuries later would come to be called Turkey. In Nicaea, the capital of this young Muslim state, Byzantine churches were still more numerous than Muslim mosques. Although the city's garrison was made up of Turkish cavalry, the majority of the population was Greek, and Kilij Arslan had few illusions about his subjects' true sentiments: as far as they were concerned, he would never be other than a barbarian chieftain. The only sovereign they recognised – the man whose name, spoken in a low whisper, was murmured in all their prayers – was the *basileus* Alexius Comnenus, 'Emperor of the Romans'. Alexius was in fact the emperor of the Greeks, who proclaimed themselves the inheritors of the Roman empire. The Arabs, indeed, recognised them as such, for in the eleventh century – as in the twentieth – they designated the Greeks by the term Rūm, or

'Romans'. The domain conquered from the Greek empire by Kilij Arslan's father was even called the Sultanate of the Rūm.

Alexius was one of the most prestigious figures of the Orient at the time. Kilij Arslan was genuinely fascinated by this short-statured quinquagenarian, always decked in gold and in rich blue robes, with his carefully tended beard, elegant manners, and eyes sparkling with malice. Alexius reigned in Constantinople, fabled Byzantium, situated less than three days' march from Nicaea. This proximity aroused conflicting emotions in the mind of the young sultan. Like all nomadic warriors, he dreamed of conquest and pillage, and was not displeased to find the legendary riches of Byzantium so close at hand. At the same time he felt threatened: he knew that Alexius had never abandoned his dream of retaking Nicaea, not only because the city had always been Greek, but also and more importantly because the presence of Turkish warriors such a short distance from Constantinople represented a permanent threat to the security of the empire.

Although the Byzantine army, torn by years of internal crisis, would have been unable to undertake a war of reconquest on its own, it was no secret that Alexius could always seek the aid of foreign auxiliaries. The Byzantines had never hesitated to resort to the services of Western knights. Many Franj, from heavily armoured mercenaries to pilgrims en route to Palestine, had visited the Orient, and by 1096 they were by no means unknown to the Muslims. Some twenty years earlier – Kilij Arslan had not yet been born, but the older emirs in his army had told him the story – one of these fair-haired adventurers, a man named Roussel of Bailleul, had succeeded in founding an autonomous state in Asia Minor and had even marched on Constantinople. The panicky Byzantines had had no choice but to appeal to Kilij Arslan's father, who could hardly believe his ears when a special envoy from the *basileus* implored him to rush to their aid. The Turkish cavalry converged on Constantinople and managed to defeat Roussel; Süleymān received handsome compensation in the form of gold, horses and land.

The Byzantines had been suspicious of the Franj ever since, but the imperial armies, short of experienced soldiers, had no choice but to recruit mercenaries, and not only Franj: many Turkish warriors also fought under the banners of the Christian empire. It was precisely from his congeners enrolled in the Byzantine army that Kilij Arslan learned, in July 1096, that thousands of Franj were approaching Constantinople. He was perplexed by the picture painted by his informants. These Occidentals bore scant resemblance to the mercenaries to whom the Turks were accustomed. Although their number included several hundred knights and a significant number of foot soldiers, there were also thousands of women, children and old people in rags. They had the air of some wretched tribe evicted from their lands by an invader. It was also reported that they all wore strips of cloth in the shape of a cross, sewn onto the backs of their garments.

The young sultan, who doubtless found it difficult to assess the danger, asked his agents to be especially vigilant and to keep him informed of the exploits of these new invaders. He had the fortifications of his capital inspected as a precaution. The walls of Nicaea, more than a *farsakh* (six thousand metres) in length, were topped by 240 turrets. South-west of the city, the placid waters of the Ascanian Lake offered excellent natural protection.

Nevertheless by early August the serious nature of the threat had become clear. Escorted by Byzantine ships, the Franj crossed the Bosporus and, despite a blazing summer sun, advanced along the coast. Wherever they passed, they were heard to proclaim that they had come to exterminate the Muslims, although they were also seen to plunder many a Greek church on their way. Their chief was said to be a hermit by the name of Peter. Informants estimated that there were several tens of thousands of them in all, but no one would hazard a guess as to where they were headed. It seemed that Basileus Alexius had decided to settle them in Civitot, a camp that had earlier been equipped for other mercenaries, less than a day's march from Nicaea.

The sultan's palace was awash with agitation. While the Turkish cavalry stood ready to mount their chargers at a moment's notice, there was a constant flow of spies and scouts, reporting the smallest movements of the Franj. It transpired that every morning hordes several thousand strong left camp to forage the surrounding countryside: farms were plundered or set alight before the rabble returned to

Civitot, where their various clans squabbled over the spoils of their raids. None of this was surprising to the sultan's soldiers, and their master saw no reason for particular concern. The routine continued for an entire month.

One day, however, towards the middle of September, there was a sudden change in the behaviour of the Franj. Probably because they were unable to squeeze anything more out of the immediate neighbourhood, they had reportedly set out in the direction of Nicaea. They passed through several villages, all of them Christian, and commandeered the harvests, which had just been gathered, mercilessly massacring those peasants who tried to resist. Young children were even said to have been burned alive.

Kilij Arslan found himself taken unawares. By the time the news of these events reached him, the attackers were already at the walls of his capital, and before sunset the citizens could see the smoke rising from the first fires. The sultan quickly despatched a cavalry patrol to confront the Franj. Hopelessly outnumbered, the Turks were cut to pieces. A few bloodied survivors limped back into Nicaea. Sensing that his prestige was threatened, Kilij Arslan would have liked to join the battle immediately, but the emirs of his army dissuaded him. It would soon be night, and the Franj were already hastily falling back to their camp. Revenge would have to wait.

But not for long. Apparently emboldened by their success, the Occidentals decided to try again two weeks later. This time the son of Süleymān was alerted in time, and he followed their advance step by step. A Frankish company, including some knights but consisting mainly of thousands of tattered pillagers, set out apparently for Nicaea. But then, circling around the town, they turned east and took the fortress of Xerigordon by surprise.

The young sultan decided to act. At the head of his men, he rode briskly towards the small stronghold, where the drunken Franj, celebrating their victory, had no way of knowing that their fate was already sealed, for Xerigordon was a trap. As the soldiers of Kilij Arslan well knew (but the inexperienced foreigners had yet to discover), its water supplies lay outside and rather far from the walls. The Turks quickly sealed off access to the water. Now they had only to take up positions around the fortress and sit and wait. Thirst would do the fighting in their stead.

An atrocious torment began for the besieged Franj. They went so far as to drink the blood of their mounts and their own urine. They were seen looking desperately up into the sky, hoping for a few drops of rain in those early October days. In vain. At the end of the week, the leader of the expedition, a knight named Reynald, agreed to capitulate provided his life would be spared. Kilij Arslan, who had demanded that the Franj publicly renounce their religion, was somewhat taken aback when Reynald declared his readiness not only to convert to Islam but even to fight at the side of the Turks against his own companions. Several of his friends, who had acceded to the same demands, were sent in captivity to various cities of Syria or central Asia. The rest were put to the sword.

The young sultan was proud of his exploit, but he kept a cool head. After according his men a respite for the traditional sharing out of the spoils, he called them to order the following day. The Franj had admittedly lost nearly six thousand men, but six times that number still remained, and the time to dispose of them was now or never. Kilij Arslan decided to attempt a ruse. He sent two Greek spies to the Civitot camp to report that Reynald's men were in an excellent position, and that they had succeeded in taking Nicaea itself, whose riches they had no intention of sharing with their coreligionists. In the meantime, the Turkish army would lay a gigantic ambush.

As expected, the carefully propagated rumours aroused turmoil in the camp at Civitot. A mob gathered, shouting insults against Reynald and his men; it was decided to proceed without delay to share in the pillage of Nicaea. But all at once, no one really knows how, an escapee from the Xerigordon expedition arrived, divulging the truth about his companions' fate. Kilij Arslan's spies thought that they had failed in their mission, for the wisest among the Franj counselled caution. Once the first moment of consternation had passed, however, excitement soared anew. The mob bustled and shouted: they were ready to set out in a trice, no longer to join in pillage, but 'to avenge the martyrs'. Those who hesitated were dismissed as cowards. The most enraged voices carried the day, and the time of departure was set for the following morning. The sultan's spies, whose ruse had been exposed but its objective attained, had triumphed after all. They sent word to their master to prepare for battle.

At dawn on 21 October 1096 the Occidentals left their camp. Kilij Arslan, who had spent the night in the hills near Civitot, was not far away. His men were in position, well hidden. From his vantage point, he could see all along the column of Franj, who were raising great clouds of dust. Several hundred knights, most of them without their armour, marched at the head of the procession, followed by a disordered throng of foot soldiers. They had been marching for less than an hour when the sultan heard their approaching clamour. The sun, rising at his back, shone directly into the eyes of the Franj. Holding his breath, he signalled his emirs to get ready. The fateful moment had arrived. A barely perceptible gesture, a few orders whispered here and there, and the Turkish archers were slowly bending their bows: a thousand arrows suddenly shot forth with a single protracted whistle. Most of the knights fell within the first few minutes. Then the foot soldiers were decimated in their turn.

By the time the hand-to-hand combat was joined, the Franj were already routed. Those in the rear ran for their camp, where the noncombatants were barely awake. An aged priest was celebrating morning mass, the women were preparing food. The arrival of the fugitives, with the Turks in hot pursuit, struck terror throughout the camp. The Franj fled in all directions. Those who tried to reach the neighbouring woods were soon captured. Others, in an inspired move, barricaded themselves in an unused fortress that had the additional advantage of lying alongside the sea. Unwilling to take futile risks, the sultan decided not to lay a siege. The Byzantine fleet, rapidly alerted, sailed in to pick up the Franj. Two or three thousand men escaped in this manner. Peter the Hermit, who had been in Constantinople for several days, was also saved. But his partisans were not so lucky. The youngest women were kidnapped by the sultan's horsemen and distributed to the emirs or sold in the slave markets. Several young boys suffered a similar fate. The rest of the Franj, probably nearly twenty thousand of them, were exterminated.

Kilij Arslan was jubilant. He had annihilated the Frankish army, in spite of its formidable reputation, while suffering only insignificant losses among his own troops. Gazing upon the immense booty amassed at his feet, he basked in the most sublime triumph of his life.

And yet, rarely in history has a victory proved so costly to those who had won it.

Intoxicated by his success, Kilij Arslan pointedly ignored the information that came through the following winter about the arrival of fresh groups of Franj in Constantinople. As far as he was concerned – and even the wisest of his emirs did not dissent – there was no reason for disquiet. If other mercenaries of Alexius dared to cross the Bosporus, they would be cut to pieces like those who had come before them. The sultan felt that it was time to return to the major preoccupations of the hour – in other words, to the merciless struggle he had long been waging against the other Turkish princes, his neighbours. It was there, and nowhere else, that his fate and that of his realm would be decided. The clashes with the Rūm or with their foreign Franj auxiliaries would never be more than an interlude.

The young sultan was well placed to feel certain about this. Was it not during one of these interminable battles among chiefs that his father, Süleymān, had laid down his life in 1086? Kilij Arslan was then barely seven years old, and he was to have succeeded his father under the regency of several faithful emirs. But he had been kept from power and taken to Persia under the pretext that his life was in danger. There he was kept: adulated, smothered in respect, waited on by a small army of attentive slaves, but closely watched, and strictly prevented from visiting his realm. His hosts – in other words, his jailers – were none other than the members of his own clan, the Seljuks.

If there was one name known to everyone in the eleventh century, from the borders of China to the distant land of the Franj, it was theirs. Within a few years of their arrival in the Middle East from central Asia, the Seljuk Turks, with their thousands of nomadic horsemen sporting long braided hair, had seized control of the entire region, from Afghanistan to the Mediterranean. Since 1055 the caliph of Baghdad, successor of the Prophet and inheritor of the renowned ʿAbbasid empire, had been no more than a docile puppet in their hands. From Isfahan to Damascus, from Nicaea to Jerusalem, it was their emirs who laid down the law. For the first time in three centuries, the entire Muslim East was united under the authority of a single dynasty which proclaimed its determination to restore the past glory of Islam. The Rūm, who were crushed by the Seljuks in 1071, would never rise again. The largest of their provinces, Asia Minor, had been invaded, and their capital itself was no longer secure. Their emperors, including Alexius himself, despatched one delegation after another to the pope in Rome, the supreme commander of the West, imploring him to declare holy war against this resurgence of Islam.

Kilij Arslan was more than a little proud to belong to such a prestigious family, but he had no illusions about the apparent unity of the Turkish empire. There was no hint of solidarity among the Seljuk cousins: to survive, you had to kill. Kilij Arslan's father had conquered Asia Minor, the vast area of Anatolia, without any help from his brothers, and when he attempted to move further south, into Syria, he was killed by one of his own cousins. While Kilij Arslan was being held forcibly in Isfahan, the paternal realm had been dismembered. In 1092, when the adolescent chief was released in the wake of a quarrel among his jailers, his authority barely extended beyond the ramparts of Nicaea. He was only thirteen years old.

The advice subsequently given him by the emirs in his army had enabled him to recover a part of his paternal heritage through war, murder and subterfuge. He could now boast that he had spent more time in the saddle than at his palace. Nevertheless, when the Franj arrived, the game was far from over. His rivals in Asia Minor were still powerful, although fortunately for Kilij Arslan, his Seljuk cousins in Syria and Persia were absorbed in their own internecine quarrels.

To the east, along the desolate highlands of the Anatolian plateau, the ruler during these uncertain days was an elusive personality called Danishmend 'the Wise'. Unlike the other Turkish emirs, most of whom were illiterate, this adventurer of unknown origin was schooled in the most varied branches of learning. He would soon become the hero of a famous epic, appropriately entitled *The Exploits of King Danishmend*, which recounted the conquest of Malaṭya, an Armenian city south-east of Ankara. The authors of this tale considered the city's fall as the decisive turning point in the Islamicisation of what would some day become Turkey. The battle of Malaṭya had already been joined in the early months of 1097, when Kilij Arslan was told that a new Frankish expedition had arrived in Constantinople. Danishmend had laid siege to Malaṭya, and the young sultan chafed at the idea that this rival of his, who had taken advantage of his father Süleymān's death to occupy north-east Anatolia, was about to score such a prestigious victory. Determined to prevent this, Kilij Arslan set out for Malaṭya at the head of his cavalry and pitched his camp close enough to Danishmend to intimidate him. Tension mounted, and there were increasingly murderous skirmishes.

By April 1097 Kilij Arslan was preparing for the decisive confrontation, which now seemed inevitable. The greater part of his army had been assembled before the walls of Malaṭya when an exhausted horseman arrived at the sultan's tent. Breathlessly, he panted out his message: the Franj were back; they had crossed the Bosporus once again, in greater numbers than the previous year. Kilij Arslan remained calm. There was no reason for such anxiety. He had already shown the Franj that he knew how to deal with them. In the end, it was only to reassure the inhabitants of Nicaea – especially his wife, the young sultana, who was about to give birth – that he sent a few cavalry detachments to reinforce the garrison of his capital. He himself would return as soon as he had finished with Danishmend.

Kilij Arslan had once again thrown himself body and soul into the battle of Malaṭya when, early in May, another messenger arrived, trembling with fear and fatigue. His words struck terror in the sultan's camp. The Franj were at the gates of Nicaea, and had begun a siege. This time, unlike the previous summer, it was not a few bands of tattered pillagers, but real armies of thousands of heavily equipped knights. And this time they were accompanied by soldiers of the *basileus*. Kilij Arslan sought to reassure his men, but he himself was tormented by anxiety. Should he abandon Malaṭya to his rival and return to Nicaea? Was he sure that he could still save his capital? Would he not perhaps lose on both fronts? After long consultations with his most trusted emirs, a solution began to emerge, a sort of compromise: he would go to see Danishmend, who was after all a man of honour, inform him of the attempted conquest undertaken by the Rūm and their mercenaries, which posed a threat to all the Muslims of Asia Minor, and propose a cessation of hostilities. Even before Danishmend had given his answer, the sultan despatched part of his army to the capital.

After several days of talks, a truce was concluded and Kilij Arslan set out westwards without delay. But the sight that awaited him as he reached the highlands near Nicaea chilled the blood in his veins. The superb city bequeathed him by his father was surrounded: a multitude of soldiers were camped there, busily erecting mobile towers, catapults and mangonels to be used in the final assault. The emirs were categorical: there was nothing to be done. The only option was to retreat to the interior of the country before it was too late. But the young sultan could not bring himself to abandon his capital in this way. He insisted on a desperate attempt to breach the siege on the city's southern rim, where the attackers seemed less solidly entrenched. The battle was joined at dawn on 21 May. Kilij Arslan threw himself furiously into the fray, and the fighting raged until sunset. Losses were equally heavy on both sides but each maintained its position. The sultan did not persevere. He realised that nothing would enable him to loosen the vice. To persist in throwing all his forces into such an ill-prepared battle might prolong the siege for several weeks, perhaps even several months, but would threaten the very existence of the sultanate. As the scion of an essentially nomadic people, Kilij Arslan felt that the source of his power lay in the thousands of warriors under his command, and not in the possession of a city, however enchanting it might be. In any event, he would soon choose as his new capital the city of Konya much further east, which his descendants would retain until the beginning of the fourteenth century. Kilij Arslan was never to see Nicaea again.

Before his departure, he sent a farewell message to the city's defenders, informing them of his painful decision and urging them to act 'in the light of their own interests'. The meaning of these words was clear to the Turkish garrison and the Greek population alike: the city must be handed over to Alexius Comnenus and not to his Frankish auxiliaries. Negotiations were opened with the *basileus*, who had taken up a position to the west of Nicaea, at the head of his troops.

The sultan's men tried to gain time, probably hoping that their master would somehow manage to return with reinforcements. But Alexius hurried them along. The Occidentals, he threatened, were preparing the final assault, and then there would be nothing he could do. Recalling the behaviour of the Franj in the environs of Nicaea the year before, the negotiators were terrified. In their mind's eye they saw their city pillaged, the men massacred, the women raped. Without further hesitation, they agreed to place their fate in the hands of the *basileus*, who would himself establish the modalities of the surrender.

On the night of 18–19 June soldiers of the Byzantine army, most of them Turks, entered the city by means of boats that slipped silently across the Ascanian Lake; the garrison capitulated without a fight. By the first glimmerings of dawn, the blue and gold banners of the emperor were already fluttering over the city walls. The Franj called off their assault. Thus did Kilij Arslan receive some consolation in his misfortune: the dignitaries of the sultanate would be spared, and the young sultana, accompanied by her newborn son, would even be received in Constantinople with royal honours – to the great consternation of the Franj.

Kilij Arslan's young wife was the daughter of a man named Chaka, a Turkish emir and adventurer of genius, famous on the eve of the Frankish invasion. Imprisoned by the Rūm after being captured during a raid in Asia Minor, he had impressed his captors with the ease with which he learned Greek, for he spoke it perfectly within a few months. Brilliant and clever, and a magnificent speaker, he had become a regular visitor at the imperial palace, which had gone so far as to bestow a noble title upon him. But this astonishing promotion was not enough for him, for he had set his sights far higher: he aspired to become the emperor of Byzantium!

The emir Chaka had devised a coherent plan in pursuit of this goal. First he left Constantinople to settle in Smyrna, on the Aegean Sea. There, with the aid of a Greek shipbuilder, he constructed a fleet of his own, including light brigantines and galleys, dromonds, biremes and triremes – nearly a hundred vessels in all. During the initial phase of his campaign, he occupied many islands, in particular Rhodes, Chios and Samos, and established his authority along the entire

Aegean coast. Having thus carved out a maritime empire, he proclaimed himself *basileus*, organising his Smyrna palace on the pattern of the imperial court. He then launched his fleet in an assault on Constantinople. Only after enormous effort did Alexius manage to repel the attack and destroy a part of the Turkish vessels.

Far from discouraged, the father of the future sultana set to work to rebuild his warships. By then it was late 1092, just when Kilij Arslan was returning from exile, and Chaka calculated that the young son of Süleymān would be an excellent ally against the Rūm. He thus offered him the hand of his daughter. But the calculations of the young sultan were quite different from those of his father-in-law. He saw the conquest of Constantinople as an absurd project; on the other hand, all in his entourage were aware of his intention to eliminate the Turkish emirs who were then seeking to carve out fiefdoms for themselves in Asia Minor, in particular Danishmend and the ambitious Chaka. The sultan did not hesitate: a few months after the arrival of the Franj, he invited his father-in-law to a banquet, plied him with drink, and stabbed him to death, with his own hand it appears. Chaka was succeeded by a son who possessed neither his father's intelligence nor his ambition. The sultana's brother was content to administer his maritime emirate until one day in 1097 when the Rūm fleet arrived unexpectedly off the coast of Smyrna with an equally unexpected messenger on board: his own sister.

She was slow to realise the reasons for the Byzantine emperor's solicitude towards her, but as she was being led to Smyrna, the city in which she had spent her childhood, everything suddenly became clear. She was told to explain to her brother that Alexius had taken Nicaea, that Kilij Arslan had been defeated, and that a powerful army of Rūm and Franj would soon attack Smyrna, supported by an enormous fleet. In exchange for his life, Chaka's son was invited to lead his sister to her husband, somewhere in Anatolia.

Once this proposition was accepted, the emirate of Smyrna ceased to exist. With the fall of Nicaea, the entire coast of the Aegean Sea, all the islands, and the whole of western Asia Minor now stood beyond the control of the Turks. And the Rūm, with the aid of their Frankish auxiliaries, seemed determined to press on further.

In his mountain refuge, however, Kilij Arslan did not lay down his arms.

Once he had recovered from the surprise of the first few days, the sultan began actively preparing his riposte. 'He set about recruiting troops and enrolling volunteers, and proclaimed *jihād*,' notes Ibn al-Qalānisi. The Damascene chronicler adds that Kilij Arslan 'asked all Turks to come to his aid, and many of them answered his call'.

In fact, the sultan's prime objective was to cement his alliance with Danishmend. A mere truce was no longer enough: it was now imperative that the Turkish forces of Asia Minor unite, as if forming elements of a single army. Kilij Arslan was certain of his rival's response. A fervent Muslim as well as a realistic strategist, Danishmend felt threatened by the advance of the Rūm and their Frankish allies. He preferred to confront them on his neighbour's lands rather than on his own, and without further ado he arrived in the sultan's camp, accompanied by thousands of cavalry. There was fraternisation and consultation, and plans were drafted. The sight of this multitude of warriors and horses blanketing the hills filled the commanders with fresh courage. They would attack the enemy at the first opportunity.

Kilij Arslan stalked his prey. Informers who had infiltrated the Rūm brought him precious information. The Franj openly proclaimed that they were resolved to press on beyond Nicaea, and that their real destination was Palestine. Even their route was known: they would march in a south-easterly direction towards Konya, the only important city still in the hands of the sultan. During their entire trek through this mountainous zone, the flanks of the Occidental army would be vulnerable to attack. The only problem was to select the proper site for the ambush. The emirs, who knew the region well, had no hesitation. Near the city of Dorylaeum, four days' march from Nicaea, there was a place at which the road narrowed to pass through a shallow valley. If the Turkish warriors gathered behind the hills, all they would have to do was bide their time.

By the last days of June 1097, when Kilij Arslan learned that the Occidentals had left Nicaea, accompanied by a small force of Rūm, the apparatus for the ambush was already in position. At dawn on

1 July the Franj loomed onto the horizon. Knights and foot soldiers advanced serenely, seemingly with no idea of what was in store for them. The sultan had feared that his stratagem might be discovered by enemy scouts. Apparently, he had nothing to worry about. Another source of satisfaction for the Seljuk monarch was that the Franj seemed less numerous than had been reported. Had some of them perhaps remained behind in Nicaea? He did not know. At first sight, however, he seemed to command numerical superiority. This, combined with the element of surprise, augured well. Kilij Arslan was anxious, but confident. The wise Danishmend, with his twenty more years of experience, felt the same.

The sun had barely risen from behind the hills when the order to attack was given. The tactics of the Turkish warriors were well practised. After all, they had assured their military supremacy in the Orient for half a century. Their army was composed almost exclusively of light cavalry who were also excellent archers. They would draw near, unleash a flood of deadly arrows on their enemy, and then retreat briskly, giving way to a new row of attackers. A few successive waves usually sufficed to bring their prey to their death agony. It was then that the final hand-to-hand combat was joined.

But on the day of the battle of Dorylaeum, the sultan, ensconced with his general staff atop a promontory, noted anxiously that the tried-and-true Turkish methods seemed to lack their usual effectiveness. Granted, the Franj lacked agility and seemed in no hurry to respond to the repeated attacks, but they were perfect masters of the art of defence. Their army's main strength lay in the heavy armour with which their knights covered their entire bodies, and sometimes those of their mounts as well. Although their advance was slow and clumsy, their men were magnificently protected against arrows. On that day, after several hours of battle, the Turkish archers had inflicted many casualties, especially among the foot soldiers, but the bulk of the Frankish army remained intact. Should they engage in hand-to-hand combat? That seemed risky: during the many skirmishes around the field of battle, the horsemen of the steppes had come nowhere near holding their own against these virtual human fortresses. Should the phase of harassment be prolonged indefinitely? Now that the element of surprise had worn off, the initiative might well shift to the other side.

Some of the emirs were already counselling retreat when a cloud of dust appeared in the distance. A fresh Frankish army was approaching, as numerous as the first. Those against whom the Turks had been fighting all morning turned out to be only the vanguard. Now the sultan had no choice but to order a retreat. Before he could do so, however, a third Frankish army came into view behind the Turkish lines, on a hill overlooking the tent of the general staff.

This time Kilij Arslan succumbed to fear. He leapt onto his charger and headed for the mountains at full gallop, even abandoning the rich treasure he carried with him to pay his troops. Danishmend was not far behind, along with most of the emirs. Taking advantage of their one remaining trump card, speed, many horsemen managed to get away without the victors' being able to give chase. But most of the soldiers remained where they were, surrounded on all sides. As Ibn al-Qalānisi was later to write: 'The Franj cut the Turkish army to pieces. They killed, pillaged, and took many prisoners, who were sold into slavery.'

During his flight, Kilij Arslan met a group of cavalry coming from Syria to fight at his side. They were too late, he told them ruefully. The Franj were too numerous and too powerful, and nothing more could be done to stop them. Joining deed to word, and determined to stand aside and let the storm pass, the defeated sultan disappeared into the immensity of the Anatolian plateau. He was to wait four years to take his revenge.

Nature alone seemed still to resist the invader. The aridity of the soil, the tiny mountain pathways, and the scorching summer heat on the shadowless roads slowed the advance of the Franj. After Dorylaeum, it took them a hundred days to cross Anatolia, whereas in normal times a month should have sufficed. In the meantime, news of the Turkish debacle spread throughout the Middle East. 'When this event, so shameful for Islam, became known,' noted the Damascene chronicler, 'there was real panic. Dread and anxiety swelled to enormous proportions.'

Rumours circulated constantly about the imminent arrival of

redoubtable knights. At the end of July there was talk that they were approaching the village of al-Balana, in the far north of Syria. Thousands of cavalry gathered to meet them, but it was a false alarm: there was no sign of the Franj on the horizon. The most optimistic souls wondered whether the invaders had perhaps turned back. Ibn al-Qalānisi echoed that hope in one of those astrological parables of which his contemporaries were so enamoured: 'That summer a comet appeared in the western sky; it ascended for twenty days, then disappeared without a trace.' But these illusions were soon dispelled. The news became increasingly detailed. From mid-September onwards, the advance of the Franj could be followed from village to village.

On 21 October 1097 shouts rang out from the peak of the citadel of Antioch, then Syria's largest city: 'They are here!' A few layabouts hurried to the ramparts to gawk, but they could see nothing more than a vague cloud of dust far in the distance, at the end of the broad plain, near Lake Antioch. The Franj were still a day's march away, perhaps more, and there was every indication that they would want to stop to rest for a while after their long journey. Nevertheless, prudence demanded that the five heavy city gates be closed immediately.

In the souks the morning clamour was stilled, as merchants and customers alike stood immobile. Women whispered, and some prayed. The city was in the grip of fear.

II

An Accursed Maker of Armour

'When Yaghi-Siyān, the ruler of Antioch, was informed of the approach of the Franj, he feared possible sedition on the part of the Christians of the city. He therefore decided to expel them.'

This event was related by the Arab historian Ibn al-Athīr, more than a century after the beginnings of the Frankish invasion, on the basis of testimony left by contemporaries:

> On the first day, Yaghi-Siyān ordered the Muslims to go out beyond the walls to clean out the trenches ringing the city. The next day, he sent only Christians on the same task. He had them work until night had fallen, and when they sought to return, he halted them, saying, 'Antioch is your city, but you must leave it in my hands until I have resolved our problem with the Franj.' They asked him, 'Who will protect our women and children?' The emir answered, 'I will take care of them for you.' He did, indeed, protect the families of those expelled, refusing to allow anyone to touch a hair of their heads.

In that October of 1097 the aged Yaghi-Siyān, for forty years an obedient servant of the Seljuk sultan, was haunted by the fear of betrayal. He was convinced that the Frankish armies gathered before Antioch would be able to enter the city only if they found accomplices within the walls. For the city could not be taken by assault, and still less starved out by a blockade. Admittedly, this white-bearded Turkish emir commanded no more than six or seven thousand soldiers, whereas the Franj had nearly thirty thousand combatants, but Antioch was practically impregnable. Its walls were two *farsakh* long (about twelve thousand metres), and had no less than 360 turrets built on three different levels. The walls themselves, solidly constructed of stone and brick on a frame of masonry, scaled Mount Ḥabīb al-Najjar to the east and crowned its peak with an inexpugnable citadel. To the west lay the Orontes, which the Syrians called al-Assi, 'the rebel river', because it sometimes seemed to flow upstream, from the Mediterranean to the interior of the country. The riverbed ran along the walls of Antioch, forming a natural obstacle not easily crossed. In the south, the fortifications overlooked a valley so steep that it seemed an extension of the city walls. It was therefore impossible for attackers to encircle the city, and the defenders would have little trouble communicating with the outside world and bringing in supplies.

The city's food reserves were unusually abundant; the city walls enclosed not only buildings and gardens, but also wide stretches of cultivated land. Before the *Fatḥ*, or Muslim conquest, Antioch was a Roman metropolis of two hundred thousand inhabitants. By 1097 its population numbered only some forty thousand, and several formerly inhabited quarters had been turned into fields and pastures. Although it had lost its past splendour, it was still an impressive city. All travellers, even those from Baghdad or Constantinople, were dazzled by their first sight of this city extending as far as the eye could see, with its minarets, churches and arcaded souks, its luxurious villas dug into the wooded slopes rising to the citadel.

Yaghi-Siyān was in no doubt as to the solidity of his fortifications and the security of his supplies. But all his weapons of defence might prove useless if, at some point along the interminable wall, the attackers managed to find an accomplice willing to open a gate to allow them access to a turret, as had already happened in the past. Hence his decision to expel most of his Christian subjects. In Antioch as elsewhere, the Christians of the Middle East – Greeks, Armenians, Maronites, Jacobites – suffered a double oppression with the arrival of the Franj: their Western coreligionists suspected them of sympathy for the Saracens and treated them as subjects of inferior rank, while their Muslim compatriots often saw them as natural allies of the invaders. Indeed, the boundary between religious and national affiliation was practically non-existent. The same term, 'Rūm', was used to refer to both Byzantines and Syrians of the Greek confession, who in any event still saw themselves as subjects of the *basileus*. The word 'Armenian' referred to a church and a people alike, and when a Muslim spoke of 'the nation', *al-umma,* he was referring to the community of believers. In the mind of Yaghi-Siyān, the expulsion of the Christians was less an act of religious discrimination than a wartime measure against citizens of an enemy power, Constantinople, to which Antioch had long belonged and which had never renounced its intention of recovering the city.

Antioch was the last of the great cities of Arab Asia to have fallen under the domination of the Seljuk Turks: in 1084 it was still a dependency of Constantinople. Thirteen years later, when the Frankish knights laid siege to the town, Yaghi-Siyān was naturally convinced that this was part of an attempt to restore the authority of the Rūm, with the complicity of the local population, the majority of whom were Christians. Faced with this danger, the emir was not troubled by any scruples. He therefore expelled the *nazara,* the adepts of the Nazarethan (for this is what Christians were called), and then took personal charge of the rationing of grain, oil and honey, ordering daily inspections of the fortifications and severely punishing any negligence. Would that suffice? Nothing was certain. But these measures were designed to enable the city to hold out until reinforcements arrived. When would they come? The question was asked insistently by everyone in Antioch, and Yaghi-Siyān was no more able to give an answer than was the man in the street. Back in the summer, when the Franj were still far away, he had despatched his son to visit the various Muslim leaders of Syria to alert them to the danger stalking his town. Ibn al-Qalānisi tells us that in Damascus Yaghi-Siyān's son spoke of holy war. But in Syria in the eleventh century, *jihād* was no more than a slogan brandished by princes in distress. No emir would rush to another's aid unless he had some personal interest in doing so. Only then would he contemplate the invocation of great principles.

Now, in that autumn of 1097, the only leader who felt directly threatened by the Frankish invasion was Yaghi-Siyān himself. If the emperor's mercenaries wanted to recover Antioch, there was nothing unnatural about that, since the city had always been Byzantine. In any case, it was thought that the Rūm would go no further. And it was not necessarily bad for his neighbours if Yaghi-Siyān was in a spot of trouble. For ten years he had toyed with them, sowing discord, arousing jealousy, overturning alliances. Now he was asking them to put their quarrels aside and rush to his aid. Why should he be surprised if they failed to come at the run?

A realistic man, Yaghi-Siyān was well aware that he would be left to languish and forced to beg for help, that he would now have to pay for his past cleverness, intrigue and betrayal. But he never imagined that his coreligionists would go so far as to hand him over, bound hand and foot, to the mercenaries of the *basileus*. After all, he was merely struggling to survive in a merciless hornets' nest. Bloody conflict was relentless in the world in which he had grown up, the world of the Seljuk Turks, and the master of Antioch, like all the other emirs of the region, had no choice but to take his stand. If he wound up on the losing side, his fate would be death, or at least imprisonment and disgrace. If he was lucky enough to pick the winning side, he would savour his victory for a time, and receive several lovely female captives as a bonus, before once again finding himself embroiled in some new conflict in which his life was at stake. Survival in such a world depended above all on backing the right horse, and on not insisting on the same horse at all times. Any mistake was fatal, and rare indeed was the emir who died in bed.

At the time of the arrival of the Franj in Syria, political life was envenomed by the 'war of the two brothers', a conflict between two bizarre personalities who seemed to have stepped out of the imagination of some popular storyteller: Riḍwān, the king of Aleppo, and his younger brother Duqāq, king of Damascus. Their mutual hatred was so obstinate that nothing, not even a common threat to both of them, could induce them even to contemplate reconciliation. Riḍwān was barely more than twenty in 1097, but his personality was already shrouded in mystery, and the most terrifying legends about him were rife. Small, thin, of severe and sometimes frightening countenance, he is said (by Ibn al-Qalānisi) to have fallen under the influence of a 'physician-astrologer' who belonged to the order of Assassins, a recently formed sect that was to play an important part in political life throughout the Frankish occupation. The king of Aleppo was accused, not without reason, of making use of these fanatics to eliminate his opponents. By means of murder, impiety and witchcraft Riḍwān aroused the distrust of nearly everyone, but it was within his own family that he provoked the most bitter odium. When he acceded to the throne in 1095 he had two of his younger brothers strangled, fearing that they might one day contest his power. A third brother escaped with his life only by fleeing the citadel of Aleppo on the very night that the powerful hands of Riḍwān's slaves were supposed to close upon his throat. This survivor was Duqāq, who subsequently regarded his elder sibling with blind hatred. After his flight, he sought refuge in Damascus, whose garrison proclaimed him king. This impulsive young man – easily influenced, inclined to fits of anger, and of fragile health – was obsessed by the idea that his brother still sought to assassinate him. Caught between these two half-crazy princes, Yaghi-Siyān had no easy task. His closest neighbour was Riḍwān, whose capital Aleppo, one of the world's oldest cities, was less than three days' march from Antioch. Two years before the arrival of the Franj, Yaghi-Siyān had given Riḍwān his daughter in marriage. But he soon realised that his son-in-law coveted his kingdom, and he too began to fear for his life. Like Duqāq, Yaghi-Siyān was obsessed by fear of the Assassins sect. Since the common danger had naturally brought the two men closer together, it was to the king of Damascus that Yaghi-Siyān now turned as the Franj advanced on Antioch.

Duqāq, however, was hesitant. It was not that he was afraid of the Franj, he assured Yaghi-Siyān, but he had no desire to lead his army into the environs of Aleppo, thus affording his brother an opportunity to strike from behind. Knowing how difficult it would be to prod his ally into a decision, Yaghi-Siyān decided to send as emissary his son Shams al-Dawla – 'Sun of the State' – a brilliant, spirited and impassioned young man who stalked the royal palace relentlessly, harassing Duqāq and his advisers, resorting by turns to flattery and threat. But it was not until December 1097, two months after the start of the battle of Antioch, that the master of Damascus finally agreed, against his better judgement, to take his army north. Shams went along, for he knew that the full week the march would take gave Duqāq plenty of time to change his mind. And indeed, the young king grew increasingly nervous as he advanced. On 31 December, when the Damascene army had already covered two-thirds of its trajectory, they encountered a foraging Frankish troop. Despite his clear numerical advantage and the ease with which he managed to surround the enemy, Duqāq declined to issue the order to attack. This allowed the Franj to overcome their initial disorientation, recover their poise, and slip away. At the day's end there was neither victor nor vanquished, but the Damascenes had lost more men than their adversaries. No more was needed to discourage Duqāq, who immediately ordered his men to turn back, despite the desperate entreaties of Shams.

The defection of Duqāq aroused the greatest bitterness in Antioch, but the defenders did not give way. Curiously, in these early days of 1098, it was among the besiegers that disarray prevailed. Many of Yaghi-Siyān's spies had managed to infiltrate the enemy army. Some of these informants were acting out of hatred of the Rūm, but most were local Christians who hoped to win the emir's favour. They had left their families in Antioch and were now seeking to guarantee their security. The information they sent back encouraged the population: although the defenders in the besieged city had abundant supplies, the Franj were vulnerable to starvation. Hundreds had died already, and most of their mounts had been slaughtered for food. The expedition encountered by the Damascene army had been sent out to find some sheep and goats, and to pilfer some granaries. Hunger was compounded by other calamities that were daily undermining the invaders' morale. A relentless rain was falling, justifying the lighthearted nickname the Syrians had bestowed upon Antioch: 'the *pissoir*'. The besiegers' camp was mired in mud. Finally, there was the earth itself, which trembled constantly. The local people of the countryside were used to it, but the Franj were terrified. The sounds of their prayers reached into the city itself, as they gathered together to plead for divine mercy, believing themselves victims of celestial punishment. It was reported that they had decided to expel all prostitutes from their camp in an effort to placate the wrath of the Almighty; they also closed down the taverns and banned dice games. There were many desertions, even among their chiefs.

News such as this naturally bolstered the combative spirit of the defenders, who organised ever more daring sorties. As Ibn al-Athīr was to say, 'Yaghi-Siyān showed admirable courage, wisdom and resolution.' Carried away by his own enthusiasm, the Arab historian added: 'Most of the Franj perished. Had they remained as numerous as they had been upon their arrival, they would have occupied all the lands of Islam!' A gross exaggeration, but one that renders due homage to the heroism of the Antioch garrison, which had to bear the brunt of the invasion alone for many long months.

For aid continued to be withheld. In January 1098, embittered by Duqāq's inertia, Yaghi-Siyān was forced to turn to Riḍwān. Once again it was Shams al-Dawla who was charged with the painful mission of presenting the most humble excuses to the king of Aleppo, of listening unflinchingly to all his sarcastic cracks, and of begging him, in the name of Islam and ties of kinship, to deign to despatch his troops to save Antioch. Shams was well aware that his royal brother-in-law was not susceptible to this type of argument, and that he would sooner lop off his own hand than extend it to Yaghi-Siyān. But events themselves were even more compelling. The Franj, whose food situation was increasingly critical, had just raided the lands of the Seljuk king, pillaging and ravaging in the environs of Aleppo itself, and for the first time Riḍwān felt his own realm threatened. More to defend himself than to aid Antioch, he decided to send his army against the Franj. Shams was triumphant. He sent his father a message informing him of the date of the Aleppan offensive and asked him to organise a massive sortie to catch the besiegers in a pincer movement.

In Antioch, Riḍwān's intervention was so unexpected that it seemed heaven-sent. Would it be the turning point of this battle, which had already been raging for more than a hundred days?

Early in the afternoon of 9 February 1098 lookouts posted in the citadel reported the approach of the Aleppan army. It included several thousand cavalry, whereas the Franj could muster no more than seven or eight hundred, so severely had their mounts been decimated by famine. The besieged, who had been anxiously awaiting the Aleppans for several days now, wanted the battle to be joined at once. But Riḍwān's troops had halted and begun to pitch their tents, and battle-orders were postponed to the following day. Preparations continued throughout the night. Every soldier now knew exactly where and when he had to act. Yaghi-Siyān was confident that his own men would carry out their side of the bargain.

What no one knew was that the battle was lost even before it began. Terrified by what he knew about the fighting abilities of the Franj, Riḍwān dared not take advantage of his numerical superiority. Instead of deploying his troops, he sought only to protect them. To avoid any threat of encirclement, he had confined them all night to a narrow strip of land wedged between the Orontes river and Lake Antioch. At dawn, when the Franj attacked, the Aleppans may as well have been paralysed. The narrowness of the land denied them any mobility. Their mounts reared, and those horsemen who fell were trampled underfoot by their comrades before they could rise. Of course, there was no longer any question of applying the traditional tactics, sending successive waves of cavalry-archers against the enemy. Riḍwān's men were forced into hand-to-hand combat in which the heavily armoured knights easily gained an overwhelming advantage. It was carnage. The king and his army, now in indescribable disarray and pursued by the Franj, dreamed only of flight.

The battle unfolded differently under the walls of Antioch itself. At first light, the defenders launched a massive sortie that compelled the attackers to fall back. The fighting was intense, and the soldiers of Yaghi-Siyān were in an excellent position. Slightly before midday, they had begun to penetrate the camp of the Franj when news came in of the Aleppans' debacle. Sick at heart, the emir ordered his men to fall back to the city. Scarcely had they completed their retreat when the knights who had crushed Riḍwān returned, carrying macabre trophies from the battle. The inhabitants of Antioch soon heard great guffaws of laughter, followed by muffled whistles. Then the fearfully mutilated severed heads of the Aleppans, hurled by catapults, began to rain down. A deathly silence gripped the city.

Yaghi-Siyān offered words of encouragement to those closest to him, but for the first time he felt the vice tighten around his city. After the debacle of the two enemy brothers, he could expect nothing more from the princes of Syria. Just one recourse remained open to him: the governor of Mosul, the powerful emir Karbūqa, who had the disadvantage of being more than two weeks' march from Antioch.

Mosul, the native city of the historian Ibn al-Athīr, was the capital of Jazīra, or Mesopotamia, the fertile plain watered by the two great rivers Tigris and Euphrates. It was a political, cultural and economic centre of prime importance. The Arabs boasted of its succulent fruit: its apples, pears, grapes and pomegranates. The fine cloth it exported – called 'muslin', a word derived from the city's name – was known throughout the world. At the time of the arrival of the Franj, the people of the emir Karbūqa's realm were already exploiting another natural resource, which the traveller Ibn Jubayr was to describe with amazement a few dozen years later: deposits of naphtha. This precious dark liquid, which would one day make the fortune of this part of the world, already offered travellers an unforgettable spectacle.

> We approach a locality called al-Qayyara [the place of tar], near the Tigris. To the right of the road to Mosul is a depression in the earth, black as if it lay under a cloud. It is there that God causes the sources of pitch, great and small, to spurt forth. Sometimes one of them hurls up pieces, as though it were boiling. Bowls have been constructed in which the pitch is collected. Around these deposits lies a black pool; on its surface floats a light black foam which washes up on the banks and coagulates into bitumen. The product looks like a highly viscous, smooth, shiny mud, giving off a sharp odour. Thus were we able to see with our own eyes a marvel of which we had heard tell, the description of which had seemed quite extraordinary to us. Not far away, on the banks of the Tigris, is another great source; we could see its smoke rising from afar. We were told that when they want to extract the bitumen it is set on fire. The flame consumes the liquid elements. The bitumen is then cut into pieces and transported. It is known throughout these lands as far as Syria, in Acre and in all the coastal regions. Allah creates whatever he wills. Praise be upon him!

The inhabitants of Mosul attributed curative powers to the dark liquid, and immersed themselves in it when they were ill. Bitumen produced from oil was also used in construction, to 'cement' bricks together. Because it was impermeable, it was used as a coating for the walls of public baths, where its appearance was similar to polished black marble. But as we shall see, it was in the military domain that oil was most widely employed.

Apart from these promising resources, Mosul was of vital strategic importance at the start of the Frankish invasion; its rulers had acquired the right to inspect Syrian affairs, a right the ambitious Karbūqa intended to exercise. He considered Yaghi-Siyān's call for help a perfect opportunity to extend his own influence. He immediately promised to raise a great army. From that moment on, Antioch was on tenterhooks anticipating Karbūqa's arrival.

This providential figure was a former slave, a condition the Turkish emirs did not consider in any sense degrading. Indeed, the Seljuk princes used to appoint their most faithful and talented slaves to posts of responsibility. Army chiefs of staff and governors of cities were often ex-slaves, or *mamlūks*, and so great was their authority that it was not even necessary to manumit them. Before the Frankish occupation was complete, the entire Muslim Middle East would be ruled by Mamluk sultans. As early as 1098 the most influential men of Damascus, Cairo and several other major cities were slaves or sons of slaves.

Karbūqa was among the most powerful of these. This authoritarian officer with the greying beard bore the Turkish title of *atabeg*, literally 'father of the prince'. Members of the ruling families suffered a staggering mortality rate in the Seljuk empire – through battles, murders and executions – and rulers often left heirs who had not yet reached their majority. Tutors were assigned to protect the interests of these heirs, and to round out his role as adoptive father, a tutor generally married his pupil's mother. These *atabegs* naturally tended to become the real holders of power, which they often subsequently transmitted to their own sons. The legitimate prince then became no more than a puppet in the hands of the *atabeg*, sometimes even a hostage. Appearances were scrupulously respected, however. Armies were often officially 'commanded' by children of three or four years of age who had 'delegated' their power to the *atabeg*.

Just such a strange spectacle was seen in the last days of April 1098, as nearly thirty thousand men gathered to set out from Mosul. The official edict announced that the valiant fighters would be waging the *jihād* against the infidels under the orders of an obscure Seljuk scion who, presumably from the depths of his swaddling clothes, had entrusted command of the army to the *atabeg* Karbūqa.

According to the historian Ibn al-Athīr, who spent his entire life in the service of the *atabegs* of Mosul, 'the Franj were seized with fear when they heard that the army of Karbūqa was on its way to Antioch, for they were vastly weakened and their supplies were slender.' The defenders, on the contrary, took heart. Once again they prepared for a sortie to coincide with the approach of the Muslim troops. With the same tenacity as before, Yaghi-Siyān, ably seconded by his son Shams al-Dawla, checked the grain reserves, inspected the fortifications and encouraged the troops, promising them a rapid end to the siege, 'with God's permission'.

But his public self-assurance was a mere facade. The real situation had been worsening for several weeks. The blockade of the city had been tightened, it was more difficult to get supplies, and – this was even more worrying – information from the enemy camp was increasingly scanty. The Franj, who had apparently realised that their every word and deed was being reported to Yaghi-Siyān, had decided on drastic action to deal with the problem. The emir's agents had occasion to watch them kill a man, roast him on a spit, and eat his flesh, while shouting that any spy who was discovered would suffer a similar fate. The terrified informants fled, and Yaghi-Siyān no longer had detailed information about his besiegers. As a seasoned military man, he considered the situation highly disquieting.

He was reassured only by the knowledge that Karbūqa was on the way. He was expected by the middle of May, with his tens of thousands of fighters. Everyone in Antioch impatiently awaited that moment. Rumours circulated day after day, propagated by citizens who mistook their desires for reality. There would be a spate of whispering and a dash to the ramparts, maternal old women asking questions of callow soldiers. The answer was always the same: no, the rescuing troops were not in sight, but it would not be long now.

The great Muslim army was a dazzling sight as it marched out of Mosul, with countless lances glinting in the sun and black banners (emblem of the ʿAbbasids and the Seljuks) waving in a sea of white-robed cavalry. Despite the heat, the pace was brisk. The army would reach Antioch in less than two weeks if it maintained its rate of advance. But Karbūqa was troubled. Shortly before the army's departure, he had received some alarming news. A troop of Franj had taken Edessa, known to the Arabs as al-Ruhāʾ, a large Armenian city situated north of the route leading from Mosul to Antioch. The *atabeg* could not help wondering whether the Franj of Edessa might not advance behind him as he approached the besieged city. Was he not running the risk of being caught in a pincer movement? In the early days of May, he assembled his principal emirs to announce that he had decided to take a different route. He would first head north and settle the problem of Edessa in a few days; then he would be able to engage the besiegers of Antioch without risk. Some protested, reminding him of Yaghi-Siyān's anxious message. But Karbūqa silenced them. Once his decision was made, he was as stubborn as a mule. While his emirs grudgingly obeyed, the army headed for the mountain passes leading to Edessa.

The situation in the Armenian city was indeed worrying. The few Muslims who had been able to leave had brought news of strange events there. In February a Frankish chief by the name of Baldwin had arrived in command of hundreds of knights and more than two thousand foot soldiers. Thoros, an old Armenian prince and ruler of the city, had appealed to him to strengthen the city garrison against repeated attacks by Turkish warriors. But Baldwin refused to act as a mere mercenary. He demanded to be formally named the legitimate successor of Thoros. The latter, aged and childless, agreed. An official ceremony was held, in accordance with Armenian custom. Thoros dressed in a loose-fitting white robe, and Baldwin, naked to the waist, slipped under his 'father's' frock and pressed their bodies together. Then it was the turn of the 'mother', the wife of Thoros, against whom Baldwin now crept, between robe and naked flesh, before the amused regard of the onlookers, who whispered that this rite, conceived for the adoption of children, seemed somewhat inappropriate when the 'son' was a great hairy knight.

The soldiers of the Muslim army laughed loud and long as they pictured the scene that had just been described to them. But the sequel of the account chilled them. A few days after the ceremony, 'father' and 'mother' were lynched by a mob urged on by the 'son', who watched impassively as they were put to death and then proceeded to proclaim himself the 'count' of Edessa. He then appointed his Frankish companions to all the important posts in the army and the administration.

Hearing his worst fears confirmed, Karbūqa decided to organise a siege of the city. His emirs again sought to dissuade him. The three thousand Frankish soldiers in Edessa would not dare to attack the Muslim army, which numbered tens of thousands of men. On the other hand, they were quite sufficient to defend the city itself, and the siege might well drag on for months. In the meantime Yaghi-Siyān, abandoned to his fate, might give way to the pressure of the invaders. But the *atabeg* would not listen. Only after a futile three weeks under the walls of Edessa did he acknowledge his mistake and set out once more for Antioch, on a forced march.

Meanwhile, within the besieged city, the high hopes of early May had given way to utter disarray. In the palace and in the streets alike, no one could understand why the troops from Mosul were taking so long. Yaghi-Siyān was in despair.

The tension reached a paroxysm just before sunset on 2 June, when the lookouts reported that the Franj had assembled their forces and were heading north-east. The emirs and soldiers could think of only one explanation: Karbūqa was in the area, and the attackers were setting out to meet him. Within a few minutes, houses and ramparts had been alerted by word of mouth. The town breathed again. By sunrise, the *atabeg* would pry the city loose. The nightmare would finally end. It was a cool and humid evening. Long hours were spent discussing the situation on the doorsteps of darkened homes. Finally Antioch drifted off to sleep, exhausted but confident.

Then at four in the morning, from the southern rim of the city, came a dull sound of rope being dragged against stone. From the peak of a great five-sided tower a man leaned out and gestured. He had not slept all night, and his beard was dishevelled. His name was Fīrūz, 'a maker of armour in charge of the defence of the towers',

Ibn al-Athīr would later report. A Muslim of Armenian origin, Fīrūz had long been part of Yaghi-Siyān's entourage, but he had lately been accused of black-market trading, and Yaghi-Siyān had slapped a heavy fine on him. Fīrūz, seeking revenge, contacted the attackers. He told them that he controlled access to a window overlooking the valley south of the city, and declared that he was prepared to escort them in. Better still, to prove that he was not leading them into a trap, he sent them his own son as hostage. For their part, the attackers promised him gold and land. Thus the plot was hatched: it would be put into action at dawn on the third day of June. The night before, in order to mislead the garrison into relaxing its vigilance, the attackers would pretend to move away from the city.

> When agreement was reached between the Franj and this accursed maker of armour [Ibn al-Athīr writes] they climbed to that small window, opened it, and hauled up many men by means of ropes. When more than five hundred of them had ascended, they sounded the dawn trumpet, while the defenders were still exhausted from their long hours of wakefulness. Yaghi-Siyān awoke and asked what was happening. He was told that the sound of the trumpets was coming from the citadel, which had surely been taken.

The noise was actually coming from Two Sisters Tower. But Yaghi-Siyān did not bother to check. He thought that all was lost. Succumbing to his fear, he ordered that one of the city gates be opened and he fled, accompanied by several guards. He rode for hours, haggard and unable to recover his spirits. After two hundred days of resistance, the ruler of Antioch had finally broken down. While reproaching him for his weakness, Ibn al-Athīr evoked his death with emotion.

> He burst into tears at having abandoned his family, his sons and the Muslims, and, in great pain, he fell unconscious from his horse. His companions tried to put him back in the saddle, but he could no longer hold himself upright. He was dying. They left him and rode off. An Armenian woodcutter who happened to be passing by recognised him. He cut off his head and brought it to the Franj in Antioch.

The city itself was a scene of blood and fire. Men, women and children tried to flee through muddy alleyways, but the knights tracked them down easily and slaughtered them on the spot. The last survivors' cries of horror were gradually extinguished, soon to be replaced by the off-key singing of drunken Frankish plunderers. Smoke rose from the many burning houses. By midday, a veil of mourning enveloped the city.

Only one man was able to keep his head amidst the bloodthirsty lunacy of 3 June 1098: the indefatigable Shams al-Dawla. The moment the city was invaded, the son of Yaghi-Siyān had barricaded himself in the citadel with a small group of fighters. The Franj tried to dislodge them on several occasions, but were repulsed each time, not without suffering heavy losses. The greatest of the Frankish commanders, Bohemond, a gigantic man with long blond hair, was himself wounded in one of these attacks. Having learned something from his misadventure, he sent Shams a message proposing that he abandon the citadel in exchange for a guarantee of safe conduct. But the young emir haughtily refused. Antioch was the fief he had always meant to inherit, and he intended to fight for it to his dying breath. There was no shortage of supplies or sharp arrows. Enthroned majestically at the summit of Mount Ḥabīb al-Najjar, the citadel could resist the Franj for months. They would lose thousands of men if they insisted on scaling its walls.

The determination of these last defenders eventually paid off. The knights abandoned their attack on the citadel, and instead established a security zone around it. Then, three days after the fall of Antioch, Shams and his companions saw to their delight that Karbūqa's army had appeared on the horizon. For Shams and his handful of diehards, there was something unreal about the appearance of the cavalry of Islam. They rubbed their eyes, wept, prayed and embraced one another. The soldiers' cries of *Allāhu akbar*, 'God is great!', rose to the citadel in a continuous roar. The Franj dug in behind the walls of Antioch. The besiegers had become the besieged.

Shams's joy was tinged with bitterness, however. When the first emirs from the rescue expedition joined him in his redoubt, he bombarded them with a thousand questions. Why had they come so late?

Why had they given the Franj time to occupy Antioch and massacre its inhabitants? To his utter astonishment, the emirs, far from defending their army's tactics, denounced Karbūqa for all these evils: Karbūqa the arrogant, the pretentious, the inept, the coward.

This was not simply a matter of personal antipathy. It was a genuine conspiracy, and the ringleader was none other than King Duqāq of Damascus, who had joined the Mosul troops as soon as they crossed into Syrian territory. The Muslim army was decidedly not a homogeneous force, but a coalition of princes whose interests were often contradictory. No one was unaware of the territorial ambitions of the *atabeg*, and Duqāq had little trouble convincing his colleagues that their real enemy was Karbūqa himself. If he emerged victorious from the battle against the infidels, he would set himself up as a saviour, and no Syrian city would escape his rule. On the other hand, if Karbūqa was beaten, the danger to the Syrian cities would be lifted. Compared to that threat, the Frankish peril was a lesser evil. There was nothing alarming about the Rūm's desire to retake their city of Antioch with the aid of their mercenaries, for it was inconceivable that the Franj would create states of their own in Syria. As Ibn al-Athīr put it, 'the *atabeg* so annoyed the Muslims with his pretensions that they decided to betray him at the battle's most decisive moment.'

This superb army, then, was a colossus with feet of clay, ready to collapse at the first fillip. Shams, who was willing to forget the decision to abandon Antioch, still sought to overcome all this pettiness. He felt that it was not yet time for accounts to be settled. But his hopes were short-lived. The very day after his arrival, Karbūqa summoned Shams to inform him that he was to be deprived of his command of the citadel. Shams was indignant. Had he not fought bravely? Had he not held out against all the Frankish knights? Was he not the rightful heir of the ruler of Antioch? The *atabeg* refused to discuss the matter. He was in charge, and he demanded obedience.

The son of Yaghi-Siyān was now convinced that the Muslim army could not win the day, in spite of its imposing size. His only consolation was the knowledge that the situation in the enemy camp was scarcely any better. According to Ibn al-Athīr, 'after conquering Antioch, the Franj went without food for twelve days. The nobles devoured their mounts, the poor ate carrion and leaves.' The Franj had suffered famine before during past months, but on those occasions they had always been able to gather provisions by raiding the surrounding countryside. Their new status as a besieged army, however, deprived them of this possibility. And Yaghi-Siyān's food reserves, on which they had counted, were practically exhausted. Desertions were running at an alarming rate.

Providence seemed unable to decide which of these two exhausted and demoralised armies to favour during that June of 1098. But then an extraordinary event brought about a decision. The Occidentals cried miracle, but the account of Ibn al-Athīr contains no hint of the miraculous.

> Among the Franj was Bohemond, their commander-in-chief, but there was also an extremely wily monk who assured them that a lance of the Messiah, peace be upon him, was buried in the Kusyan, a great edifice of Antioch. He told them: 'If you find it, you will be victorious; otherwise, it means certain death.' He had earlier buried a lance in the soil of the Kusyan and erased all his tracks. He ordered the Franj to fast and to make penance for three days. On the fourth day, he had them enter the building with their valets and workers, who dug everywhere and found the lance. The monk then cried out, 'Rejoice, for victory is certain!' On the fifth day, they began exiting from the city gates in small groups of five or six. The Muslims said to Karbūqa, 'We should slip up to the gate and slaughter all who come out. It would be easy, for they are dispersed.' But he answered, 'No. Wait for all of them to leave, and we will kill them all, every last one.'

The calculation of the *atabeg* was less absurd than it may appear. With such indisciplined troops, and with his emirs waiting for the earliest excuse to desert him, he could not afford to prolong the siege. If the Franj were ready to join the battle, he did not want to frighten them with an excessively massive attack, which would threaten to drive them back into the city. What Karbūqa had failed to anticipate, however, was that his decision to temporise would be seized upon by those who sought his downfall. While the Franj continued their deployment, desertions began in the Muslim camp. There were accusations of treason and cowardice. Sensing that he was losing control of his troops and that he had probably underestimated the size of the besieged army as well, Karbūqa asked the Franj for a truce. This merely demolished the last of his prestige in the eyes of his own army and emboldened the enemy. The Franj charged without even responding to his offer, forcing Karbūqa in turn to unleash a wave of cavalry-archers upon them. But Duqāq and most of his emirs were already serenely withdrawing with their troops. Realising his mounting isolation, the *atabeg* ordered a general retreat, which immediately degenerated into a rout.

Thus did the powerful Muslim army disintegrate 'without a stroke of sword or lance, without the firing of a single arrow'. The Mosul historian was hardly exaggerating. 'The Franj themselves feared a trick,' he wrote, 'for there had not yet been any battle justifying such a flight. They therefore preferred not to pursue the Muslims.' Karbūqa was thus able to return to Mosul safe and sound, with the tatters of his troops. All his great ambitions vanished for ever before the walls of Antioch, and the city he had sworn to save was now firmly in the hands of the Franj. It would remain so for many a year.

Most serious of all was that after this day of shame, there was no longer any force in Syria capable of checking the invaders' advance.

III

The Cannibals of Maʿarra

'I know not whether my native land be a grazing ground for wild beasts or yet my home!' This cry of grief by an anonymous poet of Maʿarra was no mere figure of speech. Sadly, we must take his words literally, and ask with him: what monstrous thing came to pass in the Syrian city of Maʿarra late in that year of 1098?

Until the arrival of the Franj, the people of Maʿarra lived untroubled lives, shielded by their circular city walls. Their vineyards and their fields of olives and figs afforded them modest prosperity. The city's affairs were administered by worthy local notables devoid of any great ambition, under the nominal suzerainty of Riḍwān of Aleppo. Maʿarra's main claim to fame was that it was the home town of one of the great figures of Arab literature, Abu'l-ʿAlāʾ al-Maʿarri, who had died in 1057. This blind poet, a freethinker, had dared to attack the mores of his age, flouting its taboos. Indeed, it required a certain audacity to write lines like these:

> The inhabitants of the earth are of two sorts:
> Those with brains, but no religion,
> And those with religion, but no brains.

Forty years after his death, a fanaticism come from afar descended on this city and seemed to prove this son of Maʿarra right, not only in his irreligion, but also in his legendary pessimism:

> Fate smashes us as though we were made of glass,
> And never are our shards put together again.

His city was to be reduced to a heap of ruins, and the poet's oft-expressed mistrust of his compatriots would find its cruellest vindication.

During the first few months of 1098 the inhabitants of Maʿarra uneasily followed the battle of Antioch, which was taking place three days' march north-west of them. After their victory, the Franj raided several neighbouring villages, and although Maʿarra was spared, several of its families decided to abandon the town for more secure residences in Aleppo, Homs and Hama. Their fears proved justified when, towards the end of November, thousands of Frankish warriors arrived and surrounded the city. Although some citizens managed to flee despite the siege, most were trapped. Maʿarra had no army, only an urban militia, which several hundred young men lacking any military experience hastily joined. For two weeks they courageously resisted the redoubtable knights, going so far as to hurl packed beehives down on the besiegers from the city walls.

> To counter such tenacity [Ibn al-Athīr wrote] the Franj constructed a wooden turret as high as the ramparts. Some Muslims, fearful and demoralised, felt that a more effective defence was to barricade themselves within the city's tallest buildings. They therefore abandoned the walls, leaving the positions they had been holding undefended. Others followed their example, and another point of the surrounding wall was abandoned. Soon the entire perimeter of the town was without defenders. The Franj scaled the walls with ladders, and when the Muslims saw them atop the walls, they lost heart.

It was 11 December, a pitch-dark night, and the Franj did not yet dare to penetrate the town. The notables of Maʿarra made contact with Bohemond, the new master of Antioch, who was leading the attackers. The Frankish commander promised to spare the lives of the inhabitants if they would stop fighting and withdraw from certain buildings. Desperately placing their trust in his word, the families gathered in the houses and cellars of the city and waited all night in fear.

The Franj arrived at dawn. It was carnage. 'For three days they put people to the sword, killing more than a hundred thousand people and taking many prisoners.' Ibn al-Athīr's figures are obviously fantastic, for the city's population on the eve of its fall was probably less than ten thousand. But the horror lay less in the number of victims than in the barely imaginable fate that awaited them.

'In Maʿarra our troops boiled pagan adults in cooking-pots; they impaled children on spits and devoured them grilled.' The inhabitants of towns and villages near Maʿarra would never read this confession by the Frankish chronicler Radulph of Caen, but they would never forget what they had seen and heard. The memory of these atrocities, preserved and transmitted by local poets and oral tradition, shaped an image of the Franj that would not easily fade. The chronicler Usāmah Ibn Munqidh, born in the neighbouring city of Shayzar three years before these events, would one day write: 'All those who were well-informed about the Franj saw them as beasts superior in courage and fighting ardour but in nothing else, just as animals are superior in strength and aggression.'

This unkind assessment accurately reflects the impression made by the Franj upon their arrival in Syria: they aroused a mixture of fear and contempt, quite understandable on the part of an Arab nation which, while far superior in culture, had lost all combative spirit. The Turks would never forget the cannibalism of the Occidentals. Throughout their epic literature, the Franj are invariably described as anthropophagi.

Was this view of the Franj unjust? Did the Western invaders devour the inhabitants of the martyred city simply in order to survive? Their commanders said so in an official letter to the pope the following year: 'A terrible famine racked the army in Maʿarra, and placed it in the cruel necessity of feeding itself upon the bodies of the Saracens.' But the explanation seems unconvincing, for the inhabitants of the Maʿarra region witnessed behaviour during that sinister winter that could not be accounted for by hunger. They saw, for example, fanatical Franj, the Tafurs, roam through the countryside openly proclaiming that they would chew the flesh of the Saracens and gathering around their nocturnal campfires to devour their prey. Were they cannibals out of necessity? Or out of fanaticism? It all seems unreal, and yet the evidence is overwhelming, not only in the facts described, but also in the morbid atmosphere it reflects. In this respect, one sentence by the Frankish chronicler Albert of Aix, who took part in the battle of Maʿarra, remains unequalled in its horror: 'Not only did our troops not shrink from eating dead Turks and Saracens; they also ate dogs!'

The ordeal of the city of Abu'l-ʿAlāʾ ended only on 13 January 1099, when hundreds of torch-bearing Franj roamed through the alleyways setting every house alight. The city walls had already been demolished stone by stone.

The Maʿarra incident was to contribute to opening a chasm between the Arabs and the Franj that would not be bridged for centuries to come. For the moment, however, the populace was paralysed by terror and ceased to resist – unless forced to do so. When the invaders resumed their southward march, leaving nothing but smoking ruins in their wake, the Syrian emirs hastened to send them emissaries laden with gifts to assure them of their goodwill, and to offer them any assistance they might require.

The first to do this was Sultan Ibn Munqidh, the uncle of the chronicler Usāmah, who ruled the small emirate of Shayzar. The Franj reached his territory very soon after their departure from Maʿarra. At their head was Raymond of Saint-Gilles, one of the commanders most frequently mentioned in the Arab chronicles. The emir despatched an embassy to him, and an agreement was quickly concluded: not only would the sultan promise to supply the Franj with provisions, he would also authorise them to buy horses on the Shayzar market and would furnish them with guides to enable them to pass unhindered through the rest of Syria.

The entire region was now aware of the advance of the Franj; their itinerary was finally known. Did they not openly proclaim that their ultimate objective was Jerusalem, where they wanted to take possession of the tomb of Jesus? Everyone who lived along the route to the holy city sought to take precautions against the Frankish scourge. The poorest hid in neighbouring woods, haunted by big game: lions, wolves, bears and hyenas. Those who had the means headed for the interior of the country. Others took refuge in the nearest fortress, as did the peasants of the rich plain of Bukaya during the first week of January 1099, when they were told that the Frankish troops were near. Gathering their cattle and their reserves of oil and grain, they climbed towards Ḥiṣn al-Akrād, the 'citadel of the Kurds', which, from the summit of an almost impregnable peak, overlooked the entire plain as far as the Mediterranean. Although the fortress had long ago fallen into disuse, its walls were intact, and the peasants hoped to find shelter there. But the Franj, ever short of provisions, laid siege. On 28 January their warriors began to scale the walls of Ḥiṣn al-Akrād. Fearing that all was lost, the peasants devised a stratagem. They threw open the doors of the citadel, allowing part of their herd to escape. The Franj, forgetting the battle, hurled themselves after the animals. So great was the chaos in their ranks that the emboldened defenders made a sortie and attacked the tent of Saint-Gilles, where the Frankish commander, abandoned by his bodyguards (who wanted their share of the cattle too), barely escaped capture.

The peasants felt more than a little satisfaction at their exploit. But they knew that the attackers would return to seek revenge. The next day, when Saint-Gilles ordered his men to assault the walls once more, they did not show themselves. The assailants wondered what new trick the peasants had come up with. In fact, it was the wisest trick of all: they had taken advantage of the darkness of night to slip away noiselessly. It was at the site of Ḥiṣn al-Akrād, forty years later, that the Franj would construct one of their most formidable fortresses. The name would change but little: 'Akrād' was deformed first into 'Crat' and then into 'Crac'. The Crac des Chevaliers, with its imposing silhouette, still dominates the plain of Bukaya today.

For several days in February 1099 the citadel became the general headquarters of the Franj. A disconcerting scene unfolded there. Delegations arrived from all the neighbouring cities, and even from several villages, leading mules carrying gold, cloth and provisions. So complete was the political fragmentation of Syria that even the smallest hamlet acted as an independent emirate. Every town knew that in defending itself and dealing with the invaders it could rely only on its own forces. No prince, no notable, no *qāḍī*, could indulge in the slightest gesture of resistance without placing his entire community in danger. Patriotic sentiments were thus held in abeyance, and the local potentates arrived, with forced smiles, to present their gifts and to pay homage. 'Kiss any arm you cannot break,' a local proverb runs, 'and pray to God to break it.'

It was this wisdom of resignation that dictated the conduct of the emir Janah al-Dawla, ruler of the city of Homs. This warrior, famous for his valour, had been the most faithful ally of the *atabeg* Karbūqa only a scant seven months ago. Ibn al-Athīr, in fact, notes that 'Janah al-Dawla was the last to flee' at Antioch. But the time for bellicosity or religious zeal was long past, and the emir was particularly accommodating to Saint-Gilles, offering him, apart from the usual presents, a large number of horses, for as the ambassadors from Homs explained mawkishly, Janah al-Dawla had heard that the knights were short of mounts.

Of all the delegations that filed through the immense unfurnished rooms of Ḥiṣn al-Akrād, the most generous came from Tripoli. Presenting one by one the splendid precious stones cut by the city's Jewish artisans, Tripoli's ambassadors welcomed the Franj in the name of the most respected prince of the Syrian coast, the *qāḍī* Jalāl al-Mulk. He belonged to the family of the Banu ʿAmmār, which had made Tripoli the jewel of the Arab East. The Banu ʿAmmār were not one of those innumerable military clans that had carved out fiefdoms for themselves by sheer force of arms, but a dynasty of scholars; their founder was a magistrate, or *qāḍī*, a title the sovereigns of the city had conserved ever since.

Thanks to the wisdom of the *qāḍī*, at the time of the Franj advance Tripoli and its environs were enjoying an age of peace and prosperity that all their neighbours envied. The pride of the citizenry was the enormous Dār al-ʿIlm, or 'House of Culture', which included a library of some one hundred thousand volumes, one of the largest collections of the era. The city was ringed with fields of olives, carobs and sugar cane, and many kinds of fruit had been amassed in the recent abundant harvests. Its port was the scene of bustling activity.

It was this very opulence that led to the city's first problems with the invaders. In the message he sent to Ḥiṣn al-Akrād, Jalāl al-Mulk invited Saint-Gilles to send a delegation to Tripoli to negotiate an alliance. This was an unpardonable error. The Frankish emissaries were amazed at the gardens, the palace, the port and the goldsmiths' souk – so much so that they paid no attention to the proposals of the *qāḍī*. They were already dreaming of the rich spoils that would be theirs if they took this city. And it seems that once they had returned to their chief, they did their best to arouse his cupidity. Jalāl al-Mulk, who was naively awaiting Saint-Gilles's response to his offer of an alliance, was more than a little surprised to discover that on 14 February the Franj had laid siege to ʿArqa, second-largest city of the principality of Tripoli. Although naturally disappointed, his stronger emotion was terror, for he was convinced that this operation by the invaders was only the first step to the conquest of his capital. How could he help remembering the fate of Antioch? Jalāl al-Mulk already saw himself in the shoes of the hapless Yaghi-Siyān, hurtling shamefully towards death or oblivion. In Tripoli, provisions were being stockpiled in preparation for a long siege. The inhabitants wondered anxiously how much time the invaders would spend at ʿArqa. Every passing day was an unexpected reprieve.

February slipped by, then March and April. In that year, as every spring, Tripoli was enveloped by the scent of orchards in blossom. The city seemed especially beautiful, for the news was comforting: the Franj had still not managed to take ʿArqa, whose defenders found this no less astonishing than did the besiegers. The town's ramparts were no more solid than those of other, more important cities that the Franj had been able to seize. ʿArqa's real strength was that from the very first moment of the battle its inhabitants were convinced that if a single breach in the walls were opened, they would all be slaughtered like their brothers in Maʿarra and Antioch. They kept watch day and night, repelling attacks and preventing the slightest infiltration. The invaders finally got tired of it all. The clamour of their disputes reached into the besieged city itself. On 13 May 1099 they finally struck camp and slid away, hanging their heads. After three months of exhausting struggle, the tenacity of the resistance had been rewarded. ʿArqa rejoiced.

The Franj began their southward march anew. They passed by Tripoli at a disquietingly leisurely pace. Jalāl al-Mulk, well aware of their irritation, hastened to send them his best wishes for the continuation of their journey. He was careful to accompany his good wishes with foodstuffs, gold, a few horses, and guides who would lead them along the narrow coastal route to Beirut. The Tripolitanian scouts were joined by many Christian Maronites from Mount Lebanon who, like the Muslim emirs, offered to cooperate with the Western warriors.

Without further attacks on the possessions of the Banu ʿAmmār, such as Jubayl (ancient Byblos), the invaders reached Nahr al-Kalb, the river of the Dog.

By crossing that river, they placed themselves in a state of war with the Fatimid caliphate of Egypt.

The strong man of Cairo, the powerful and corpulent vizier al-Afḍal Shāhinshāh, had not concealed his satisfaction when, in April 1097, emissaries from Alexius Comnenus had informed him that a massive contingent of Frankish knights had arrived in Constantinople and were about to launch an offensive in Asia Minor. Al-Afḍal, 'the Best', a thirty-five-year-old former slave who was the sole ruler of an Egyptian nation of seven million, had sent the emperor his best wishes for success and asked to be kept informed, as a friend, of the progress of the expedition.

'Some say that when the masters of Egypt saw the expansion of the Seljuk empire, they took fright and asked the Franj to march on Syria and to establish a buffer between them and the Muslims. God alone knows the truth.' Ibn al-Athīr's singular explanation of the origin of the Frankish invasion says a great deal about the deep divisions in the Islamic world between the Sunnis, whose allegiance was to the Baghdad caliphate, and the Shiʿis, who recognised the Fatimid caliphate of Cairo. The schism, which dates back to a conflict within the Prophet's family during the seventh century, has always aroused bitter conflict among Muslims. Even men of state like Saladin considered the struggle against the Shiʿis as at least as important as the war against the Franj. 'Heretics' were regularly blamed for all the evils besetting Islam, and it is not surprising that the Frankish invasion itself should be attributed to their intrigues. Nevertheless, although the alleged Fatimid appeal to the Franj is pure fiction, the Cairene leaders' elation at the arrival of the Western warriors was undoubtedly real. The vizier al-Afḍal warmly congratulated the *basileus* upon the fall of Nicaea, and three months before the invaders took Antioch, an Egyptian delegation bearing gifts visited the camp of the Franj to wish them a speedy victory and to propose an alliance with them. The ruler of Cairo, a soldier of Armenian origin, had no sympathy for the Turks, and in this his personal sentiments squared with the interests of Egypt. Since the middle of the century, Seljuk advances had been eroding the territory of the Fatimid caliphate and the Byzantine empire alike. While the Rūm watched as Antioch and Asia Minor escaped their control, the Egyptians lost Damascus and Jerusalem, which had belonged to them for a century. A firm friendship developed between al-Afḍal and Alexius, and between Cairo and Constantinople. There were regular consultations and exchanges of information; common projects were elaborated. Shortly before the arrival of the Franj, Alexius and al-Afḍal observed with satisfaction that the Seljuk empire was being undermined by internal quarrels. In Asia Minor, as in Syria, many small rival states had been established. Had the time come to take revenge against the Turks? Would the Rūm and the Egyptians now both recover their lost possessions? Al-Afḍal dreamed of a concerted operation by the two allied powers, and when he learned that the *basileus* had received a large reinforcement of troops from the lands of the Franj, he felt that revenge was at hand.

The delegation he despatched to the besiegers of Antioch made no mention of a non-aggression pact. That much was obvious, thought the vizier. What he proposed to the Franj was a formal partition: northern Syria for the Franj; southern Syria (meaning Palestine, Damascus and the coastal cities as far north as Beirut) for him. Al-Afḍal was careful to present his offer at the earliest possible date, before the Franj were certain that they would be able to take Antioch. He was convinced that they would accept with alacrity.

Their answer had been curiously evasive, however. They asked for explanations and the clarification of details, in particular as to the future of Jerusalem. Although they treated the Egyptian diplomats amicably, even offering to show them the severed heads of three hundred Turks killed near Antioch, they refused to conclude any agreement. Al-Afḍal did not understand. Was his proposal not realistic, even generous? Could it be that the Rūm and their auxiliaries seriously intended to take Jerusalem, as his envoys suspected? Could Alexius have lied to him?

The strong man of Cairo was still uncertain what policy to adopt when, in June 1098, he received the news of the fall of Antioch, followed three weeks later by that of Karbūqa's humiliating defeat. The vizier then decided to take immediate action in an effort to take friend and foe alike by surprise. 'In July,' Ibn al-Qalānisi reports, 'it was announced that the generalissimo al-Afḍal, emir of the armies, had left Egypt at the head of a powerful army and had laid siege to Jerusalem, where the emirs Sokman and Ilghazi, sons of Artuk, resided. He attacked the city and erected mangonels.' The two Turkish brothers who administered Jerusalem had just arrived from the north, where they had participated in Karbūqa's ill-fated expedition. After a forty-day siege, the city capitulated. 'Al-Afḍal treated the two emirs generously, and set them and their entourage free.'

For several months, events seemed to prove the master of Cairo right. It seemed as though the Franj, now facing an accomplished fact, had given up any idea of pressing ahead. The poets of the Fatimid court outdid themselves in composing eulogies of the famous exploit of the man of state who had wrenched Palestine from the Sunni 'heretics'. But in January 1099, when the Franj relaunched their resolute march to the south, al-Afḍal became uneasy.

He despatched one of his confidants to Constantinople to consult Alexius, who responded, in a celebrated letter, with a stunning confession: the *basileus* no longer exercised the slightest control over the Franj. Incredible as it might seem, these people were acting on their own account, seeking to establish their own states, refusing to hand Antioch back to the empire, contrary to their sworn promises. They seemed determined to take Jerusalem by any means. The pope had summoned them to a holy war to take possession of the tomb of Christ, and nothing could deter them from their objective. Alexius added that for his part he disavowed their action and would strictly observe his alliance with Cairo.

Despite this latter assertion, al-Afḍal had the impression that he had been caught in a mortal trap. Being himself of Christian origin, he found it easy to understand that the Franj, whose faith was ardent and naive, might be determined to press their armed pilgrimage through to the end. He now regretted having thrown himself into this Palestinian adventure. Would it not have been better to let the Franj and the Turks fight for Jerusalem instead of having gratuitously interposed himself across the route of these knights, as courageous as they were fanatical?

Realising that it would take him several months to raise an army capable of confronting the Franj, he wrote to Alexius, imploring him to do all he could to slow the march of the invaders. In April 1099, during the siege of ʿArqa, the *basileus* sent the Franj a message asking that they postpone their departure for Palestine, saying – and this was his pretext – that he would soon be arriving in person to join them. For his part, the ruler of Cairo sent the Franj fresh proposals for an agreement. In addition to the partition of Syria, he now explained his policy on the holy city: freedom of worship was to be strictly respected, pilgrims were to be granted the right to visit whenever they desired, so long, of course, as they were unarmed and travelled in small groups. The response of the Franj was scathing: 'We will go all of us to Jerusalem, in combat formation, our lances raised!'

It was a declaration of war. On 19 May 1099, matching word and deed, the invaders unhesitatingly crossed Nahr al-Kalb, the northern limit of the Fatimid domain.

But the river of the Dog was a largely fictitious border, for al-Afḍal had done no more than reinforce the garrison in Jerusalem, abandoning the Egyptian possessions of the littoral to their fate. All the coastal cities, virtually without exception, hastened to reach some accommodation with the invader.

The first was Beirut, four hours' march from Nahr al-Kalb. Its inhabitants despatched a delegation to the knights, promising to supply them with gold, provisions and guides, if only they would respect the harvests of the surrounding plain. The Beirutis added that they would be prepared to recognise the authority of the Franj if they succeeded in taking Jerusalem. Saida, ancient Sidon, reacted differently. Its garrison effected several daring sorties against the invaders, who took their revenge by ravaging its orchards and pillaging nearby villages. That was to be the last act of resistance. The ports of Tyre and Acre, although they would have been easy to defend, followed the example of Beirut. In Palestine most towns and villages were evacuated by their inhabitants even before the Franj arrived. At no time did the invaders encounter any serious resistance, and on the morning of 7 June 1099 the inhabitants of Jerusalem saw them in the distance, on a hill, near the mosque of the prophet Samuel. They could almost hear the sounds of their march. By late afternoon the Franj were already camped at the walls of the city.

General Iftikhār al-Dawla, 'Pride of the State', who was commander of the Egyptian garrison, observed them with equanimity from atop the Tower of David. During the past several months he had made all the necessary arrangements to sustain a long siege. A section of the city walls damaged during al-Afḍal's attack on the Turks the previous summer had been repaired. Enormous stocks of provisions had been amassed to avert any threat of shortages while waiting for the vizier, who had promised to arrive by the end of July to lift the siege. The general had even prudently followed the example of Yaghi-Siyān and expelled the Christian inhabitants liable to collaborate with their Frankish coreligionists. During these past few days, he had poisoned water sources and wells in the environs of the city, to prevent the enemy from tapping them. Life would not be easy for those besieging the city under the June sky in this mountainous and arid landscape, with olive trees scattered here and there.

Iftikhār therefore felt that the battle would be joined in the best possible conditions. With his Arab cavalry and Sudanese archers solidly entrenched within the thick fortifications that crept up hills and dipped into ravines, he felt he would be able to hold the line. True enough, the Western knights were renowned for their bravery, but their behaviour before the walls of Jerusalem was somewhat disconcerting to an experienced officer. Iftikhār had expected that as soon as they arrived, they would begin constructing mobile towers and the various other instruments of siege, digging trenches to protect themselves against sorties by the city garrison. Far from making such arrangements, however, they had begun by organising a procession around the walls, led by bare-headed praying and chanting priests; they then threw themselves against the walls like madmen, without carrying even a single ladder. Al-Afḍal had told the general that these Franj wanted to seize the city for religious reasons, but such blind fanaticism nevertheless astonished him. He himself was a devoted Muslim, but if he was fighting in Palestine, it was to defend the interests of Egypt, and – why deny it – to advance his own military career.

He knew that this was a city unlike any other. Iftikhār had always called it by its common name, Īliyāʾ, but the *ʿulamāʾ* (the doctors of Muslim law) dubbed it al-Quds, Bait al-Maqdis or Bait al-Muqaddas – 'site of holiness'. They described it as the third holy city of Islam, after Mecca and Medina, for it was here that, one miraculous night, God led the Prophet to a meeting with Moses and Jesus, son of Mary. Since then, every Muslim had considered al-Quds the symbol of the continuity of the divine message. Many believers came to gather in al-Aqṣā mosque, under the enormous sparkling dome that dominates the squat houses of the city.

Although heaven seemed present at every street corner in this town, Iftikhār himself was quite down to earth. He believed that military techniques were always the same, whatever the city. These processions of singing Franj were irritating, but they did not worry him. It was only at the end of the second week of the siege that he began to feel uneasy, when the enemy enthusiastically set to work building two huge wooden towers. By the beginning of July they were already erect, ready to carry hundreds of fighters to the top of the ramparts. Their menacing silhouettes loomed ominously from the heart of the enemy camp.

Iftikhār had issued the strictest orders: if either of these contraptions made the slightest move towards the walls, it was to be inundated in a flood of arrows. If the tower managed to draw near nevertheless, Greek fire would be used, a mixture of oil and sulphur that was poured into jugs, set alight, and hurled at the attackers by catapult. When it spattered, the liquid caused fires that were not easily extinguished. With this formidable weapon Iftikhār's soldiers repelled several successive assaults during the second week of July, even though the besiegers, in an effort to protect themselves from the flames, had lined their mobile towers with freshly flayed animal skins soaked in vinegar. In the meantime, rumours were rife that al-Afḍal's arrival was imminent. The attackers, afraid of being trapped between the defenders and the arriving army, redoubled their efforts.

> Of the two mobile towers constructed by the Franj [Ibn al-Athīr writes] one was on the side of Zion, to the south, while the other was placed to the north. The Muslims managed to burn the first one, killing all those inside. But barely had they finished destroying it when a messenger arrived calling for help, for the city had been penetrated on the opposite side. In fact, it was taken from the north, one Friday morning, seven days before the end of Shaʿbān, in the year 492.

On that terrible day of July 1099, Iftikhār was ensconced in the Tower of David, an octagonal citadel whose foundations had been welded with lead. It was the strongest point of the system of defensive fortifications. He could have held out for a few more days, but he knew that the battle was lost. The Jewish quarter had been invaded, the streets were strewn with bodies, and fighting was already raging alongside the great mosque. He and his men would soon be completely surrounded. Nevertheless, he continued to fight. What else could he do? By afternoon, fighting had practically ceased in the centre of the city. The white banner of the Fatimids now waved only over the Tower of David.

Suddenly the Frankish attack was halted and a messenger approached. He was carrying an offer from Saint-Gilles, who proposed that the Egyptian general and his men be allowed to leave the city alive if they would surrender the tower to him. Iftikhār hesitated. The Franj had already broken their commitments more than once, and there was no indication that Saint-Gilles would now act in good faith. On the other hand, he was described as a white-haired sexagenarian respected by all, which suggested that his word could be trusted. In any event, Iftikhār was sure that Saint-Gilles would eventually have to negotiate with the garrison, since his wooden tower had been destroyed and all his attacks repelled. Indeed, he had been dithering on the walls since morning, while his colleagues, the other Frankish commanders, were already plundering the city and arguing about who would get which houses. Carefully weighing the pros and cons, Iftikhār finally announced that he was ready to yield, provided that Saint-Gilles would promise, on his honour, to guarantee his safety and that of all his men.

'The Franj kept their word,' Ibn al-Athīr notes conscientiously, 'and let them depart by night for the port of Ascalon, where they camped.' And then he adds: 'The population of the holy city was put to the sword, and the Franj spent a week massacring Muslims. They killed more than seventy thousand people in al-Aqṣā mosque.' Ibn al-Qalānisi, who never reported figures he could not verify, says only: 'Many people were killed. The Jews had gathered in their synagogue and the Franj burned them alive. They also destroyed the monuments of saints and the tomb of Abraham, may peace be upon him!'

Among the monuments sacked by the invaders was the mosque of ʿUmar, erected to the memory of the second successor of the Prophet, the caliph ʿUmar Ibn al-Khaṭṭāb, who had taken Jerusalem from the Rūm in February 638. The Arabs would later frequently invoke this event, to highlight the difference between their conduct and that of the Franj. ʿUmar had entered Jerusalem astride his famous white camel, and the Greek patriarch of the holy city came forward to meet him. The caliph first assured him that the lives and property of the city's inhabitants would be respected, and then asked the patriarch to take him to visit the Christian holy places. The time of Muslim prayer arrived while they were in the church of Qiyāma, the Holy Sepulchre, and ʿUmar asked his host if he could unroll his prayer mat. The patriarch invited ʿUmar to do so right where he stood but the caliph answered: 'If I do, the Muslims will want to appropriate this site, saying "ʿUmar prayed here." ' Then, carrying his prayer mat, he went and knelt outside. He was right, for it was on that very spot that the mosque that bore his name was constructed. The Frankish commanders, alas, lacked ʿUmar's magnanimity. They celebrated their triumph with an ineffable orgy of killing, and then savagely ravaged the city they claimed to venerate.

Not even their coreligionists were spared. One of the first measures taken by the Franj was to expel from the Church of the Holy Sepulchre all the priests of Oriental rites – Greeks, Georgians, Armenians, Copts and Syrians – who used to officiate jointly, in accordance with an old tradition respected by all previous conquerors. Dumbfounded by this degree of fanaticism, the dignitaries of the Oriental Christian communities decided to resist. They refused to tell the occupiers where they had hidden the True Cross, on which Christ died. In the minds of these men, religious devotion to the relic was compounded by patriotic pride. Indeed, were they not fellow citizens of the Nazarene? But the invaders were not impressed. They arrested the priests who had been entrusted with custody of the Cross and tortured them to make them reveal the secret. Thus did the Franj manage to forcibly deprive the Christians of the holy city wherein lay their most precious relics.

While the Occidentals were completing the massacre of a few hidden survivors and laying their hands on the riches of Jerusalem, the army raised by al-Afḍal was advancing slowly across Sinai. It reached Palestine twenty days after the tragedy. The vizier, who was personally in command, hesitated to march on the holy city directly. Although he had nearly thirty thousand men, he did not consider his position strong, for he lacked the *matériel* for a siege and was frightened by the determination shown by the Frankish knights. He therefore decided to camp with his troops in the environs of Ascalon and to despatch an embassy to Jerusalem to sound out the enemy's intentions. When they reached the occupied city, the Egyptian emissaries were led to a knight with long hair and a blond beard, a big man who was introduced to them as Godfrey of Bouillon, the new master of Jerusalem. It was to him that they delivered the vizier's message, which accused the Franj of having abused his good faith and proposed to negotiate some arrangement with them if they would promise to leave Palestine. The Occidentals' response was to assemble their forces and set out without delay on the route to Ascalon.

So rapid was their advance that they arrived near the Muslim camp before the scouts had even reported their presence. With the very first engagement, 'the Egyptian army gave way and fell back towards the port of Ascalon,' Ibn al-Qalānisi relates. 'Al-Afḍal also withdrew. The sabres of the Franj triumphed over the Muslims. Neither foot soldiers, nor volunteers, nor the people of the city were spared in the killing. About ten thousand souls perished, and the camp was sacked.'

It was probably several days after the Egyptian debacle that the group of refugees led by Abū Ṣaʿad al-Ḥarawi reached Baghdad. The *qāḍī* of Damascus was not yet aware that the Franj had just won another victory, but he knew that the invaders were now masters of Jerusalem, Antioch and Edessa, that they had beaten Kilij Arslan and Danishmend, that they had crossed all of Syria from north to south, massacring and pillaging at will and with impunity. He felt that his people and his faith had been scorned and humiliated, and he meant to raise such a great cry that the Muslims would finally awake. He would shake his brothers out of their torpor, provoke them, scandalise them.

On Friday 19 August 1099 he led his companions into the great mosque of Baghdad. In the afternoon, as the faithful were converging from all over the city to pray, he began eating ostentatiously, although it was Ramaḍān, the month of obligatory fasting. Within a few moments an angry crowd pressed around him, and soldiers approached to arrest him. But al-Ḥarawi then rose and calmly asked those surrounding him how it was that they could feel so indignant at the violation of the fast whereas the massacre of thousands of Muslims and the destruction of the holy places of Islam met with their complete indifference. Having thus silenced the crowd, he proceeded to describe in detail the evils that had overwhelmed Syria, *Bilād al-Sham*, and especially those that had just befallen Jerusalem. 'The refugees wept, and they made others weep,' Ibn al-Athīr writes.

Leaving the street, al-Ḥarawi carried the scandal into the palaces. 'I see that the supporters of the faith are weak!' he cried out in the *dīwān* of the prince of the faithful al-Mustaẓhir Billāh, a young, twenty-two year-old caliph. Light-skinned, with a short beard and round face, he was a jolly and easy-going sovereign, his outbursts of anger brief and his threats rarely carried out. At a time when cruelty seemed the prime attribute of leaders, this young Arab caliph boasted that he had never wronged anyone. 'He felt genuine joy when he was told that the people were content,' Ibn al-Athīr candidly noted. Sensitive, refined and of agreeable bearing, al-Mustaẓhir had a taste for the arts. He was especially interested in architecture, and personally supervised the construction of a wall ringing the entire quarter of his residence, the Ḥārim, situated east of Baghdad. In his ample spare time, he composed love poems: 'When I stretch out my hand to bid my beloved adieu, the ardour of my passion melts ice.'

Unfortunately for his subjects, 'this man of good will, to whom any act of tyranny was alien' (as al-Qalānisi described him), had no real power, although he was constantly surrounded by complex ceremonies of veneration and the chroniclers evoke his name with deference. The refugees of Jerusalem, who placed their hopes in him, seem to have forgotten that his authority extended no further than the walls of his own palace and that in any case politics bored him.

Nevertheless, he was the legatee of a glorious history. From 632 to 833, across the two centuries that followed the death of the Prophet, his predecessors the caliphs were the spiritual and temporal commanders of a vast empire which, at its apogee, stretched from the Indus river in the east to the Pyrenees in the west and even thrust towards the Rhône and Loire valleys. The ʿAbbasid dynasty, to which al-Mustaẓhir belonged, had made Baghdad the fabulous city of the Thousand and One Nights. At the beginning of the ninth century, during the reign of his ancestor Hārūn al-Rashīd, the caliphate had been the world's richest and most powerful state, its capital the centre of the planet's most advanced civilisation. It had a thousand physicians, an enormous free hospital, a regular postal service, several banks (some of which had branches as far afield as China), an excellent water-supply system, a comprehensive sewage system and a paper mill. Indeed, it was in Syria that the Occidentals, who until their arrival in the Orient used only parchment, learned the art of manufacturing paper from straw.

But in that bloodstained summer of 1099, when al-Ḥarawi came to tell the *dīwān* of al-Mustaẓhir about the fall of Jerusalem, this golden age was long gone. Ḥārūn al-Rashīd had died in 809. A quarter of a century later, his successors had lost all real power, Baghdad was half destroyed, and the empire had disintegrated. All that remained was the myth of an era of unity, grandeur and prosperity that would haunt the dreams of the Arabs for ever. Although the ʿAbbasids were to rule in name for another four centuries, they no longer actually governed. They were no more than hostages in the hands of their Turkish or Persian soldiers, who were able to make or break sovereigns at will, often resorting to murder in the process. To escape that fate, most of the caliphs renounced any political activity. Cloistered in their harems, they devoted themselves exclusively to the pleasures of existence, becoming poets or musicians and collecting graceful perfumed female slaves.

The prince of the faithful, who had long embodied the glory of the Arabs, now became the living symbol of their decay. Al-Mustaẓhir, from whom the Jerusalem refugees expected a miracle, was the very epitome of this race of idle caliphs. Even had he wanted to, he would have been incapable of going to the aid of the holy city, for his only army was a personal guard of several hundred eunuchs, both black and white. Not that there was any lack of soldiers in Baghdad. Thousands of them roamed the streets aimlessly, often drunk. To protect themselves against the consequent depredations, the citizens had taken to blocking access to the residential quarters every night, erecting heavy barriers of wood or iron.

Of course, this pestilence in uniform, whose systematic plunder had condemned the souks to ruin, did not obey the orders of al-Mustaẓhir. In fact, their commander barely spoke Arabic. For Baghdad, like all the cities of Muslim Asia, had fallen under the yoke of the Seljuk Turks forty years earlier. The strong man of the ʿAbbasid capital, the young sultan Barkiyaruq, a cousin of Kilij Arslan, was theoretically the suzerain of all the princes of the region. In reality, however, each province of the Seljuk empire was practically independent, and the members of the ruling family were wholly absorbed in their own dynastic quarrels.

In September 1099, when al-Ḥarawi left the ʿAbbasid capital, he had been unable even to meet Barkiyaruq, for the sultan was away in northern Persia, waging a campaign against his own brother Muḥammad. The struggle was going badly for Barkiyaruq, for in the middle of October Muḥammad managed to take Baghdad itself. But that did not bring this absurd conflict to an end. As the bemused Arabs watched, having given up any attempt to understand, the struggle took a decidedly burlesque turn. In January 1100 Muḥammad fled Baghdad in haste, and Barkiyaruq re-entered the city in triumph. But not for long, for in spring he lost it yet again, only to return in force in April 1101, after an absence of one year, to crush his brother. Once more his name was pronounced in the Friday sermon in the mosques of the capital, but in September the situation was again reversed. Defeated by a coalition of two of his brothers, Barkiyaruq seemed out of the battle for good. But no. Despite his defeat, he returned obstinately to Baghdad and took possession of it for several days, before being evicted once again in October. This absence, too, was brief, for in December an agreement restored the city to his authority. Control of Baghdad had changed hands eight times in thirty months: on average, the city had known a new master every hundred days. This while the Western invaders were consolidating their grip on the conquered territories. 'The sultans did not agree among themselves,' Ibn al-Athīr wrote in a masterpiece of understatement, 'and it was for this reason that the Franj were able to seize control of the country.'

Part Two

OCCUPATION (1100–28)

Every time the Franj took one fortress, they would attack another. Their power mounted relentlessly until they occupied all of Syria and exiled the Muslims of that country.

FAKHR AL-MULK IBN ʿAMMĀR
Ruler of Tripoli

IV

Tripoli's Two Thousand Days

After so many successive defeats, such great disappointment and humiliation, three pieces of unexpected news that reached Damascus in the summer of 1100 aroused considerable hope, not only among the religious militants now groaned around the *qāḍī* al-Ḥarawi, but also in the souks. Here, under the arcades of Law Street, seated in the shadows of the creeping vines, the merchants of raw silk, gilded brocades, damask linen and inlaid furniture passed the word from one booth to the next, over the heads of passers-by, excitedly hailing the coming of an auspicious day.

The first rumour, at the beginning of July, was soon confirmed: old Saint-Gilles, who had never concealed his designs on Tripoli, Homs and all of central Syria, had suddenly left for Constantinople after a dispute with the other Frankish commanders. The word was that he would never return.

A second piece of news, even more extraordinary, came at the end of July. In a matter of moments it spread from mosque to mosque, alleyway to alleyway. 'While he was besieging the city of Acre, Godfrey, ruler of Jerusalem, was struck by an arrow, which killed him,' Ibn al-Qalānisi relates. There was also talk that poisoned fruit had been offered to the Frankish chief by a Palestinian notable. Some believed that he had died a natural death in an epidemic. But it was the version reported by the Damascene chronicler that found favour with the public: Godfrey was believed to have fallen under the blows of the defenders of Acre. Did not such a victory, coming a year after the fall of Jerusalem, suggest that the tide was beginning to turn?

This impression seemed confirmed a few days later when it was learned that Bohemond, the most formidable of the Franj, had just been captured. It was Danishmend 'the Wise' who had bested him. Just as he had done three years earlier before the battle of Nicaea, the

Turkish chief had encircled the Armenian city of Malaṭya. 'Upon hearing the news,' says Ibn al-Qalānisi, 'Bohemond, king of the Franj and ruler of Antioch, assembled his men and marched out against the Muslim army.' A reckless undertaking it was too, for to reach the besieged city the Frankish commander had to ride for a week through mountainous countryside firmly in the hands of the Turks. Informed of his approach, Danishmend laid an ambush. Bohemond and the five hundred knights accompanying him were met with a barrage of arrows that rained down upon them in a pathway so narrow that they could not form up into ranks. 'God granted victory to the Muslims, who killed a great number of Franj. Bohemond and several of his companions were captured.' They were led in chains to Niksar, in northern Anatolia.

The successive elimination of Saint-Gilles, Godfrey and Bohemond, the three principal architects of the Frankish invasion, seemed to everyone a sign from heaven. Those who had been amazed by the apparent invincibility of the Occidentals took heart. Was it not the moment to deal them a decisive blow? One man, in any event, longed to do so, and that was Duqāq.

Let there be no mistake: the young king of Damascus was no zealous defender of Islam. Had he not amply demonstrated, during the battle of Antioch, that he was prepared to betray his own people to further his local ambitions? Moreover, it was not until the spring of 1100 that the Seljuk suddenly found it necessary to wage a holy war against the infidels. One of his vassals, a Bedouin chief from the Golan Heights, had complained of repeated incursions by Franj from Jerusalem, who were pillaging harvests and pilfering livestock, and Duqāq decided to intimidate them. One day in May, as Godfrey and his right-hand man Tancred, a nephew of Bohemond, were returning with their men from a particularly fruitful raid, they were attacked by the army of Damascus. Weighed down by their booty, the Franj were unable to fight back. Instead they fled, leaving several dead behind. Tancred himself barely escaped.

In revenge, he organised a reprisal raid on the outskirts of the Syrian metropolis itself. Orchards were devastated, villages plundered and burned. Taken unawares by the scope and rapidity of the riposte,

The Seljuk Turks, from Central Asia, whose nomadic horsemen sported 'long braided hair', united the Middle East under 'the authority of a single dynasty'

The early Arab army was composed almost entirely of light cavalry: they would attack the enemy with wave after wave of mounted archers, who would unleash a flood of arrows before retreating and giving way to a new group

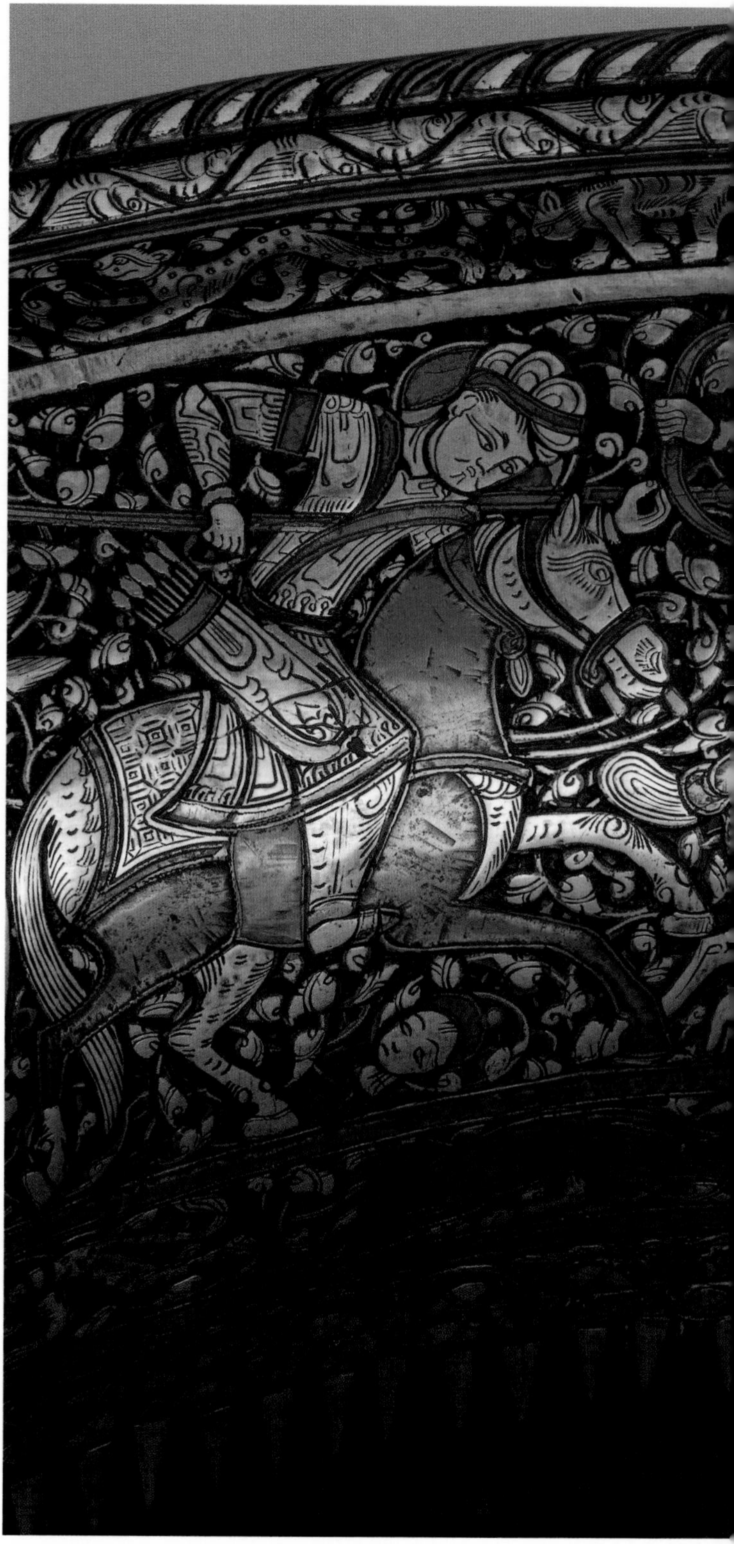

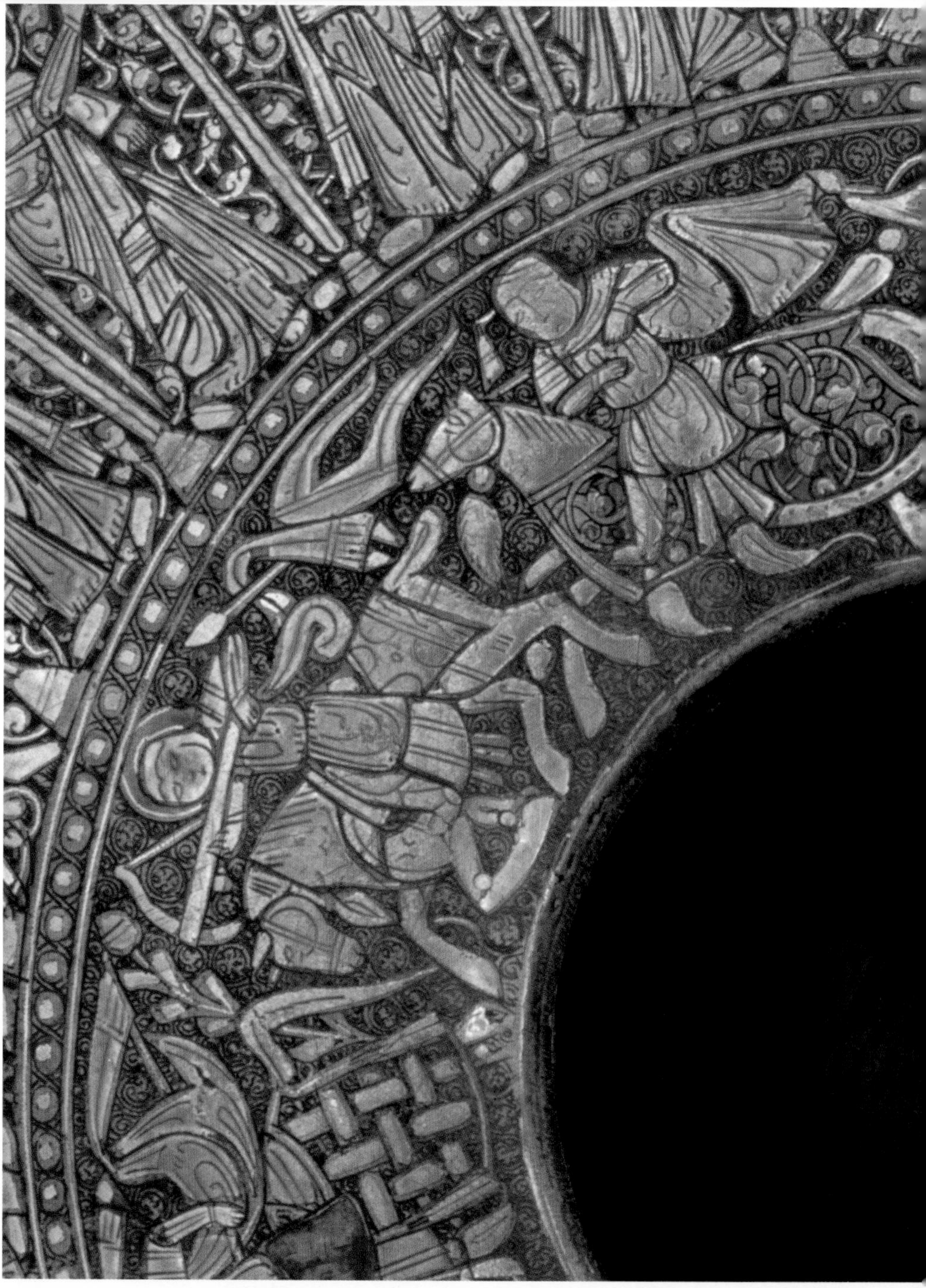

Detail of a group of warriors on horseback, from the reverse of the Freer Canteen. The Franj army, with its mastery of the art of defence, proved to be a formidable adversary to the lightly armoured Arab forces

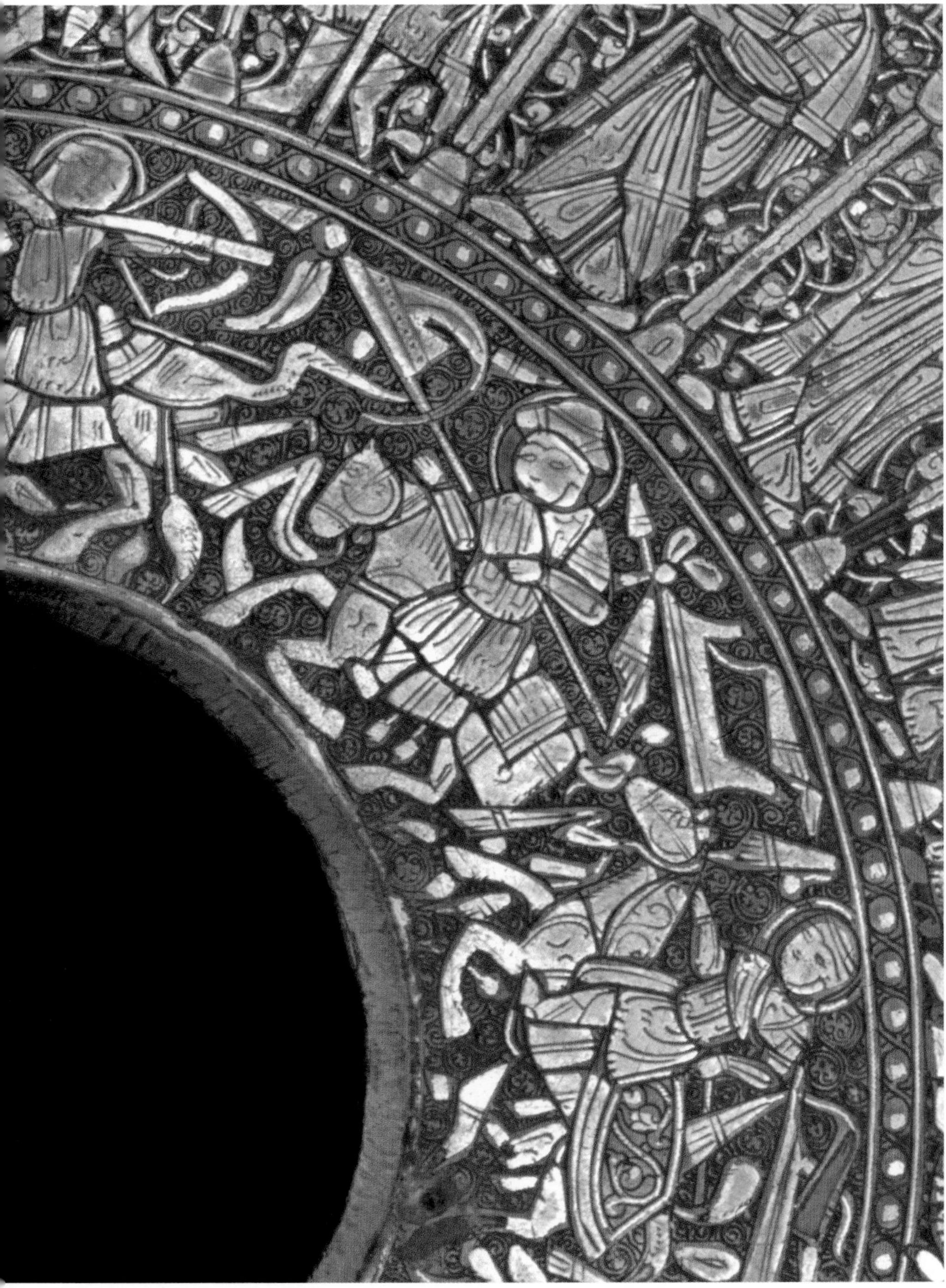

Arab warrior depicted on a pottery bowl, from thirteenth-century Aleppo. *Below,* the library in Basra. Libraries, including the Dār al-ʿIlm (House of Culture) at Tripoli, were the pride of the citizenry in an age that enjoyed both peace and prosperity

وَصِفَةُ الرَّجَّالَةِ الَّذِيَ مَتَ وَالتَّرَاسِيمُ بِالتَّبَابِيسِ الرَّتِّي

كَانَتِ الْمُلُوكُ مِنْ قَدِيمِ الزَّمَانِ مَا بَرَحُوا الْحَرْبَ إِلَّا بِالْحِيَلِ لِأَنَّ النَّبِيَّ صَلَّى اللهُ عَلَيْهِ وَسَلَّمَ قَالَ الْحَرْبُ خُدْعَةٌ فَاسْتُعْمِلَتْ ذَلِكَ إِلَى زَمَانِ هَلَاوُنْ فَاسْتَعْمَلَتْ أَهْلُ مِصْرَ

Warriors holding fire-propelling weapons: the mounted knight carries a lance to which gunpowder cartridges are attached, and all three are wearing fireproof clothing, with yet more cartridges. Explosives, such as Greek fire, a mixture of oil and sulphur, were used effectively by Iftikhār against the mobile towers of the Franj during the defence of al-Quds in July 1099

An *imām* preaching in a mosque. On 19 August 1099, Abū Ṣaʿad al-Ḥarawi, the *qāḍi* of Damascus, led his group of refugees into the great mosque of Baghdad, violated the Ramadan fast and announced the fall of Jerusalem

Duqāq did not dare intervene. With his customary versatility, and now bitterly regretting his Golan operation, he even proposed to pay Tancred a tidy sum if he would agree to withdraw his men. This offer only hardened the determination of the Frankish prince. Believing, quite logically, that the king was now at bay, he sent him a six-man delegation, which called upon him to convert to Christianity or hand over Damascus. Nothing less. Offended by the arrogance of this demand, the Seljuk ordered the arrest of the emissaries. Spluttering with rage, he in turn enjoined them to embrace Islam. One of them agreed. The other five were immediately beheaded.

As soon as he heard the news, Godfrey rushed to join Tancred. With all the men at their command, they threw themselves into ten days of systematic destruction of the environs of the Syrian metropolis. The rich plain of Ghūṭa, which 'rings Damascus as a halo rings the moon', as Ibn Jubayr put it, became a scene of desolation. Duqāq did not budge. Barricaded in his palace in Damascus, he waited for the storm to pass – especially since his Golan vassal had now rejected his suzerainty and would henceforth pay his annual tribute to the masters of Jerusalem. Even more serious, the people of the Syrian metropolis were beginning to complain about their leaders' inability to protect the city. They grumbled about all the Turkish soldiers who strutted like peacocks through the souks but disappeared the moment an enemy appeared at the city gates. Duqāq now had a single obsession: he wanted revenge, and as quickly as possible, if only to rehabilitate himself in the eyes of his own subjects.

In these circumstances, one may well imagine the Seljuk's immense joy at hearing of the death of Godfrey, although three months earlier he would hardly have cared less. The capture of Bohemond just a few days later emboldened him to undertake some spectacular action.

His opportunity came in October. 'When Godfrey was killed,' writes Ibn al-Qalānisi, 'his brother Count Baldwin, master of Edessa, set out for Jerusalem with five hundred knights and foot soldiers. At the news of his passage, Duqāq assembled his troops and marched out against him. He met him near the coastal locality of Beirut.' Baldwin was visibly striving to succeed Godfrey. He was a knight known for his brutality and lack of scruples, as the murder of his 'adoptive parents' in Edessa had shown. But he was also a courageous and crafty warrior whose presence in Jerusalem would constitute a permanent threat to Damascus and indeed to all of Muslim Syria. To kill or capture him at this critical moment would leave the invading army leaderless and challenge the very presence of the Franj in the Orient. If the date of the attack was well chosen, the site was no less ideal.

Baldwin was moving down from the north, along the Mediterranean coast, and was expected to reach Beirut around 24 October. Before that, he would have to cross Nahr al-Kalb, the old Fatimid frontier. Near the mouth of the river of the Dog the route narrowed, skirting cliffs and steep hills. An ideal spot for an ambush, it was here that Duqāq had decided to wait for the Franj, deploying his men in the grottoes and wooded slopes. His scouts supplied regular reports of the enemy's advance.

Nahr al-Kalb had been the bane of conquerors since remote antiquity. Whenever one of them managed to get through the pass unscathed, his pride would be such that he would chisel an account of his exploit into the walls of the cliff. Vestiges of several of these boasts could still be admired back in Duqāq's time, from the hieroglyphs of the pharaoh Ramses II and cuneiform characters of the Babylonian Nebuchadnezzar to the Latin eulogies that Septimius Severus, the Roman emperor of Syrian origin, had addressed to his valiant Gallic legionnaires. But apart from the handful of victors, how many warriors had seen their dreams shattered without trace on these rocks! The king of Damascus had no doubt whatever that 'the accursed Baldwin' would soon be added to that cohort of the vanquished. Duqāq had every reason for optimism. His troops outnumbered those of the Frankish commander by six or seven to one, and most important of all, the element of surprise was on his side. He would not only avenge the affront he had suffered, but would resume his pre-eminent place among the princes of Syria. Once again he would exercise the authority that had been undermined by the irruption of the Franj.

No one was more aware of the stakes of the battle than the new ruler of Tripoli, the *qāḍī* Fakhr al-Mulk, who had succeeded his brother Jalāl al-Mulk one year earlier. He had more than one reason to fear Baldwin's defeat, for the ruler of Damascus had coveted his city even before the arrival of the Occidentals, and if Duqāq was able to portray himself as the champion of Islam and the liberator of Syrian land, it would then be necessary to recognise his suzerainty and submit to his whims.

Fakhr al-Mulk was bothered by no scruples in seeking to avert this. When he learned that Baldwin was approaching Tripoli on his way to Beirut and then Jerusalem, he had wine, honey, bread and meat sent to him, as well as lavish gifts of gold and silver. He also despatched a messenger who insisted on seeing Baldwin in private and informed him of the ambush planned by Duqāq. He provided him with much detailed information about the disposition of the Damascene troops and offered him advice as to the best tactics for countering the ambush. The Frankish chief thanked the *qāḍī* for his collaboration, as precious as it was unexpected, and then set out again for Nahr al-Kalb.

The unsuspecting Duqāq was preparing to swoop down upon the Franj as soon as they had entered the narrow coastal strip that his archers were keeping in their sights. In fact, the Franj made their appearance on the side adjacent to the town of Jūnīya and advanced with apparent nonchalance. A few more steps and they would be caught in the trap. But suddenly they halted, and then slowly began to retreat. Nothing had yet been decided, but Duqāq was disconcerted when he saw the enemy avoid his trap. Harassed by his emirs, he finally ordered his archers to unleash a few salvoes of arrows, but without daring to send his cavalry against the Franj. As night fell, the morale of the Muslim troops sank. Arabs and Turks hurled mutual accusations of cowardice and scuffles broke out. The next morning, after a brief confrontation, the Damascene troops withdrew to the Lebanese mountains, while the Franj calmly continued on their way to Palestine.

The *qāḍī* of Tripoli had deliberately decided to save Baldwin, believing that the main threat to his city came from Duqāq, who had himself acted in just this way against Karbūqa two years before. At the decisive moment, each of them felt that the Frankish presence was the lesser evil. But the evil was to spread swiftly. Three weeks after the abortive ambush of Nahr al-Kalb, Baldwin proclaimed himself king of Jerusalem and initiated a programme of organisation and conquest designed to consolidate the gains of the invasion. Nearly a century later, when Ibn al-Athīr tried to comprehend what had induced the Franj to come to the East, he attributed the initiative to King Baldwin, 'al-Bardawīl', whom he considered a sort of commander of the Occident. He was not far wrong, for although this knight was only one of the many leaders responsible for the invasion, the Mosul historian was correct in calling him the principal architect of the occupation. Given the incorrigible fragmentation of the Arab world, the Frankish states – with their determination, warlike qualities and relative solidarity – appeared as a genuine regional power.

The Muslims nevertheless still held a powerful trump card: the extreme numerical weakness of their enemies. Most of the Franj had headed back to their own countries after the fall of Jerusalem. When he acceded to the throne, Baldwin could count on no more than several hundred knights. This apparent weakness was eliminated, however, when it was learned in the spring of 1101 that new Frankish armies far more numerous than any of those yet seen were being assembled in Constantinople.

The first to become alarmed were Kilij Arslan and Danishmend, who had not forgotten the previous passage of the Franj through Asia Minor. They immediately decided to unite their forces in an attempt to bar the route of the new invasion. The Turks no longer dared to venture into the vicinity of Nicaea and Dorylaeum, now firmly in the hands of the Rūm. They preferred to attempt a new ambush much further away, in south-eastern Anatolia. Kilij Arslan, who had gained in age and experience, had all the water sources poisoned along the route that had been taken by the previous expedition.

In May 1101 the sultan learned that nearly a hundred thousand men had crossed the Bosporus under the command of Saint-Gilles, who had been living in Byzantium for the past year. He tried to follow their movements step by step in order to decide when to surprise them. Their first port of call was thought to be Nicaea. But curiously, the scouts posted near the sultan's former capital saw no sign of their arrival. No news about them was heard from the Sea of Marmara, nor even from Constantinople. Kilij Arslan got word of them only at the end of June, when they suddenly appeared before the walls of another of his cities, Ankara, in the middle of Anatolia, right in Turkish territory, a place where no one had ever expected an attack. The Franj took the city even before Kilij Arslan could arrive. Kilij Arslan felt that he had been transported four years back in time, to the fall of Nicaea. But this was not the time for lamentation, for the Occidentals were now threatening the very heart of his domain. He decided to lay an ambush for them as soon as they left Ankara to resume their march south. This turned out to be a further mistake. Turning their backs on Syria, the invaders resolutely headed north-east, towards Niksar, the powerful citadel in which Danishmend was holding Bohemond. So that was it! The Franj were trying to rescue the former ruler of Antioch!

With disbelief, the sultan and his allies began to understand the curious itinerary of the invaders. In one sense they felt reassured, for they could now choose the site of the ambush. They settled on the village of Merzifun, which the Occidentals, stupefied by the leaden sun, reached early in August. Their army was hardly impressive. A few hundred knights advanced heavily, weighed down by their burning armour; behind them came a motley crowd including more women and children than genuine fighters. The Franj gave way as soon as the first wave of Turkish cavalry swooped down. It was not a battle, but a slaughter, which continued the entire day. As night fell, Saint-Gilles fled with his aides, without even informing the bulk of the army. The survivors were finished off the next day. Thousands of young women were captured and would stock the harems of Asia.

Barely was the Merzifun massacre over when messengers arrived to warn Kilij Arslan: a fresh Frankish expedition was already advancing through Asia Minor. This time there was nothing unusual about their itinerary. The warriors of the Cross had taken the southern route, and not until they had been on the road for several days did they realise their mistake. At the end of August, when the sultan arrived with his cavalry, the Franj were racked by thirst, already in their death agony. They were decimated without offering any resistance.

It was not over yet. Just one week later, a third Frankish expedition followed the second, along the same route. Knights, foot soldiers, women and children arrived, in a state of almost complete dehydration, near the city of Heraclea. When they glimpsed a glistening body of water, they hurled themselves towards it in complete disarray. Kilij Arslan was waiting for them on the banks.

The Franj never fully recovered from this triple massacre. Given their expansionist objectives during these decisive years, such a large number of new arrivals, whether combatants or not, would likely have enabled them to colonise the entire Arab East before the region had time to pull itself together. Yet it was precisely the shortage of men caused by their losses that was responsible for the most lasting and spectacular achievement of the Franj in Arab lands: the construction of fortresses. To mitigate their numerical weakness they built fortresses which were so well protected that a handful of defenders could hold off a multitude of attackers. Despite the handicap of numbers, however, for many years the Franj commanded a weapon even more formidable than their fortresses, and that was the torpor of the Arab world. There is no better illustration of this state of affairs than Ibn al-Athīr's description of the extraordinary battle that unfolded before Tripoli at the beginning of April 1102.

> Saint-Gilles, may God curse his name, returned to Syria after having been crushed by Kilij Arslan. He had only three hundred men left. Fakhr al-Mulk, the lord of Tripoli, sent word to King Duqāq and to the governor of Homs: 'Now is the time to finish off Saint-Gilles for ever, for he has so few troops!' Duqāq despatched two thousand men, and the governor of Homs came in person. The troops of Tripoli joined them before the gates of the city, and together they marched into battle against Saint-Gilles. The latter threw a hundred of his soldiers against the Tripolitanians, a hundred against the Damascenes, and fifty against the troops of Homs; he kept fifty behind with him. At the mere sight of the enemy, the troops of Homs fled, and the Damascenes soon followed. Only the Tripolitanians held their ground, and when he saw this, Saint-Gilles attacked them with his two hundred other soldiers, defeating them and killing seven thousand of them.

Three hundred Franj triumphing over several thousand Muslims? But the unlikely account of the Arab historian seems to match the facts. The most probable explanation is that Duqāq wanted to make the *qāḍī* of Tripoli pay for the attitude he had taken during the Nahr al-Kalb ambush. At that time, Fakhr al-Mulk's betrayal had prevented the elimination of the founder of the kingdom of Jerusalem. The revenge of the king of Damascus was to permit the creation of a fourth Frankish state: the county of Tripoli.

Six weeks after this humiliating defeat came a fresh demonstration of the negligence of the region's leaders, who despite their numerical superiority proved incapable of taking advantage of victory even on the occasions when they triumphed.

The scene unfolded in May 1102. An Egyptian army of nearly twenty thousand men, commanded by Sharaf, son of the vizier al-Afḍal, arrived in Palestine and managed to take Baldwin's troops by surprise in Ramlah, near the port of Jaffa. The king himself barely avoided capture by hiding flat on his stomach among the reeds. Most of his knights were killed or captured. The Cairene army could perfectly well have retaken Jerusalem that same day, for as Ibn al-Athīr would later note, the town was undefended and the Frankish king in flight. 'Some of Sharaf's men said to him: "Let us take the holy city!" Others said: "Let us instead take Jaffa!" Sharaf could not make up his mind. While he hesitated, the Franj received reinforcements by sea, and Sharaf had to return to his father's home in Egypt.'

Realising that he had come within a hair's breadth of victory, the ruler of Cairo decided to launch a fresh offensive the following year, and another the year after that. But some unforeseen event robbed him of victory at each attempt. On one occasion the Egyptian fleet fell out with the land army. On another, the commander of the expedition was accidentally killed, and his death sowed disarray among the troops. He was a courageous general, but very superstitious, Ibn al-Athīr tells us. 'It had been predicted that he would die as the result of a fall from his horse, and when he was named governor of Beirut, he ordered all paving-stones removed from the streets, for fear that his mount might stumble. But prudence is no protection against fate.' During the battle, his horse reared without having been attacked, and the general fell dead among his troops.

Bad luck, want of imagination, lack of courage: every one of al-Afḍal's successive expeditions ended unhappily. In the meantime, the Franj were steadily continuing their conquest of Palestine.

In May 1104, after taking Haifa and Jaffa, they attacked the port of Acre, whose well-protected natural harbour made it the only place where ships could moor winter and summer alike. 'Despairing of receiving any assistance, the Egyptian king asked that his life and those of the people of the city be saved,' writes Ibn al-Qalānisi. Baldwin promised that they would not be harmed. But the moment the Muslims exited from the city carrying their property, the Franj attacked, plundering them and killing many. Al-Afḍal swore that he would redress this new humiliation. He sent powerful armies against the Franj year after year, but each one met with some fresh disaster. The lost opportunity of Ramlah in May 1102 was never again on offer.

The negligence of the Muslim emirs also saved the Franj from annihilation in the north. The principality that Bohemond had founded in Antioch remained leaderless (and practically without an army) for seven months after his capture in August 1100, but none of the neighbouring monarchs – neither Riḍwān, nor Kilij Arslan, nor Danishmend – dreamed of taking advantage of the situation. They allowed the Franj the time to select a new regent for Antioch, Bohemond's nephew Tancred as it happened. He took possession of his fiefdom in March 1102, and in an effort to assert his presence, set to ravaging the environs of Aleppo as he had those of Damascus the year before. Riḍwān's reaction was even more cowardly than that of his brother Duqāq. He sent word to Tancred that he was prepared to satisfy his every whim if he would only leave him in peace. More arrogant than ever, the Franj demanded that an enormous cross be placed on the minaret of the great mosque at Aleppo. Riḍwān did so. It was a humiliation which, as we shall see, was not without sequel.

In the spring of 1103 Danishmend, who was by no means unaware of Bohemond's ambitions, nevertheless decided to release him without any political recompense. 'He demanded of him a ransom of 100,000 dinars and the release of the daughter of Yaghi-Siyān, the former master of Antioch, who was then being held captive.' Ibn al-Athīr was scandalised. 'Once out of prison, Bohemond returned to Antioch. His people took heart, and before long he had recovered the ransom from the people of the neighbouring towns. Thus did the Muslims suffer such harm as caused them to forget the boon of the capture of Bohemond.'

After thus 'reimbursing' himself at the expense of the local population, the Frankish prince set about enlarging his domain. In the spring of 1104 a joint operation by the Franj of Antioch and Edessa was launched against the stronghold of Ḥarrān, which overlooks the vast plain stretching to the edge of the Euphrates and in practice controls communications between Iraq and northern Syria.

The city itself was of no great interest. Ibn Jubayr, who visited it several years after these events, described it in particularly depressing terms. 'Water is never cool in Ḥarrān; intense heat, like a furnace, scorches its territory relentlessly. Here one finds no shaded corner for a siesta; one breathes in oppressive gasps. Ḥarrān gives the impression of having been abandoned on the bare plain. It lacks the brilliance of a city, and no trace of elegance adorns its environs.'

Its strategic value was considerable, however. If the Franj took Ḥarrān, they would be able to advance towards Mosul and even Baghdad itself. In the short run, its fall would mean the encirclement of the kingdom of Aleppo. Admittedly, these were ambitious objectives, but the invaders did not lack daring – especially since the divisions of the Arab world encouraged their undertakings. The murderous struggle between the two enemy brothers Barkiyaruq and Muḥammad was once more in full swing, Baghdad passing from one Seljuk sultan to the other. In Mosul the *atabeg* Karbūqa had just died, and his successor, the Turkish emir Jekermish, had not yet managed to assert his authority.

The situation was chaotic in Ḥarrān itself. The governor had been assassinated by one of his officers during a bout of heavy drinking, and the city was mired in blood and fire. 'It was then that the Franj marched on Ḥarrān,' Ibn al-Athīr explains. When Jekermish, the new ruler of Mosul, and his neighbour Sokman, the former governor of Jerusalem, learned of this, they were at war with each other.

> Sokman was trying to avenge one of his nephews who had been killed by Jekermish, and both were preparing for the confrontation. But in the face of this new event, they called upon each other to unite their forces to save the situation in Ḥarrān, each stating his willingness to offer his life to God and to seek only the glory of the Almighty. They united, sealed their alliance, and set out against the Franj, Sokman with seven thousand horsemen and Jekermish with three thousand.

The two allies met the enemy in May 1104 on the banks of the river Balīkh, a tributary of the Euphrates. The Muslims pretended to flee, allowing the Franj to pursue them for more than an hour. Then, on a signal from their emirs, they spun around, encircling their pursuers and cutting them to pieces.

> Bohemond and Tancred split away from the bulk of their troops and hid behind a hill, from which they hoped to assault the Muslims from behind. But when they saw that their troops were defeated, they decided to stay where they were. They waited there until nightfall and then fled, pursued by the Muslims, who killed and captured a good number of their companions. They themselves escaped, along with six knights.

Among the Frankish chiefs participating in the battle of Ḥarrān was Baldwin II, a cousin of the king of Jerusalem who had succeeded him at the head of the county of Edessa. He, too, tried to flee, but his mount slipped in the mud while he was fording the Balīkh. The soldiers of Sokman took him prisoner and led him to the tent of their master. According to the account of Ibn al-Athīr, this aroused the jealousy of their allies.

> Jekermish's men said to him: 'What will we look like if the others take all the booty and we sit here empty-handed?' And they persuaded him to seek out the count in Sokman's tent. When the latter returned, he seemed deeply moved. His companions were already in the saddle, prepared for battle, but he restrained them, saying: 'The joy our victory has aroused among the Muslims must not be spoiled by our dispute. I do not want to soothe my anger by granting satisfaction to the enemy at

the expense of the Muslims.' He then assembled all the weapons and banners he had taken from the Franj, dressed his men in their clothing, ordered them to mount up, and then headed for the fortresses held by the Franj. It was their custom, whenever they saw their companions returning victorious, to rush out to meet them. They did so this time too, and Sokman massacred them and seized the fortress. He repeated this stratagem in several places.

The victory of Ḥarrān had profound repercussions, as Ibn al-Qalānisi's unusually enthusiastic tone testifies.

For the Muslims it was an unequalled triumph. The morale of the Franj was deeply affected, their numbers were reduced, their offensive capacity undermined, and their arsenal depleted. The morale of the Muslims rose, their ardour in defence of their religion was enhanced. People congratulated one another on this victory, feeling certain that success had forsaken the Franj.

One Franj – and not one of the less important either – was indeed demoralised by his defeat, and that was Bohemond. A few months later he sailed away, never again to set foot on Arab land.

The battle of Ḥarrān thus removed from the scene the invasion's principal architect, this time for good. More important, it halted the Franj drive to the east for ever. The victors, however, like the Egyptians in 1102, proved unable to reap the fruit of their success. Instead of advancing together against Edessa, only two days' march from the battlefield, they separated in a fresh outbreak of their dispute. Although Sokman's trick had enabled him to seize a few relatively unimportant fortresses, Jekermish was soon taken by surprise by Tancred, who managed to capture several leading members of his entourage. Among them was a young princess of rare beauty; the ruler of Mosul was so enamoured of her that he sent word to Bohemond and Tancred that he was prepared either to exchange her for Baldwin II of Edessa or to buy her back for 15,000 gold dinars. Uncle and nephew consulted and then informed Jekermish that, on balance, they preferred to take the money and to leave their companion in captivity – where he remained for another three years. It is not known how the emir felt about this less than chivalrous response from the Frankish chiefs. He nevertheless paid them the agreed sum, recovered his princess, and kept Baldwin.

But the affair was not over yet. Indeed, it was ultimately to give rise to one of the most curious episodes of the Frankish wars.

The scene occurred four years later, at the beginning of October 1108, in a field of plum trees where the last of the dark fruit was ripening. The surrounding lightly wooded hills seemed to stretch out endlessly. On one of them rose the majestic ramparts of Tel Bāshir, alongside which the two opposing armies offered an unusual spectacle.

In one camp stood Tancred of Antioch, ringed by fifteen hundred Frankish knights and foot soldiers wearing *cervellières* that covered head and nose, firmly gripping their swords, maces and sharpened battleaxes. Alongside them stood six hundred long-haired Turkish cavalry sent from Aleppo by Riḍwān.

In the other camp stood Jawali, the emir of Mosul, his coat of mail covered by a flowing robe with brocade sleeves. His army was composed of two thousand men divided into three battalions: Arabs on the left, Turks on the right, and in the centre Frankish knights, among them Baldwin of Edessa and his cousin Joscelin, master of Tel Bāshir.

Could the participants in the titanic battle of Antioch possibly have believed that, a mere ten years later, a governor of Mosul, successor of the *atabeg* Karbūqa, would make an alliance with a Frankish count of Edessa and that the two would fight side by side against a coalition made up of a Frankish prince of Antioch and the Seljuk king of Aleppo? It had decidedly not taken the Franj long to become full partners in the murderous game of the Muslim petty kings. The chroniclers do not seem in the least astonished. The hint of an amused grin may just be detected in Ibn al-Athīr, but he mentions the quarrels and alliances of the Franj without any change in tone, just as he speaks, throughout his *Perfect History*, of the innumerable conflicts among the Muslim princes. The Arab historian explains that while Baldwin was being held prisoner in Mosul, Tancred took Edessa, which suggests that he was not all that eager for his companion to recover his freedom. In fact, he had intrigued with Jekermish to have him held as long as possible.

In 1107, however, this emir was overthrown, and the count now fell into the hands of the new master of Mosul, Jawali, a Turkish adventurer of remarkable intelligence, who immediately understood the advantage he could draw from the dispute between the two Frankish chiefs. He therefore freed Baldwin, offered him vestments of honour, and concluded an alliance with him. 'Your Edessa fiefdom is threatened,' he told him in substance, 'and my position in Mosul is scarcely secure. Let us aid one another.'

> As soon as he was released [Ibn al-Athīr relates] Count Baldwin ('al-Comes Bardawīl') went to see 'Tankri' in Antioch and asked him to restore Edessa to him. Tancred offered him 30,000 dinars, horses, arms, clothing and many other things, but refused to restore the city to him. When Baldwin left Antioch, in a fury, Tancred tried to follow him to prevent him from uniting with his ally Jawali. There were a number of clashes between them, but after each battle they came together again to eat and chat!

These Franj are crazy, the Mosul historian seems to be saying. And he continues:

> Since they had not succeeded in settling this problem, an attempt at mediation was made by the patriarch, who is a sort of *imām* for them. He appointed a commission of bishops and priests, who testified that before returning to his home country, Bohemond, the uncle of Tancred, had advised Tancred to restore Edessa to Baldwin if he were released from captivity. The master of Antioch accepted the arbitration and the count again took possession of his domain.

Believing that his victory was due less to Tancred's goodwill than to his fear of intervention by Jawali, Baldwin quickly released all the Muslim prisoners in his territory, going so far as to execute one of his Christian functionaries, who had publicly insulted Islam.

Tancred was not the only leader exasperated by the curious alliance between the count and the emir. King Riḍwān of Aleppo wrote to the master of Antioch to warn him against the ambitions and perfidy of Jawali. He told him that the emir coveted Aleppo, and that if he succeeded in taking it, the Franj would be unable to maintain their positions in Syria. The Seljuk king's concern for the security of the Franj seems somewhat ludicrous, but among princes understanding is always possible, regardless of religious or cultural barriers. A new Islamo-Frankish coalition was therefore formed to counter the earlier one. Thus it was that in October 1108 these two armies stood opposite one another near the ramparts of Tel Bāshir.

The men of Antioch and Aleppo soon gained the advantage. 'Jawali fled, and a large number of Muslims sought refuge in Tel Bāshir, where Baldwin and his cousin Joscelin treated them with kindness; they cared for the wounded, gave them clothing, and led them home.' The Arab historian's tribute to Baldwin's chivalrous spirit stands in sharp contrast to the opinion the Christian inhabitants of Edessa had formed of the count. Upon learning that he had been defeated, and presumably believing him dead, the Armenians of the city thought that the time had come to rid themselves of Frankish domination. On his return, Baldwin found the city being administered by a kind of commune. Uneasy at his subjects' desire for independence, he had the principal notables arrested, among them several priests, and ordered their eyes put out.

His ally Jawali would dearly have liked to take similar action against the notables of Mosul, who had likewise taken advantage of his absence to revolt. But he had to forgo the urge, for his defeat had discredited him too thoroughly. His subsequent fate was unenviable. He lost his fief, his army and his treasure, and the sultan Muḥammad put a price on his head. But Jawali did not admit defeat. He disguised himself as a merchant, travelled to the palace of Isfahan, and threw himself suddenly and humbly before the throne of the sultan, holding his own shroud in his hands. Muḥammad was touched, and agreed to pardon him. Some time later, he named him governor of a province in Persia.

As for Tancred, his victory of 1108 brought him to the apogee of his glory. The principality of Antioch became a regional power feared by all its neighbours, be they Turk, Arab, Armenian or Frank. King Riḍwān was now no more than a cringing vassal. The nephew of Bohemond dubbed himself 'the grand emir'!

Just a few weeks after the battle of Tel Bāshir, which sanctioned the presence of the Franj in northern Syria, it was the turn of the kingdom of Damascus to sign an armistice with Jerusalem. Under the terms of the agreement, the revenue from the agricultural lands lying between the two capitals would be split in three, 'one-third for the Turks, one-third for the Franj, and one-third for the peasants', notes Ibn al-Qalānisi. 'A protocol was drafted on that basis.' Several months later, the Syrian metropolis signed a new treaty acknowledging the loss of an even more important zone: the rich plain of Bekaa, east of the Lebanese mountains, was in turn divided with the kingdom of Jerusalem. In fact, the Damascenes were reduced to impotence. Their harvests were at the mercy of the Franj, and their trade passed through the port of Acre, now ruled by Genoese merchants. In southern and northern Syria alike, the Frankish occupation was a daily reality.

But the Franj did not stop there. In 1108 they stood on the eve of the most sweeping territorial expansion they had attempted since the fall of Jerusalem. All the great coastal cities were threatened, and the local potentates had neither the strength nor the will to defend them.

The initial target was Tripoli. Saint-Gilles had camped on the outskirts of the city back in 1103, and had ordered the construction of a fortress which the citizens still knew by his name. The well-preserved 'Qalʿat Saint-Gilles' is still visible in the twentieth century, in the centre of the modern city of Tripoli. At the time of the arrival of the Franj, however, the city extended no further than the Mināʾ quarter, the port, which lay at the end of a peninsula access to which was controlled by this famous fortress. No caravan could reach or leave Tripoli without being intercepted by Saint-Gilles's men.

The *qāḍī* Fakhr al-Mulk wanted at all costs to destroy this citadel, which threatened to strangle his capital. Night after night his soldiers attempted daring raids, stabbing a guard or damaging a wall under construction, but it was in September 1104 that the most spectacular operation was mounted. The entire garrison of Tripoli effected a sortie en masse, led by the *qāḍī* himself. Several Frankish warriors were massacred and a wing of the fortress was burned. Saint-Gilles himself was caught by surprise atop one of the flaming roofs. Suffering from severe burns, he died five months later, in terrible agony. As he lay dying, he asked to see emissaries from Fakhr al-Mulk and proposed a deal: the Tripolitanians would stop their assault on the citadel, and in exchange the Frankish chief would promise never again to interfere with the flow of travellers and goods. The *qāḍī* agreed.

It was a strange compromise. Is not the aim of a siege precisely to prevent the circulation of people and foodstuff? And yet, one has the impression that besiegers and besieged had established something approaching normal relations. The port of Tripoli suddenly enjoyed a spurt of activity, as caravans came and went after paying a tax to the Franj, and Tripolitanian notables crossed enemy lines with safe-conduct passes. In fact, however, the belligerents were simply waiting each other out. The Franj anticipated the arrival of a Christian fleet, from Genoa or Constantinople, which would enable them to assault the besieged city. The Tripolitanians, not unaware of this, were expecting a Muslim army to speed to their rescue. The most effective support should logically have come from Egypt, for the Fatimid caliphate was a great maritime power whose intervention would suffice to discourage the Franj. But once again, relations between the lords of Tripoli and Cairo were disastrous. Al-Afḍal's father had been a slave in the *qāḍī*'s household, and it seems that he had been on very bad terms with his masters. The vizier had never concealed his rancour and his desire to humiliate Fakhr al-Mulk, who for his part would have preferred to abandon his city to Saint-Gilles rather than place his fate in the hands of al-Afḍal. The *qāḍī* could rely on no ally in Syria either. He had to seek help elsewhere.

When news of the Ḥarrān victory reached him in June 1104, he immediately despatched a message to the emir Sokman begging him to complete his triumph by driving the Franj from Tripoli. He sweetened his request with a gift of a great quantity of gold, and also promised to cover all the expedition's expenses. The victor of Ḥarrān was tempted. Assembling a powerful army, he set out for Syria. But when he was less than four days' march from Tripoli, he was halted by an attack of angina. His troops dispersed. The morale of the *qāḍī* and his subjects collapsed.

Nevertheless, in 1105 a ray of hope appeared. Sultan Barkiyaruq had just died of tuberculosis, which put an end to the interminable fratricidal warfare that had paralysed the Seljuk empire since the beginning of the Frankish invasion. Henceforth Iraq, Syria and western Persia were supposed to have but a single master, 'the sultan, saviour of the world and of religion, Muḥammad Ibn Malikshāh'. This twenty-four-year-old Seljuk sultan's title was taken literally by the Tripolitanians. Fakhr al-Mulk sent the sultan message after message, and received endless promises in return. But there was no sign of any rescuing army.

In the meantime, the blockade of the city was tightened. Saint-Gilles was replaced by one of his cousins, 'al-Cerdani', the count of Cerdagne, who stepped up the pressure on the besieged. It was increasingly difficult to get food through overland. The prices of foodstuffs within the city spiralled dizzyingly: a pound of dates was sold for a gold dinar, a coin that would normally suffice to feed an entire family for several weeks. Many citizens sought to emigrate to Tyre, Homs or Damascus. Hunger led to betrayals. One day some Tripolitanian notables sought out al-Cerdani and, in exchange for his favours, revealed how the city was still managing to receive some provisions. Fakhr al-Mulk then offered his adversary a fabulous sum if he would deliver the traitors. But the count refused. The next morning the notables were found inside the enemy camp itself; their throats had been cut.

Despite this exploit, the situation in Tripoli continued to deteriorate. There was still no sign of rescue, and persistent rumours suggested the imminent approach of a Frankish fleet. In despair, Fakhr al-Mulk decided to go in person to Baghdad to plead his cause before the sultan Muḥammad and the caliph al-Mustaẓhir Billāh. In his absence, one of his cousins was entrusted with the interim government of the city, and the troops were given six months' pay in advance. A large escort had been prepared, five hundred cavalry and foot soldiers, plus many servants bearing gifts of every description: engraved swords, thoroughbred horses, brocaded robes of honour, as well as various products of the goldsmiths' craft, Tripoli's speciality. Thus it was that towards the end of March 1108 Fakhr al-Mulk left the city with his long cortège. 'He left Tripoli by land,' reports Ibn al-Qalānisi unambiguously, the only chronicler who actually lived through these events, thus suggesting that the *qāḍī* obtained permission from the Franj to pass through their lines in order to go and preach holy war against them! Given the curious relations between the besiegers and the besieged, that is not impossible. But it seems more plausible that the *qāḍī* reached Beirut by boat and only then took the land route.

However that may be, Fakhr al-Mulk stopped first in Damascus. The ruler of Tripoli had a marked aversion for Duqāq, but the inept Seljuk king had died some time earlier, probably poisoned, and the city was now in the hands of his tutor, the *atabeg* Tughtigin, a lame former slave whose ambiguous relations with the Franj were to dominate the Syrian political scene for more than twenty years. Ambitious, wily and unscrupulous, this Turkish officer, like Fakhr al-Mulk himself, was a mature and realistic man. In contrast with the vindictive stance adopted by Duqāq, Tughtigin received the master of Tripoli warmly, held a great banquet in his honour, and even invited him to his own private bath. The *qāḍī* appreciated these attentions, but preferred to be lodged outside the walls – confidence has its limits!

In Baghdad his reception was even more sumptuous. So great was Tripoli's prestige in the Muslim world that the *qāḍī* was treated as a powerful monarch. Sultan Muḥammad took him across the Tigris in his own boat. The officers of protocol led the master of Tripoli through a floating salon to where had been placed a brocade cushion on which the sultan usually sat. Fakhr al-Mulk settled himself next to it, in the place usually allotted to visitors, but the dignitaries rushed forward and took him by the arm: the monarch had personally insisted that his guest be seated on his own cushion. The *qāḍī* was welcomed in one palace after another, and was asked many questions by the sultan, the caliph and their collaborators. They wanted to know everything about the siege, and all Baghdad praised Fakhr al-Mulk's bravery in the *jihād* against the Franj.

But when it finally came to political matters, and Fakhr al-Mulk asked Muḥammad to send an army to lift the siege of Tripoli, 'the sultan,' Ibn al-Qalānisi spitefully reports, 'ordered several of his principal emirs to go with Fakhr al-Mulk to help repel those who were besieging the city. He instructed the expeditionary force to stop briefly in Mosul to take the city from Jawali, and told them to head for Tripoli once that was done.'

Fakhr al-Mulk was devastated. The situation in Mosul was so muddled that it would take years to sort out. Moreover, the city was situated north of Baghdad, whereas Tripoli lay due west. If the army made such a detour, it would never arrive in time to save his capital, which, he insisted, was liable to collapse any day now. But the sultan would not hear of it. The interests of the Seljuk empire required that the problem of Mosul be given priority. The *qāḍī* tried everything, even buying some of the sultan's counsellors at inflated prices, but in vain: the army would go first to Mosul. When Fakhr al-Mulk set out to return to Tripoli after a four-month stay in Baghdad, he left without any ceremony. He was now convinced that he would no longer be able to hold his city. What he did not know was that he had already lost it.

He was told the sad news when he arrived in Damascus in August 1108. Demoralised by his long absence, the notables of Tripoli had decided to entrust the city to the ruler of Egypt, who promised to defend it against the Franj. Al-Afḍal sent his vassals food, as well as a governor to take charge of the city's affairs; his first mission was to arrest the family of Fakhr al-Mulk and his supporters, to seize his treasury, furniture and personal property, and to send them all to Egypt by ship.

While the vizier was thus persecuting the unfortunate *qāḍī*, the Franj were preparing the final assault on Tripoli. One after the other, their commanders had arrived at the walls of the besieged city. King Baldwin of Jerusalem, their supreme commander, was there. Baldwin of Edessa and Tancred of Antioch, who had been reconciled for the occasion, were both there, as were two counts from the family of Saint-Gilles, who had just arrived from his country with dozens of Genoese vessels. Both coveted Tripoli, but the king of Jerusalem ordered them to halt their quarrels. Ibn Saint-Gilles would await the end of the battle to have his rival assassinated.

In March 1109 everything seemed ready for a concerted attack by land and sea. The terrified Tripolitanians observed all these preparations, but did not lose hope. Had not al-Afḍal promised to send a fleet more powerful than any they had ever seen, with enough food, fighters and *matériel* to hold out for a year?

The Tripolitanians had no doubt that the Genoese vessels would flee the moment the Fatimid fleet sailed into view. Let it only arrive in time!

At the beginning of the summer, Ibn al-Qalānisi says,

> the Franj launched an attack on Tripoli with all their forces, driving their mobile towers towards the city walls. When the people of the city saw what violent assaults they would have to face, they lost heart, for they understood that their defeat was inevitable. Food supplies were exhausted, and the Egyptian fleet was nowhere in sight. The winds were blowing against them, for such was the will of God, who determines what things will come to pass. The Franj redoubled their efforts and took the city by storm [on 12 July 1109].

After two thousand days of resistance, the city of goldsmiths and libraries, of intrepid seamen and learned *qāḍīs,* was sacked by the warriors of the West. The hundred thousand volumes of the Dār al-ʿIlm were pillaged and burned, so that 'impious' books would be destroyed. According to the chronicler of Damascus, 'the Franj decided that one-third of the city would go to the Genoese, the other two-thirds to the son of Saint-Gilles. All that King Baldwin desired was set aside for him.' Most of the inhabitants were sold into slavery, the rest were despoiled of their property and expelled. Many headed for the port of Tyre. Fakhr al-Mulk ended his life in the vicinity of Damascus.

And the Egyptian fleet? 'It arrived in Tyre eight days after the fall of Tripoli,' Ibn al-Qalānisi relates, 'when all had been lost, because of the divine punishment that had struck the inhabitants.'

The Franj selected Beirut as their second target. Lying next to the

Lebanese mountains, the city was ringed by pine forests, in particular in the suburbs of Mazrat al-ʿArab and Raʾs al-Nabah. There the invaders would find the wood they needed to construct the instruments of siege. Beirut had none of the splendour of Tripoli, and its modest villas could not easily be compared to the Roman palaces whose marble ruins were still scattered across the grounds of ancient Berytus. But because of its port, it was a relatively prosperous city, situated on the rocky slope where, according to tradition, St George had slain the dragon. Coveted by the Damascenes, 'held negligently by the Egyptians', Beirut finally had to confront the Franj on its own, beginning in February 1110. Its five thousand inhabitants fought with an ardour born of despair, as they destroyed the siege towers one after another. 'Never before or since did the Franj face such a harsh battle,' Ibn al-Qalānisi exclaimed. The invaders were unforgiving. On 13 May, when the city was taken, they threw themselves into a blind massacre. To set an example.

The lesson was well learned. The following summer, 'a certain Frankish king [the Damascene chronicler may be forgiven for failing to recognise Sigurd, the sovereign of distant Norway] arrived by sea with more than sixty vessels packed with fighters intent on making their pilgrimage and waging war in the lands of Islam. They headed towards Jerusalem, Baldwin joined them, and together they laid siege, by land and sea, to the port of Saida,' the ancient Phoenician city of Sidon. The walls of this city, destroyed and rebuilt more than once in the course of history, are impressive even today, their enormous blocks of stone lashed relentlessly by the Mediterranean. But the inhabitants, who had shown great courage at the beginning of the Frankish invasion, no longer had the heart to fight, since, according to Ibn al-Qalānisi, 'they feared that they would suffer the same fate as Beirut. They therefore sent their *qāḍī* with a delegation of notables to ask Baldwin to spare their lives. He accepted their request.' The city capitulated on 4 December 1110. This time there was no massacre, but a massive exodus to Tyre and Damascus, which were already bulging with refugees.

In the space of eighteen months three of the most renowned cities of the Arab world – Tripoli, Beirut and Saida – had been taken and sacked, their inhabitants massacred or deported, their emirs, *qāḍīs* and experts on religious law killed or forced into exile, their mosques profaned. Could any power now prevent the Franj from pressing on to Tyre, Aleppo, Damascus, Cairo, Mosul, or – why not? – even Baghdad? Did any will to resist remain? Among the Muslim leaders, probably not. But among the population of the most seriously threatened cities, the relentless holy war waged for the past thirteen years by the pilgrim-fighters of the West was beginning to have its effect: the idea of *jihād*, which had long been no more than a slogan used to enliven official speeches, was being reasserted. Groups of refugees, poets and even men of religion were now preaching it anew.

It was one of these religious figures – ʿAbdu Faḍ Ibn al-Khashāb, a *qāḍī* of Aleppo, small of stature but loud of voice – who resolved, by sheer tenacity and strength of character, to waken the sleeping giant of the Arab world. His first public initiative was to rekindle, twelve years on, the scandal that al-Ḥarawi had aroused in the streets of Baghdad. This time, however, there would be a genuine riot.

V

Turban-Clad Resistance

On Friday 17 February 1111, the *qāḍī* Ibn al-Khashāb burst into the sultan's mosque in Baghdad accompanied by a large group of Aleppans, among them a Hashemite *sharīf* (a descendant of the Prophet) and a number of Sufi ascetics, *imāms* and merchants. Ibn al-Qalānisi describes what happened next.

> They forced the preacher to descend from the pulpit, which they smashed. They then began to cry out, to bewail the evils that had befallen Islam because of the Franj, who were killing men and enslaving women and children. Since they were preventing the faithful from saying their prayers, the officials present made various promises, in the name of the sultan, in an effort to pacify them: armies would be sent to defend Islam against the Franj and all the infidels.

But these fine words were not enough to soothe the rebels. The following Friday, they restaged their demonstration, this time in the mosque of the caliph. When guards tried to bar their way, they quickly thrust them aside, smashed the wooden *minbar*, which was adorned with carved arabesques and verses of the Koran, and hurled insults at the prince of the faithful himself. Baghdad was plunged into the greatest confusion.

> At the same moment [relates the Damascene chronicler in a disingenuously naive tone] the princess, sister of Sultan Muḥammad and wife of the caliph, arrived in Baghdad from Isfahan with a magnificent retinue: there were precious stones, sumptuous robes, all sorts of saddlery and beasts of burden, servants, slaves of both sexes, attendants and many other things that would defy estimation and enumeration. Her arrival coincided with the scenes described above. The joy and security of the

> royal arrival were disrupted. The caliph al-Mustaẓhir Billāh manifested considerable discontent. He wanted to prosecute those responsible for the incident, and to punish them severely. But the sultan prevented him from doing so, pardoned the actions of these people, and ordered the emirs and military officers to return to their provinces to prepare a *jihād* against the infidels, the enemies of God.

If the worthy al-Mustaẓhir was thus moved to anger, it was not only because of the disagreeable effects of the turmoil on his young wife, but also because of the terrifying slogan that had been shouted so deafeningly in the streets of the capital: 'The king of the Rūm is a better Muslim than the prince of the faithful!' For he was well aware that this was no gratuitous accusation. The demonstrators, led by Ibn al-Khashāb, were alluding to a message received a few weeks earlier by the caliph's *dīwān*. It came from the emperor Alexius Comnenus and insistently called upon the Muslims to unite with the Rūm 'to struggle against the Franj and expel them from our lands'.

If the powerful master of Constantinople and the humble *qāḍī* of Aleppo seemed to have made common cause in their initiatives in Baghdad, it was because they both felt that they had been humiliated by the same man: Tancred. When Byzantine ambassadors were sent to remind Tancred that the knights of the West had promised to restore Antioch to the *basileus* and that thirteen years after the fall of the city they had yet to do so, the 'great emir' of the Franks had insolently shown them the door. As for the Aleppans, Tancred had recently imposed a particularly discreditable treaty upon them: they were to pay him an annual tribute of 20,000 dinars, hand over two important fortresses in the immediate vicinity of their city, and give him, as a gift and sign of allegiance, their ten finest horses. Riḍwān, fearful as ever, dared not refuse. But the streets of his capital had been seething ever since the terms of the treaty had been revealed.

It had always been the custom in Aleppo for people to gather in small groups to hold lively discussions of the dangers threatening them at critical moments in their history. The notables would get together in the great mosque, sitting cross-legged on the red carpets, sometimes in the courtyard, in the shade of the minaret that overlooked the ochre-coloured houses of the city. The merchants would meet during the day, along the old colonnaded avenue built by the Romans, which ran across Aleppo from west to east, from the Gate of Antioch to the forbidden quarter of the citadel, where the sullen Riḍwān resided. This major artery had long been closed to wagons and processions. The roadway had been taken over by hundreds of little booths in which cloth, amber, trinkets, dates, pistachio nuts and condiments were amassed. The avenue and its neighbouring alleyways were covered with a wooden ceiling to protect passers-by from sun and rain; at the intersections, it rose up into high stucco domes. At the corners of the alleys, especially those leading to the souks of the makers of straw mats, the blacksmiths and the sellers of wood for heating, the Aleppans would gossip before the many low-class eating houses. Amidst a persistent odour of boiling oil, grilled meat and spices, these places offered meals at moderate prices: chunks of grilled mutton, doughnuts, lentils. Families of modest means would buy their food ready-made in the souks; only the rich cooked at home. Not far from the food stalls, the characteristic tinkle of the *sharab* sellers could be heard; these cold drinks of concentrated fruit the Franj would later borrow from the Arabs in liquid and frozen forms, calling them 'sirops' and 'sorbets'.

In the afternoon people of all walks of life would meet in the *ḥammām*, or public bath, that special meeting place where one cleansed oneself before the sunset prayer. As night fell, the citizens would desert the centre of Aleppo to return to their own quarters, away from drunken soldiers. There too, news and rumours would circulate, passed on by men and women alike, and ideas would wend their way through the city. Anger, enthusiasm, discouragement would daily stir this hive, which had buzzed in just this way for more than three millennia.

Ibn al-Khashāb was the most respected man in the quarters of Aleppo. Born of a family of rich wood-merchants, he played a primordial role in the administration of the city. As a Shiʿi *qāḍī*, he enjoyed great religious and moral authority; he was responsible for resolving disputes involving the people and property of his community, the largest in Aleppo. In addition, he was a *raʾīs*, or chief of the city, which made him simultaneously provost of the merchants, representative of the interests of the population before the king, and commandant of the urban militia.

But Ibn al-Khashāb's activities went beyond the already wide competence of his official functions. Ever since the arrival of the Franj, he had, through his numerous coterie, encouraged a patriotic and pietistic current of public opinion that demanded a firmer attitude against the invaders. He was not afraid to tell King Riḍwān what he thought of his conciliatory, even servile, policy. When Tancred obliged the Seljuk monarch to affix a cross to the minaret of the great mosque, the *qāḍī* organised a riot and had the crucifix transferred to the cathedral of Saint Helen. Since then, Riḍwān had avoided any conflict with the irascible *qāḍī*. Entrenched in the citadel with his harem and bodyguard, with his own mosque, his own source of water and his grassy racecourse, the Turkish king preferred to spare the sensibilities of his subjects. So long as his own authority was not challenged, he tolerated public opinion.

In 1111, however, Ibn al-Khashāb turned up at the citadel to tell Riḍwān once again of the citizens' extreme discontent. The faithful, he explained, were scandalised at having to pay tribute to infidels implanted in the land of Islam, and the merchants' businesses had been in peril ever since the intolerable prince of Antioch had seized control of all the routes from Aleppo to the Mediterranean, for he was holding caravans to ransom. Since the city could no longer defend itself with its own resources, the *qāḍī* proposed that a delegation of Sunni and Shiʿi notables, merchants and men of religion, be sent to Baghdad to seek the aid of Sultan Muḥammad. Riḍwān had no desire to involve his Seljuk cousin in the affairs of his kingdom. He still preferred to deal with Tancred. But in view of the futility of all missions hitherto despatched to the ʿAbbasid capital, he felt that the least risky course of action would be to accede to his subjects' request.

In this he was mistaken. Against all expectations, the Baghdad demonstrations of February 1111 produced just the effect sought by Ibn al-Khashāb. The sultan, who had just been informed of the fall of Saida and the treaty imposed on the Aleppans, felt growing unease at the ambitions of the Franj. Yielding to Ibn al-Khashāb's entreaties, he ordered the latest in the line of governors of Mosul, the emir Mawdūd, to march without delay at the head of a powerful army and to rescue Aleppo. When Ibn al-Khashāb returned to Aleppo and informed Riḍwān of the success of his mission, the king pretended to rejoice, while praying that nothing would come of it. He even informed his cousin of his eagerness to participate in the *jihād* at his side. But in July, when he was told that the sultan's troops were actually approaching the city, he could no longer conceal his consternation. He ordered the gates of the city to be barricaded, arrested Ibn al-Khashāb and his major supporters, and imprisoned them in the citadel. The Turkish soldiers were ordered to patrol the residential quarters day and night to prevent any contact between the populace and the 'enemy'. The sequel of events was to justify Riḍwān's volte-face, at least in part. Deprived of the supplies the king was supposed to procure for them, the sultan's troops took their revenge by savagely plundering the environs of Aleppo. Then, following dissension between Mawdūd and the other emirs, the army disintegrated without fighting a single battle.

Mawdūd returned to Syria two years later, under orders from the sultan to assemble all the Muslim princes, except Riḍwān, against the Franj. Since Aleppo was off limits to him, he quite naturally established his general headquarters in Damascus, that other great city, in preparation for a large-scale offensive against the kingdom of Jerusalem. His host, the *atabeg* Tughtigin, pretended to be thrilled by the honour that the sultan's envoy had thus bestowed upon him, but in fact he was as terrified as Riḍwān had been. He feared that Mawdūd sought only to take over his capital, and resented the emir's every deed as a threat to his own future.

On 2 October 1113, the Damascene chronicler tells us, the emir Mawdūd left his camp, situated near the Gate of Iron, one of the eight entrances to the city. He walked, as he did every day, to the Umayyad mosque, in the company of the lame *atabeg*.

> When the prayer was over and Mawdūd had performed several supplementary devotions, they both departed, Tughtigin walking ahead out of respect for the emir. They were surrounded by soldiers, guards and

militiamen bearing arms of all varieties; the slender sabres, sharp épées, scimitars and unsheathed daggers gave an impression of thick undergrowth. All around them, crowds pressed forward to admire their arsenal and their magnificence. When they reached the courtyard of the mosque, a man emerged from the crowd and approached the emir Mawdūd as if to pray to God on his behalf and to ask alms of him. Suddenly he seized the belt of his mantle and struck him twice with his dagger, just above the navel. The *atabeg* Tughtigin took a few steps backwards, and his companions quickly surrounded him. As for Mawdūd, who never lost his head, he walked as far as the north gate of the mosque and then collapsed. A surgeon was summoned and managed to suture some of the wounds, but the emir died several hours later, may God have mercy upon him!

Who killed the governor of Mosul on the very eve of his offensive against the Franj? Tughtigin lost no time in accusing Riḍwān and his friends of the Assassins sect. But most contemporaries believed that no one but the master of Damascus himself could have armed the killer. According to Ibn al-Athīr, King Baldwin was so shocked by the murder that he sent Tughtigin a particularly contemptuous message: 'A nation that kills its leader in the house of its God deserves to be annihilated.' As for Sultan Muḥammad, he howled with rage when he learned of the death of his lieutenant. He considered the heinous crime a personal insult, and he decided to bring all the Syrian leaders into line once and for all, those of Aleppo as well as those of Damascus. He raised an army of several tens of thousands of soldiers commanded by the best officers of the Seljuk clan and curtly ordered all the Muslim princes to join it in its sacred duty of waging *jihād* against the Franj.

When the sultan's powerful expedition arrived in central Syria in the spring of 1115, a great surprise awaited it. Baldwin of Jerusalem and Tughtigin of Damascus stood side by side, supported not only by their own troops but also by those of Antioch, Aleppo and Tripoli. The princes of Syria, Muslims and Franj alike, felt equally threatened by the sultan, and they had decided to join forces. Within several months, the Seljuk army was forced shamefully to withdraw. Muḥammad swore that never again would he concern himself with the Frankish problem. He kept his word.

While the Muslim princes were thus offering fresh evidence of their utter irresponsibility, two Arab cities demonstrated, in the space of a few months, that it was nevertheless still possible to resist the foreign occupation. With the surrender of Saida in December 1110 the Franj were masters of the entire littoral, the *sāḥil*, from Sinai in the south to 'the land of the son of the Armenian', north of Antioch. With the exception, however, of two coastal enclaves: Ascalon and Tyre. Encouraged by his successive victories, Baldwin decided to settle their fate without delay. The Ascalon region was noted for the cultivation of reddish onions, called 'ascalonians', a word the Franj distorted into *échalote* (shallot). But its real importance was military, for it served as the assembly point for Egyptian troops during every attempted expedition against the kingdom of Jerusalem.

In 1111 Baldwin paraded his army before the walls of the city. Shams al-Khalīfa ('Sun of the Caliphate'), the Fatimid governor of Ascalon – 'more inclined to commerce than to war', was Ibn al-Qalānisi's judgement of him – was terrified by the Occidentals' show of force. Without offering any resistance whatsoever, he agreed to pay them a tribute of 7,000 dinars. The Palestinian population of the city, humiliated by this unexpected capitulation, sent emissaries to Cairo to ask that the governor be removed. Upon learning this, and fearing that the vizier al-Afḍal meant to chastise him for his cowardice, Shams al-Khalīfa tried to ward off that eventuality by expelling the Egyptian functionaries and placing himself squarely under the protection of the Franj. Baldwin sent him three hundred men, who took charge of the citadel of Ascalon.

Though scandalised, the inhabitants did not lose heart. Secret meetings were held in the mosques. Plots were hatched, until one day in July 1111, as Shams al-Khalīfa was leaving the grounds of his residence on horseback, a group of conspirators attacked him, riddling his body with dagger-strokes. That was the signal for revolt. Armed citizens, joined by Berber soldiers of the governor's guard, threw themselves against the citadel. The Frankish warriors were hunted down in the towers and along the walls. None of Baldwin's three hundred men survived. The city was to escape domination by the Franj for another forty years.

Seeking revenge for his humiliation at the hands of the Ascalon rebels, Baldwin turned against Tyre, the ancient Phoenician city from which Prince Cadmus, brother of Europa (who was to give her name to the continent of the Franj), had set out to spread the alphabet throughout the Mediterranean. The impressive walls of Tyre still recalled its glorious history. The city was surrounded on three sides by the sea, and only a narrow coastal road built by Alexander the Great linked it to the mainland. Reputed to be impregnable, in 1111 it was home to a large number of refugees from the recently occupied territories. Their role in the defence of the city was primordial, as Ibn al-Qalānisi, whose account is clearly based on first-hand testimony, reports.

> The Franj had erected a mobile tower to which they affixed a battering-ram of redoubtable force. The walls were shaken, some of the stones crumbled, and the besieged found themselves on the brink of disaster. It was then that a sailor from Tripoli, who was acquainted with metallurgy and had some experience in the affairs of war, undertook to manufacture iron grapnels designed to grip the battering-ram from the top and sides, by means of ropes held by the defenders. The latter then pulled so vigorously that the wooden tower was wrenched off balance. On several occasions, the Franj had to break their own battering-ram to prevent the tower from collapsing.

Renewing their attempts, the attackers succeeded in drawing their tower near the walls and fortifications, which they then proceeded to hammer with a new battering-ram sixty cubits long, whose head was a chunk of cast iron weighing more than twenty pounds. But the Tripolitanian sailor did not give up.

> With the aid of several skilfully installed joists [the Damascene chronicler continues] he had jars of excrement and rubbish raised high and poured over the Franj. Choked by the odours enveloping them, the latter could no longer handle their battering-ram properly. The sailor then

had grape baskets and large straw trunks filled with oil, bitumen, firewood, resin and the bark of reeds. After setting them on fire, he tilted them onto the Franj tower. The top of the tower burst into flames, and as the Franj hurried to extinguish the blaze with vinegar and water, the Tripolitanian quickly hurled other baskets filled with boiling oil to feed the flames. Fire now swept through the whole upper part of the tower and spread little by little to the lower levels, feeding on the wood of which the structure was made.

Unable to bring the fire under control, the attackers finally evacuated the tower and fled. The defenders took advantage of the situation to make a sortie, seizing a large number of abandoned weapons. 'When they saw this,' Ibn al-Qalānisi concludes triumphantly, 'the Franj lost heart and beat a retreat, after setting fire to the barracks they had erected in their camp.'

It was 12 April 1112. After 132 days of siege, the population of Tyre had inflicted a stinging defeat on the Franj.

After the Baghdad riots, the Ascalon insurrection and the resistance in Tyre, a wind of revolt began to surge through the region. A growing number of Arabs felt an equally intense hatred for the invaders and for the majority of the Muslim leaders, whom they accused of negligence or even treason. In Aleppo more than elsewhere, this attitude soon went beyond a mere change of mood. Under the leadership of the *qāḍī* Ibn al-Khashāb, the citizens decided to take their fate into their own hands. They chose their own leaders and forced them to carry out the policy they wanted.

Admittedly, many defeats, many disappointments, were yet to come. The expansion of the Franj was not over, and their arrogance knew no bounds. But from this point on, a ground-swell would slowly rise, beginning in the streets of Aleppo. Little by little it would inundate the Arab East, eventually carrying to power just, courageous and devoted men who would be capable of reconquering the lost territory.

Before that, however, Aleppo was to pass through the most erratic period of its long history. At the end of November 1113 Ibn al-Khashāb learned that Riḍwān lay seriously ill at his palace in the citadel.

He gathered his friends together and told them to prepare for action. The king died on 10 December. As soon as the news was known, groups of armed militiamen fanned through the quarters of the city, occupied the major buildings, and seized many of Riḍwān's supporters, notably the adherents of the Assassins sect, who were immediately put to death for their collaboration with the Frankish enemy.

The *qāḍī*'s aim was not to seize power himself but to make an impression on the new king, Alp Arslan, the son of Riḍwān, so as to induce him to follow a policy different from that of his father. At first this young man of sixteen, who stuttered so badly that he was nicknamed 'the Mute', seemed to endorse the militant stance of Ibn al-Khashāb. With unconcealed delight, he had all Riḍwān's collaborators arrested and beheaded forthwith. The *qāḍī* became uneasy. He urged the young monarch not to subject the city to a bloodbath but simply to punish the traitors so as to set an example. But Alp Arslan paid him no heed. He executed two of his own brothers, several officers, a few servants, and in general anyone to whom he took a dislike. Little by little, the citizenry realised the horrible truth: the king was mad! The best available source dealing with this period is the chronicle by Kamāl al-Dīn, an Aleppan author-diplomat, written a century after the events but based on the testimony of contemporaries.

> One day [he recounts] Alp Arslan assembled some emirs and notables and took them to visit a sort of cellar dug into the citadel. Once they were inside, he asked them, 'What would you say if I had all your heads cut off right here?'
>
> 'We are slaves subject to your majesty's orders,' answered one of the unfortunates, pretending to consider the threat a good joke.
>
> And it was thus, in fact, that they escaped death.

It was not long before the demented young king was being given a wide berth. Only one man still dared to approach him, his eunuch Luʾluʾ, 'Pearls'. But finally he too began to fear for his life. In September 1114 he killed his sleeping master and installed another of Riḍwān's sons, aged six, on the throne.

Aleppo was sinking deeper into anarchy day by day. While uncontrollable groups of slaves and soldiers cut one another to pieces in the citadel, armed citizens patrolled the streets of the city to protect themselves against marauders. During this initial period, the Franj of Antioch did not seek to take advantage of the chaos paralysing Aleppo. Tancred had died a year before Riḍwān, and his successor Sir Roger, whom Kamāl al-Dīn calls Sirjal, lacked sufficient self-assurance to engage in action of any real scope. But the respite was of brief duration. In 1116 Roger of Antioch, now sure of his control over all the routes to Aleppo, occupied the major fortresses ringing the city one after another. In the absence of any resistance, he even managed to impose a tax on every Muslim pilgrim leaving for Mecca.

In April 1117 the eunuch Luʾluʾ was assassinated. According to Kamāl al-Dīn, 'the soldiers of his escort had hatched a plot against him. While he was walking east of the city one day, they suddenly drew their bows, crying, "After the hare! After the hare!", to make him believe that they were hunting that animal. In fact, it was Luʾluʾ himself who was riddled with arrows.' After his death, power passed to another slave, who, unable to assert his authority, asked Roger to come to his aid. The subsequent chaos was indescribable. While the Franj prepared to lay siege to the city, the military officers continued to fight among themselves for control of the citadel. Ibn al-Khashāb also decided to act without delay. He assembled the principal notables of the city to propose a plan of action whose consequences were to be weighty. As a border town, he explained, Aleppo ought to be in the vanguard of the *jihād* against the Franj. It should therefore offer its government to a powerful emir, perhaps even the sultan himself, and should never again allow itself to be governed by a local kinglet who placed his personal interests above those of Islam. The *qāḍī*'s proposal was approved, though not without some reluctance, for the Aleppans were jealously attached to their particularism. The major candidates were then reviewed. The sultan? He refused to have anything further to do with Syria. Tughtigin? He was the only Syrian prince with some degree of personal strength, but the Aleppans would never accept a Damascene. Ibn al-Khashāb then proposed the Turkish emir Ilghazi, governor of Mardin in Mesopotamia. True, his conduct had not always been exemplary. Two years earlier, he had supported the Islamo-Frankish alliance against the sultan, and he was known for his frequent drunkenness. 'When he drank wine', Ibn al-Qalānisi tells us, 'Ilghazi would remain in a state of hebetude for days on end, not even rousing himself sufficiently to issue an order or directive.' But a long search indeed would be required to find a sober military man. On the other hand, Ibn al-Khashāb argued, Ilghazi was a courageous fighter, his family had governed Jerusalem for quite some time, and his brother Sokman had won the victory of Ḥarrān against the Franj. A majority finally rallied to this view, and Ilghazi was invited to come to Aleppo. The *qāḍī* himself opened the city gates to him during the summer of 1118. The emir's first act was to marry the daughter of King Riḍwān, a gesture that symbolised the union between the city and its new master and simultaneously asserted the latter's legitimacy. Ilghazi then called his troops to arms.

Twenty years after the beginning of the invasion, the capital of northern Syria for the first time had a commander who really wanted to fight. The result was stunning. On Saturday 28 June 1119 the army of the new ruler of Aleppo confronted the forces of Antioch on the plain of Sarmada, midway between the two cities. A *khamsīn*, a hot, dry and sand-laden wind, was blowing in the eyes of the combatants. Kamāl al-Dīn describes the scene.

> Ilghazi made his emirs swear that they would fight bravely, that they would hold their positions, that they would not retreat, and that they would give their lives for the *jihād*. The Muslims were then deployed in small waves, and managed to take up night-time positions alongside Sir Roger's troops. At daybreak the Franj suddenly saw the Muslim banners approach, surrounding them on all sides. The *qāḍī* Ibn al-Khashāb advanced astride his mare, and gestured with one hand, urging our forces into battle. Seeing him, one of the soldiers shouted contemptuously, 'Have we come all the way from our home country to follow a turban?' But the *qāḍī* marched towards the troops, moved through their ranks, and addressed them, trying to rouse their energy and lift their spirits, delivering a harangue so eloquent that men wept with emotion

and felt great admiration for him. Then they charged. Arrows flew like a cloud of locusts.

The army of Antioch was decimated. Sir Roger himself was found among the bodies, his head cleaved to the nose. 'Word of the victory reached Aleppo just as the Muslims, all in rows, were coming to the end of the midday prayer in the great mosque. A great clamour was heard from the west, but no fighter entered the city before the afternoon prayer.'

Aleppo spent days celebrating its victory. There was singing and drinking, sheep were slaughtered, people wandered about looking at the crossed banners, helmets and coats of mail brought back by the troops, or watching some poor prisoner being decapitated – the rich ones were ransomed. People listened as improvised poems in honour of Ilghazi were recited in the city squares: 'After God, it is you whom we trust.' For years the Aleppans had lived in terror of Bohemond, Tancred and then Roger of Antioch, and many had come to expect that they, like their brothers in Tripoli, would some day inevitably be forced to choose between death and exile. After the Sarmada victory, they felt as though life had begun anew. Ilghazi's exploit aroused enthusiasm throughout the Arab world. 'Never in past years has such a triumph been bestowed upon Islam,' exclaimed Ibn al-Qalānisi.

These exaggerated words reflect the extremely low morale that had prevailed on the eve of Ilghazi's victory. The arrogance of the Franj had indeed come to border on the absurd. At the beginning of March 1118 King Baldwin had sought to invade Egypt with exactly 216 knights and four hundred foot soldiers. He crossed Sinai at the head of his meagre forces, occupied the city of al-Faramā' without meeting any resistance, and went as far as the banks of the Nile, 'where he bathed', notes Ibn al-Athīr mockingly. He would have gone further had he not suddenly been taken ill. Carried back to Palestine as quickly as possible, he died en route, at al-ʿArīsh in north-east Sinai. Despite Baldwin's death, al-Afḍal would never recover from this fresh humiliation. Rapidly losing control of the situation, he was assassinated three years later in a Cairo street. As for the king of the Franj, he was replaced by his cousin, Baldwin II of Edessa.

The Sarmada victory, coming so soon after the spectacular raid across Sinai, seemed like revenge, and a number of optimists thought it signalled the beginning of the reconquest. They expected Ilghazi to march on Antioch without delay, for the city now had neither prince nor army. Indeed, the Franj themselves were preparing for a siege. Their first decision was to disarm the Syrian, Armenian and Greek Christians of the city and to forbid them to leave their homes, for the Franj feared that they would ally with the Aleppans. Tension was running high between the Occidentals and their Oriental coreligionists, who complained that the former were contemptuous of their rites and had confined them to subordinate roles in their own city. But the precautions taken by the Franj proved unnecessary. Ilghazi did not even dream of pressing his advantage. Wallowing in drunkenness, he refused to leave the former residence of Riḍwān, where he seemed intent on celebrating his victory without end. So much fermented liquor did he consume that he was seized by a violent attack of fever. It took him twenty days to recover, just in time to be told that the army of Jerusalem, under the command of the new King Baldwin II, had that moment arrived in Antioch.

His health ruined by alcohol, Ilghazi died three years later, never having managed to exploit his success. The Aleppans were grateful to him for saving their city from the Frankish danger, but they were hardly distressed at his death, for they were already turning their attention to his successor, an exceptional man whose name was on everyone's lips: Balak. He was Ilghazi's nephew, but a man of quite another stamp. Within a few months he would become the adored hero of the Arab world, his exploits celebrated in the mosques and public squares.

In September 1122, through a brilliant manoeuvre, Balak succeeded in capturing Joscelin, who had replaced Baldwin II as count of Edessa. According to Ibn al-Athīr, 'he wrapped him in a camel skin, had it sewn shut, and then, rejecting all offers of ransom, locked him in a fortress.' Following the death of Roger of Antioch, a second Frankish state had now lost its leader. The king of Jerusalem, uneasy at these developments, decided to go north himself. Some knights of Edessa led him to the place where Joscelin had been seized, a swampy area alongside the Euphrates. After a quick reconnoitre, Baldwin II ordered the tents pitched for the night. The next day he rose early to take part in his favourite sport, falconry, which he had learned from Oriental princes. Suddenly Balak and his men, who had approached noiselessly, surrounded the camp. The king of Jerusalem threw down his arms. He, in turn, was taken into captivity.

In June 1123 Balak made a triumphant entrance into Aleppo, his prestige vastly inflated as a result of all these exploits. Following in Ilghazi's footsteps, his first act was to marry the daughter of Riḍwān. Then, without suffering a single setback, he swiftly and systematically reconquered the Frankish possessions around the city. The military skill of this forty-year-old Turkish emir, his spirit of determination, his rejection of any compromise with the Franj, his sobriety, and finally, the roll of honour of his successive victories, were in sharp contrast to the disconcerting mediocrity of the other Muslim princes.

One city in particular saw him as its providential saviour: Tyre, to which the Franj had again laid siege despite the capture of their king. The defenders' position proved far more delicate than it had been during their victorious resistance twelve years earlier, for this time the Occidentals had control of the seas. An impressive Venetian squadron comprising more than 120 vessels had appeared off the Palestinian coast in the spring of 1123. The Egyptian fleet, lying at anchor in Ascalon, was taken by surprise and destroyed. In February 1124, after signing an agreement with Jerusalem on the division of the booty, the Venetians blockaded the port of Tyre, while the Frankish army pitched its camp to the east of the city. The outlook for the defenders was not encouraging. The Tyrians, of course, fought on obstinately. One night, for example, a group of accomplished swimmers slid up to a Venetian ship guarding the entrance to the port and managed to draw it to the city, where it was disarmed and destroyed. But despite such stunning operations, the chances of success were minimal. The debacle of the Fatimid fleet made any rescue from the sea impossible. Moreover, it was becoming difficult to supply the city with drinking water. Tyre – and this was its major weakness – had no source within its walls. In peacetime, water was brought in from outside through pipelines. In time of war, the city relied on its cisterns and on intensive provisioning by small boats. But the tight Venetian blockade made this impossible. If the vice was not loosened, the city would be forced to capitulate within a few months.

Since they expected nothing from their usual protectors the Egyptians, the defenders turned to the hero of the hour, Balak. The emir was then laying siege to a fortress called Manbij in the Aleppo region, where one of his vassals had rebelled. When the appeal from Tyre reached him, he immediately decided, according to Kamāl al-Dīn, to turn over command of the siege to one of his lieutenants and to go to Tyre's rescue himself. On 6 May 1124 he made a last tour of inspection before setting out.

> Helmeted and with his shield on his arm [the chronicler of Aleppo continues] Balak approached the fortress of Manbij to choose the site for the placement of his mangonels. As he was giving his orders, an arrow shot from the ramparts struck him under the left clavicle. He wrenched the shaft out himself and, spitting in the air in contempt, murmured, 'That blow will be fatal for all the Muslims.' Then he fell dead.

Balak was right. When news of his death reached Tyre, the inhabitants lost heart. They now saw no course open to them but to negotiate the terms of their surrender. 'On 7 July 1124,' Ibn al-Qalānisi relates, 'they filed out of Tyre between the two ranks of soldiers, without being molested by the Franj. All soldiers and civilians left the city, in which only the infirm remained. Some of the exiles went to Damascus, while the others scattered through the countryside.'

Although a bloodbath was thereby averted, the admirable resistance of Tyre nevertheless ended in humiliation.

The people of Tyre were not alone in suffering the consequences of Balak's death. In Aleppo power fell to Timurtash, the son of Ilghazi, a young man of nineteen who, according to Ibn al-Athīr, 'was interested only in having fun and was eager to leave Aleppo for his native city, Mardin, because he felt that there had been too many wars with the Franj in Syria'. Not content merely to abandon his capital, the inept Timurtash hastened to release the king of Jerusalem in exchange for a ransom of 20,000 dinars. He presented him with robes of honour, a gold helmet and ornamented ankle boots, and even gave him back the horse he had been riding on the day of his capture. Princely behaviour no doubt, but completely irresponsible, since several weeks after his release, Baldwin II arrived at the gates of Aleppo with the firm intention of seizing it.

The defence of the city devolved entirely upon Ibn al-Khashāb, who had only a few hundred armed men. When he saw thousands of enemy fighters deployed around his city, the *qāḍī* despatched a messenger to Ilghazi's son. The emissary risked his life slipping through enemy lines by night. Upon his arrival in Mardin, he repaired to the emir's *dīwān* and insistently implored him not to abandon Aleppo. But Timurtash, as impudent as he was cowardly, found the messenger's complaints annoying, and ordered him thrown into prison.

Ibn al-Khashāb then turned to another potential saviour, al-Borsoki, an old Turkish officer who had just been named governor of Mosul. Renowned not only for his rectitude and religious zeal, but also for his political skill and ambition, al-Borsoki quickly accepted the *qāḍī*'s invitation and set out forthwith. His arrival at the besieged city in January 1125 surprised the Franj, who fled, abandoning their tents. Ibn al-Khashāb rushed out to meet al-Borsoki, urging him to pursue the fleeing Franj, but the emir was weary from his long ride, and more importantly, was impatient to visit his new possession. Like Ilghazi five years earlier, he dared not press his advantage, and thus allowed the enemy time to recover their wits. Nevertheless, his intervention assumed great significance, because the union of Aleppo and Mosul in 1125 became the nucleus of a powerful state that would soon be able to respond successfully to the arrogance of the Franj.

We now know that the astonishing perspicacity and tenacity of Ibn al-Khashāb not only saved the city from occupation, but also contributed more than anything else to preparing the way for the great leaders of the *jihād* against the invaders. But the *qāḍī* would not live to see these events. One day in the summer of 1125, as he was leaving the great mosque of Aleppo after the midday prayer, a man disguised as an ascetic leapt upon him and sunk a dagger into his chest. It was an act of revenge by the Assassins. Ibn al-Khashāb had been the sect's most intransigent opponent, had spilled buckets of its adherents' blood, and had never repented of his actions. He must have known that some day he would pay with his life. For a third of a century, no enemy of the Assassins had ever managed to elude them.

This sect, the most terrifying ever seen, had been founded in 1090 by a man of immense culture, a devotee of poetry profoundly interested in the latest advances of science. Ḥasan Ibn al-Ṣabbāḥ was born around 1048 in the city of Rayy, close by the site where the town of Tehran would be founded a few dozen years later. Was he really, as legend claims, an inseparable companion of the young poet Omar Khayyam, himself a devotee of mathematics and astronomy? It is not known with certainty. On the other hand, the circumstances that led this brilliant man to dedicate his life to organising his sect are known in detail.

At the time of Ḥasan's birth, the Shiʿi doctrine, to which he adhered, was dominant in Muslim Asia. Syria belonged to the Fatimids of Egypt, and another Shiʿi dynasty, the Buwayhids, controlled Persia and dictated orders at will to the ʿAbbasid caliph in Baghdad itself. During Ḥasan's youth, however, the situation was radically reversed. The Seljuks, upholders of Sunni orthodoxy, took control of the entire region. Shiʿism, triumphant only a short time before, was now only a barely tolerated, often persecuted, doctrine.

Ḥasan, who grew up in a milieu of religious Persians, was indignant at this state of affairs. Towards 1071 he decided to settle in Egypt, the last bastion of Shiʿism. But what he discovered in the land of the Nile was hardly cause for elation. The aged Fatimid caliph al-Mustanṣir was even more of a puppet than his ʿAbbasid rival. He no longer dared even to leave his palace without the permission of his Armenian vizier, Badr al-Jamālī, the father and predecessor of al-Afḍal. In Cairo Ḥasan met many religious fundamentalists who shared his apprehension and sought, like him, to reform the Shiʿi caliphate and to take revenge on the Seljuks.

A movement soon took shape, headed by Nizār, the older son of the caliph. The Fatimid heir as pious as he was courageous, had no intention of abandoning himself to the pleasures of the court, nor of acting as a puppet in the hands of some vizier. When his elderly father died, which could not now be long, he meant to succeed him and, with the aid of Ḥasan and his friends, to inaugurate a new golden age for the Shiʿis. A detailed plan was prepared, of which Ḥasan was the principal architect. The Persian militant would return to the heart of the Seljuk empire to pave the way for the reconquest that Nizār would most assuredly undertake upon his accession to power.

Ḥasan succeeded beyond his wildest dreams, but by methods very different from those imagined by the virtuous Nizār. In 1090 he took the fortress of Alamūt by surprise. This bastion, the 'eagle's nest', was situated in a practically inaccessible region of the Albruz mountains near the Caspian Sea. Once he commanded this inviolable sanctuary, Ḥasan set about establishing a politico-religious organisation whose effectiveness and spirit of discipline would be unequalled in all history.

All members, from novices to the grand master, were ranked according to their level of knowledge, reliability and courage. They underwent intensive courses of indoctrination as well as physical training. Ḥasan's favourite technique for sowing terror among his enemies was murder. The members of the sect were sent individually – or more rarely, in small groups of two or three – on assignments to kill some chosen personality. They generally disguised themselves as merchants or ascetics and moved around in the city where the crime was to be perpetrated, familiarising themselves with the habits of their victims. Then, once their plan was ready, they struck. Although the preparation was always conducted in the utmost secrecy, the execution had to take place in public, indeed before the largest possible crowd. That was why the preferred site was a mosque, the favourite day Friday, generally at noon. For Ḥasan, murder was not merely a means of disposing of an enemy, but was intended primarily as a twofold lesson for the public: first, the punishment of the victim and, second, the heroic sacrifice of the executioner, who was called *fidāʾī* (plural: *fidāʾīn*, or fedayeen), or 'suicide commando', because he was almost always cut down on the spot.

The serenity with which the members of the sect accepted their own death led their contemporaries to believe that they were drugged with hashish, which is why they were called *ḥashashūn*, or *ḥashīshīn*, a word that was distorted into 'Assassin' and soon incorporated into many languages as a common noun. The hypothesis is plausible, but like everything else to do with this sect, it is difficult to separate legend from reality. Did Ḥasan encourage the adherents to drug themselves so that they had a sense of being in paradise for a short time, which would thus encourage them to seek martyrdom? Or, more prosaically, was he trying to accustom them to a narcotic in order to keep them dependent on him? Was he simply urging them towards a state of euphoria so that they would not falter at the moment of the murder? Or did he instead rely on their blind faith? Whatever the answer, merely to list the hypotheses is to pay tribute to the exceptional organiser Ḥasan must have been.

Indeed, his success was stunning. The first murder, committed in 1092, two years after the sect was founded, was an epic unto itself. The Seljuks were at the apogee of their power. The pillar of their empire, the man who over thirty years had created a state out of the lands conquered by the Turkish warriors, the architect of the renaissance of Sunni power and of the struggle against Shiʿism, was an old vizier whose name itself evoked his deeds: Niẓām al-Mulk, or 'Order of the Realm'. On 14 October 1092 one of Ḥasan's adherents killed him with a sword-stroke. 'When Niẓām al-Mulk was assassinated,' Ibn al-Athīr wrote, 'the state disintegrated.' Indeed, the Seljuk empire never recovered its unity. Its history would now be punctuated not by further conquests, but by interminable wars of succession. 'Mission accomplished,' Ḥasan may well have told his comrades in Egypt. The road was now open to a Fatimid reconquest: it was up to Niẓār. In Cairo, however, the insurrection had run aground. Al-Afḍal, who inherited the vizierate from his father in 1094, mercilessly crushed the associates of Nizār, who was himself buried alive.

Ḥasan thus found himself in an unforeseen situation. He had not renounced his goal of reviving the Shiʿi caliphate, but he knew that it would take time. He therefore modified his strategy. While continuing to undermine official Islam and its religious and political representatives, he also tried to find a place where he could establish an autonomous fiefdom. What country offered better prospects for such a project than Syria, carved up as it was into a multitude of minuscule rival states? The sect had only to establish a base, to play one city against another, one emir against his brother, and it would survive until the Fatimid caliphate emerged from its torpor.

Ḥasan sent a Persian preacher into Syria, an enigmatic 'physician-astrologer' who settled in Aleppo and managed to win the confidence of Riḍwān. Adherents began to converge on the city, to preach their doctrine, to form cells. To preserve the friendship of the Seljuk king, they agreed to do some small favours for him, in particular to assassinate some of his political opponents. Upon the death of the 'physician-astrologer' in 1103, the sect immediately sent Riḍwān a new Persian adviser, Abū Ṭāhir, a goldsmith. His influence soon became more overwhelming than that of his predecessor. Riḍwān fell completely under his spell, and according to Kamāl al-Dīn, no Aleppan could obtain the slightest favour from the monarch or settle any administrative problem without dealing with one of the innumerable members of the sect scattered through the king's entourage.

But the Assassins were hated precisely because of their power. Ibn al-Khashāb in particular relentlessly demanded an end to their activities. He detested them not only for the way they bought and sold influence, but also and above all for their alleged sympathy for the Western invaders. However paradoxical it may seem, the accusation was justified. When the Franj arrived, the Assassins, who had barely begun to settle in Syria, were called Bāṭinis, 'those who adhere to a faith other than that which they profess in public'. The appellation suggested that the adherents were Muslims only in appearance. The Shiʿis, like Ibn al-Khashāb, had no sympathy for the disciples of Ḥasan because of their break with the Fatimid caliphate, which, however weak, remained the formal protector of the Shiʿis of the Arab world.

Detested and persecuted by all Muslims, the Assassins were not displeased at the arrival of a Christian army that was inflicting one defeat after another on both the Seljuks and al-Afḍal, the murderer of Nizār. There is no doubt that Riḍwān's outrageously conciliatory attitude towards the Occidentals was due in large part to the counsel of the Bāṭinis.

As far as Ibn al-Khashāb was concerned, the connivance between the Assassins and the Franj amounted to treason. He acted accordingly. During the massacres that followed Riḍwān's death at the end of 1113, the Bāṭinis were tracked down street by street and house by house. Some were lynched by mobs, others leapt to their death from the ramparts of the city walls. Nearly two hundred members of the sect perished in this manner, among them Abū Ṭāhir the goldsmith. Nevertheless, Ibn al-Qalānisi reports that 'several managed to flee and sought refuge among the Franj or dispersed in the countryside.'

Even though Ibn al-Khashāb had thus deprived the Assassins of their major bastion in Syria, their astonishing career had only just begun. Drawing lessons from their failure, the sect altered its tactics. Ḥasan's new envoy to Syria, a Persian propagandist by the name of Bahram, decided to call a temporary halt to all spectacular actions and to return to careful and discreet organisation and infiltration. 'Bahram', the Damascene chronicler relates, 'lived in the greatest secrecy and seclusion, changing his dress and appearance so cleverly that he moved through the cities and strongholds without anyone suspecting his identity.'

Within a few weeks, he had organised a network powerful enough to contemplate emerging from clandestinity. He found an excellent protector in Riḍwān's replacement.

> One day [says Ibn al-Qalānisi] Bahram arrived in Damascus, where the *atabeg* Tughtigin received him quite correctly, as a precaution against his misdeeds and those of his gang. He was shown great respect and assured of vigilant protection. The second-ranking personality of the Syrian metropolis, the vizier Ṭāhir al-Mazdaghāni, came to an understanding with Bahram, although he did not belong to the sect, and helped him to plant the snares of his malfeasance wherever he willed.

In fact, despite the death of Ḥasan Ibn al-Ṣabbāḥ in his Alamūt retreat in 1124, there was a sharp recrudescence of the activity of the Assassins. The murder of Ibn al-Khashāb was not an isolated act. A year later, another 'turbaned resister' of the first importance fell under their blows. All the chroniclers relate his assassination with the utmost solemnity, for the man who, in August 1099, had led the first manifestation of popular outrage against the Frankish invasion had become one of the Muslim world's leading religious authorities. It was announced from Iraq that the *qāḍī of qāḍīs* of Baghdad, the splendour of Islam, Abū Ṣaʿad al-Ḥarawi, had been attacked by Bāṭinis in the great mosque of Hamadān. They had stabbed him to death and fled immediately, leaving no clue or trace behind them. So great was the fear they inspired that no one dared pursue them. The crime aroused great indignation in Damascus, where al-Ḥarawi had lived for many years. The activities of the Assassins were by now provoking mounting hostility, especially in religious circles. The best of the faithful were furious, but they held their tongue, because the Bāṭinis had begun killing those who resisted them and supporting those who approved their aberrations. No one dared to criticise them publicly, neither emir, nor vizier, nor sultan.

This terror was understandable. On 26 November 1126 al-Borsoki himself, the powerful master of Aleppo and Mosul, suffered the terrible vengeance of the Assassins.

> And yet [wrote Ibn al-Qalānisi in astonishment] the emir had been on his guard. He wore a coat of mail that could not be penetrated by sabre or knife-blade, and he was always surrounded by soldiers armed to the teeth. But there is no escape from fate. Al-Borsoki had gone, as usual, to the great mosque of Mosul to say his Friday prayers. The scoundrels were there, dressed as Sufis, praying in a corner without arousing any suspicion. Suddenly they leapt upon him and struck him several blows, though without piercing his coat of mail. When the Bāṭinis saw that the daggers had not harmed the emir, one of them cried: 'Strike high, at his head!' They struck him in the throat and knife thrusts rained down upon him. Al-Borsoki died a martyr, and his murderers were put to death.

Never had the threat represented by the Assassins been so serious. They were no longer simply pests, but had become a plague torturing the Arab world at a time when all its energies were required to confront the Frankish occupation. Moreover, the skein of killings was not yet fully unravelled. A few months after the death of al-Borsoki, his son, who had just succeeded him, was in turn assassinated. Four rival emirs then contended for power in Aleppo, and Ibn al-Khashāb was no longer on the scene to maintain a minimum of cohesion. In autumn 1127, as the city sank into anarchy, the Franj reappeared at the walls. Antioch had a new prince, the young son of the great Bohemond, a huge blond man of eighteen who had just arrived from his homeland to take possession of the familial heritage. He bore his father's first name and also possessed his impetuous character. The Aleppans lost no time in paying tribute to him, and the most defeatist already saw him as the future conqueror of their city.

The situation in Damascus was no less tragic. The *atabeg* Tughtigin, ageing and sick, no longer exercised the slightest control over the Assassins. They had their own armed militia, the city administration was in their hands, and the vizier al-Mazdaghāni, who was devoted to them body and soul, had established close contacts with Jerusalem. For his part, Baldwin II made no secret of his intention to crown his career by taking the Syrian metropolis. Only the presence of the aged Tughtigin seemed still to prevent the Assassins from handing the city over to the Franj. But the reprieve was to be brief. By early 1128 the *atabeg* was visibly wasting away and could no longer rise from his bed. Plots were being hatched at his bedside. He finally expired on 12 February, after designating his son Būri as his successor. The Damascenes were convinced that the fall of their city was now only a matter of time.

Discussing this critical period of Arab history a century later, Ibn al-Athīr would write with good reason: 'With the death of Tughtigin, the last man capable of confronting the Franj was gone. The latter then seemed in a position to occupy all of Syria. But God in his infinite kindness took pity on the Muslims.'

Part Three

RIPOSTE (1128–46)

I was about to begin the prayer when a Franj threw himself upon me, seized me, and turned my face to the East, telling me, 'That's how you pray!'

USĀMAH IBN MUNQIDH
Chronicler (1095–1188)

VI

The Damascus Conspiracies

> The vizier al-Mazdaghāni [Ibn al-Qalānisi relates] went, as he did every day, to the Pavilion of Roses, in the palace of the citadel, in Damascus. All the emirs and military officers were gathered there. The meeting dealt with various matters. Būri, son of Tughtigin, who was now master of the city, exchanged views with all those present, whereupon they rose to return to their residences. According to custom, the vizier was supposed to leave after the others. As he stood, Būri gestured to one of his associates, who promptly struck al-Mazdaghāni several sabre blows on his head. He was then beheaded, and his body, in two pieces, was carried to the Gate of Iron that all might see what God had in store for those who had recourse to deceit.

News of the death of the Assassins' protector spread through the souks of Damascus within a few minutes, and was immediately followed by a manhunt. A huge crowd fanned out through the streets, brandishing sabres and daggers. All the Bāṭinis, their relatives, their friends and anyone suspected of sympathy for them were tracked through the city, followed home and mercilessly slaughtered. Their leaders were crucified on the battlements of the city ramparts. Several members of Ibn al-Qalānisi's family took an active part in the massacre. It might be thought that the chronicler himself, who was a fifty-seven-year-old high-ranking functionary in that September of 1129, would not have mixed with the populace. But his tone speaks volumes about his state of mind during those bloody hours: 'By morning, the public squares were rid of the Bāṭinis, and howling dogs vied for their corpses.'

The Damascenes were visibly outraged by the Assassins' hold on their city, and none more so than the son of Tughtigin, who refused to play his allotted role of puppet in the hands of the sect and of the vizier al-Mazdaghāni. For Ibn al-Athīr, however, this was not a mere power struggle, but a fight to save the Syrian metropolis from imminent disaster: 'al-Mazdaghāni had written to the Franj proposing to hand over Damascus to them if they would give him the city of Tyre in return. Agreement had been reached. They had even set the date, a Friday.' Indeed, the troops of Baldwin II were expected at any minute at the city walls; groups of armed Assassins planned to throw open the gates for them, while other commandos were sent to guard the exits of the great mosque to prevent dignitaries and officers from leaving the building until the Franj had occupied the city. A few days before the scheduled execution of this plan, Būri, who had learned of it, hurried to eliminate the vizier, thus giving the signal that unleashed the population against the Assassins.

Had there really been such a plot? One is tempted to doubt it, since Ibn al-Qalānisi himself, despite his evident hatred of the Bāṭinis, never accused them of seeking to deliver the city to the Franj. Nevertheless, Ibn al-Athīr's account is not implausible. The Assassins and their ally al-Mazdaghāni felt threatened not only by mounting popular hostility, but also by the intrigues of Būri and his entourage. Moreover, they knew that the Franj had decided to take Damascus regardless of the cost. Rather than have to fight too many enemies at once, the sect might well have decided to establish a sanctuary such as Tyre from which preachers and killers could be sent into Fatimid Egypt, now the principal target of the disciples of Ḥasan Ibn al-Ṣabbāḥ.

The sequel to these events lends credence to the hypothesis that there had in fact been a plot. The few Bāṭinis who survived the massacre went to settle in Palestine, under the protection of Baldwin II, to whom they delivered Baniyās, a powerful fortress situated at the foot of Mount Hermon that controls the route from Jerusalem to Damascus. Moreover, several weeks later, a powerful Frankish army appeared in the environs of the Syrian metropolis. It included nearly ten thousand knights and foot soldiers, who came not only from Palestine but also from Antioch, Edessa and Tripoli; there were also several hundred warriors freshly arrived from the land of the Franj, who loudly proclaimed their intention to seize Damascus. The most fanatical of them belonged to the order of the Templars, a religio-military society founded ten years earlier in Palestine.

Since he lacked sufficient troops to confront the invaders, Būri hastily appealed to a number of Turkish nomadic bands and a few Arab tribes of the region, promising them lucrative recompense if they would help to repel the attack. The son of Tughtigin was well aware that he would be unable to rely on these mercenaries for very long, for they would quickly desert to indulge their lust for plunder. His prime concern was therefore to join the battle as soon as possible. One day in November his scouts informed him that several thousand Franj had begun foraging in the rich plain of Ghūṭa. Without delay he despatched his entire army to give chase. The Occidentals, taken by surprise, were quickly surrounded. Some of their knights did not even have time to retrieve their mounts.

> The Turks and the Arabs returned to Damascus late in the afternoon, [Ibn al-Qalānisi relates]. They were triumphant, joyous and laden with booty. The populace rejoiced, morale soared, and the army decided to attack the Franj in their own camp. At dawn the next day, many horsemen set out at full gallop. When they saw great clouds of rising smoke, they thought they had found the Franj, but when they drew near, they discovered that the enemy had decamped after setting fire to their equipment, for they had no more beasts of burden to carry it.

Despite this setback, Baldwin II reassembled his troops for a fresh attack on Damascus. At the beginning of September the region was suddenly engulfed by torrential rains. The Franj camp was transformed into a sea of mud in which men and horses alike were soon hopelessly mired. Broken-hearted, the king of Jerusalem ordered his men to retreat.

Būri, who upon his accession to the throne had been considered a frivolous and timorous emir, had saved Damascus from the two major dangers threatening it, the Franj and the Assassins. Drawing the lessons of his defeat, Baldwin II definitively renounced any new expedition against the city he coveted.

*

But Būri had not silenced all his enemies. One day two individuals dressed in the Turkish style, with robes and pointed calottes, arrived in Damascus. They said they were seeking work at a fixed salary, and the son of Tughtigin hired them for his personal bodyguard. One morning in May 1131, while the emir was returning to his palace from his *ḥammām*, the two men sprang upon him and wounded him in the stomach. Before their execution they confessed that the master of the Assassins had sent them from the fortress of Alamūt to seek vengeance for their brothers who had been exterminated by the son of Tughtigin.

Many physicians were summoned to the victim's bedside, in particular, Ibn al-Qalānisi reports, 'surgeons expert in the treatment of wounds'. The medical care then available in Damascus was among the best in the world. Duqāq had founded a hospital, a *muristan,* and a second one would be built in 1154. The traveller Ibn Jubayr, who visited both of them several years later, described how they worked. 'Each hospital has administrators who keep the records, which list the names of the patients, the expenses required for their care and nourishment, and various other sorts of information. The physicians come every morning to examine the patients and prescribe the remedies and diets that can cure them, depending on what is required for each individual.'

After the visit of these surgeons, Būri, who begun to feel better, insisted on returning home on horseback to receive his friends for the usual day's chat and drinking. But this excessive enthusiasm eventually proved fatal to the patient, for his wound never healed properly. He died in June 1132, after thirteen months of terrible suffering. Once again, the Assassins had had their revenge.

Būri was the first architect of a victorious riposte by the Arab world to the Frankish occupation, although his all-too-brief reign bequeathed no lasting memory, for it coincided with the rise of a personality of a wholly different stamp: the *atabeg* ʿImād al-Dīn Zangī, the new ruler of Aleppo and Mosul, a man Ibn al-Athīr considered no less than 'the gift of divine providence to the Muslims'.

At first glance, this dark-skinned officer with the bristly beard looked little different from the many Turkish military commanders who had preceded him in this interminable war against the Franj. Frequently dead drunk and, like them, prepared to resort to any amount of cruelty and perfidy to achieve his ends, Zangī often combated the Muslims with greater obstinacy than he did the Franj. What was known of him on that eighteenth day of June 1128, when he solemnly entered Aleppo, was scarcely encouraging. He had acquired his principal claim to fame the previous year, when he had suppressed a revolt by the caliph of Baghdad against his Seljuk protectors. The light-hearted al-Mustaẓhir had died in 1118, passing the throne to his son al-Mustarshid Billāh, a young man of twenty-five with blue eyes, red hair and a freckled face. It was his ambition to revive the glorious tradition of his earliest ʿAbbasid ancestors. The moment seemed propitious, for Sultan Muḥammad had just died, and the usual war of succession had broken out. The young caliph seized the opportunity to take direct control of his troops, an act unprecedented for more than two centuries. A talented orator, al-Mustarshid won the support of the population of his capital.

Paradoxically, just when the prince of the faithful had broken with a long tradition of caliphal lethargy, the sultanate had fallen to a fourteen-year-old boy interested only in hunting and in the pleasures of the harem. Maḥmūd, the son of Muḥammad, was treated with condescension by al-Mustarshid, who frequently advised him to go back to Persia. It was a genuine revolt by the Arabs against the Turks, those foreign military officers who had dominated them for so long. Unable to deal with the insurrection, the sultan appealed to Zangī, who was then governor of the rich port of Basra, at the north-west tip of the Gulf. His intervention was decisive: defeated near Baghdad, the caliph's troops surrendered their weapons, and the prince of the faithful retreated to his palace to await better days. Several months later, to repay Zangī for his precious aid, the sultan entrusted him with the government of Mosul and Aleppo.

One could well have imagined more glorious military exploits for this future hero of Islam. But it was with good reason that Zangī would one day be hailed as the first great combatant of the *jihād* against the Franj. Before him, Turkish generals would arrive in Syria accompanied by troops anxious to engage in plunder and depart with as much money and booty as possible. The effects of their victories were rapidly wiped out by subsequent defeats. Troops were demobilised one year only to be remobilised the next. All this changed with Zangī. For eighteen years this indefatigable warrior would travel the length and breadth of Syria and Iraq, sleeping on a straw mat to protect himself from the mud, fighting with some, sealing pacts with others, and intriguing against everyone. Never did he dream of residing peacefully in one of the many palaces of his vast fiefdom.

His entourage was made up not of courtesans and flatterers but of seasoned political advisers whom he had learned to heed. He ran a network of informers who kept him regularly apprised of what was afoot in Baghdad, Isfahan, Damascus, Antioch and Jerusalem, as well as in his own cities of Aleppo and Mosul. Unlike the other armies that had fought the Franj, his was not commanded by a multitude of autonomous emirs ever ready for treason or internecine quarrels. Discipline was strict, punishment merciless at the slightest infraction. According to Kamāl al-Dīn, 'the soldiers of the *atabeg* seemed to march between two ropes' – in an effort not to step into any cultivated fields. 'Once,' Ibn al-Athīr reports, 'one of Zangī's emirs who had been granted a small city as a fiefdom took over the residence of a rich Jewish merchant. The latter asked to see the *atabeg* and set out his objections. Zangī glanced once at the emir, who evacuated the house immediately.' Moreover, the master of Aleppo made the same demands on himself as he did on others. When he arrived at a city, he would sleep outside the walls in his tent, contemptuous of the many palaces at his disposal. 'Zangī', the Mosul historian says, 'was also very concerned about the honour of women, especially of the wives of his soldiers. He used to say that if they were not well looked after, they would soon be corrupted, because of the long absences of their husbands during campaigns.'

Zangī was possessed of severity, perseverance and a strong sense of state, all qualities tragically lacking in the leaders of the Arab world. Even more important for the future, Zangī was greatly concerned about legitimacy. Upon his arrival in Aleppo he took three initiatives, made three symbolic gestures. The first was by now classic: he married the daughter of Riḍwān, already the widow of Ilghazi and Balak.

The second was to transfer his father's remains to the city, to demonstrate his family's new roots in the fiefdom. The third was to obtain from the sultan undisputed authority over the whole of Syria and northern Iraq. Zangī thereby clearly indicated that he was no mere peripatetic adventurer, but the founder of a state that was expected to survive him. This element of cohesion that he introduced in the Arab world would not have its effects for several years yet. Intestine quarrels were to paralyse the Muslim princes – and indeed the *atabeg* himself – for a long time to come.

Nevertheless, the time seemed ripe to organise a sweeping counter-offensive, for the unshakeable solidarity that had hitherto been the great strength of the Occidentals now seemed seriously in doubt. 'It is said that discord has arisen among the Franj, something unusual for them.' Ibn al-Qalānisi says no more about it, except: 'It has even been said that they have fought among themselves and that several were killed.' But the chronicler's astonishment pales before that felt by Zangī the day he received a message from Alix, daughter of Baldwin II, king of Jerusalem, offering him an alliance against her own father.

This strange affair began in February 1130, when Prince Bohemond II of Antioch, then fighting in the north, fell into an ambush laid by Ghāzī, the son of the emir Danishmend, who had captured Bohemond I thirty years before. Bohemond II, who lacked his father's luck, was killed in the fighting, and his blond head, carefully embalmed and enclosed in a silver box, was sent to the caliph as a gift. When news of his death reached Antioch, his widow, Alix, organised what amounted to a coup d'état. It appears that she had the support of the Armenian, Greek and Syrian populations of Antioch; she first secured her control of the city and then made contact with Zangī. It was a curious attitude for her to have taken, one that heralded the advent of a new, second generation of Franj, who had little in common with the pioneers of the invasion. The young princess, whose mother was Armenian and who had never set eyes on Europe, felt Oriental and acted as such. Informed of his daughter's rebellion, the king of Jerusalem immediately marched north at the head of his army. Shortly before reaching Antioch, he happened upon a knight of dazzling appearance, whose pure white charger wore shoes of silver and was barded, from mane to breast, with superb chiselled armour. The horse was a gift from Alix to Zangī and was accompanied by a letter in which the princess asked the *atabeg* to come to her aid, promising to recognise his suzerainty in return. After having the messenger hanged, Baldwin II continued on his way to Antioch, where he rapidly re-established his control. Alix capitulated after purely symbolic resistance in the citadel. Her father exiled her to the port of Latakia.

Shortly afterwards, however, in August 1131, the king of Jerusalem died. He received a proper obituary from the Damascene chronicler – a sign of the times, for by then the Franj were no longer an undifferentiated mass among whom it was just possible to identify a few commanders, as had been the case during the initial period of the invasion. Ibn al-Qalānisi's chronicle now pays attention to detail, and even sketches out an analysis.

> Baldwin [he writes] was an old man polished by time and misfortune. He had fallen into the hands of the Muslims but escaped by dint of his celebrated ruses. With his death, the Franj lost their most perceptive politician and their most competent administrator. Royal power fell to the count of Anjou, recently arrived by sea from their country. But his judgement was unsound and his administration ineffective, so the loss of Baldwin plunged the Franj into turmoil and disorder.

The third king of Jerusalem – Fulk of Anjou, a stocky, red-haired quinquagenarian who was married to Melisende, the elder sister of Alix – was indeed a newcomer. Baldwin, like the great majority of the Frankish princes, had no male heir. Because of their worse than primitive health standards and their failure to adapt to the living conditions of the Orient, the Occidentals suffered a very high infant mortality rate, which according to a well-known natural law affects boys more than girls. It was only with time that they learned to improve conditions by regular visits to the *ḥammām* and by resorting more frequently to the services of Arab physicians.

Ibn al-Qalānisi was justified in expressing contempt for the political capacities of the heir from the West, for it was under Fulk's reign that the 'disorder among the Franj' would be most severe. As soon as he came to power he was faced with a new insurrection led by Alix, which was repressed only with great difficulty. Revolt then rumbled in Palestine itself. A persistent rumour had it that Fulk's wife, Queen Melisende, had initiated an amorous liaison with a certain young knight, one Hugh of Le Puiset. The subsequent conflict between the partisans of the husband and those of the lover caused a cleavage within the Franj nobility, who were now racked by altercations, duels and rumours of assassination. When Hugh felt threatened, he sought refuge in Ascalon among the Egyptians, who greeted him warmly. He was even offered the use of Fatimid troops, with which he seized the port of Jaffa. It took weeks to dislodge him.

In December 1132 Fulk assembled his forces to reoccupy Jaffa. Meanwhile the new master of Damascus, the young *atabeg* Ismāʿīl, son of Būri, had just taken the fortress of Baniyās by surprise, the same fortress the Assassins had handed over to the Franj three years before. This reconquest, however, was an isolated incident. The Muslim princes, absorbed in their own quarrels, were unable to take advantage of the dissension afflicting the Occidentals. Zangī himself was practically invisible in Syria. Once again he had been forced to throw himself into a merciless struggle against the caliph, leaving one of his lieutenants in charge of the government of Aleppo. But this time it was al-Mustarshid who seemed to have gained the upper hand.

The sultan Maḥmūd, an ally of Zangī, had just died at the age of twenty-six, and once again a war of succession had erupted within the Seljuk clan. The prince of the faithful had seized upon the opportunity to rise again. Promising each of the pretenders that he would say the Friday prayers in his name, al-Mustarshid became the arbiter of the situation. Zangī was alarmed. Gathering his troops, he marched on Baghdad, intending to inflict as crushing a defeat on al-Mustarshid as he had during their first confrontation five years earlier. But the caliph rode out to meet him at the head of several thousand men, near the town of Takrīt, on the Tigris, north of the ʿAbbasid capital. Zangī's troops were cut to pieces and the *atabeg* himself was on the point of falling into the hands of his enemies when at the last minute a man intervened and saved his life. It was the governor of Takrīt, a young Kurdish officer by the as yet unknown name of Ayyūb. Instead of currying favour with the caliph by delivering his adversary to him, this officer helped the *atabeg* cross the river to escape his pursuers and return in haste to Mosul. Zangī would never forget this magnanimous gesture. He pledged indefectible friendship to Ayyūb and his family. Many years later, this friendship would be decisive in the career of Ayyūb's son Yūsuf, better known by his surname Ṣalāḥ al-Dīn, or Saladin.

After his victory over Zangī, al-Mustarshid stood at the pinnacle of his glory. The Turks, feeling threatened, united around a single Seljuk pretender, Masʿūd, brother of Maḥmūd. In January 1133 the new sultan went to Baghdad to obtain his crown from the prince of the faithful. This ceremony was usually a mere formality, but al-Mustarshid transformed it in his own manner. Ibn al-Qalānisi, our 'journalist' of the epoch, recounts the scene.

> The *imām*, prince of the faithful, was seated. Sultan Masʿūd was led into his presence and paid him the homage due to his rank. The caliph presented him successively with seven stately robes, the last of which was black, a jewel-encrusted crown and golden bracelets with a necklace of gold, saying to him: 'Receive this favour with gratitude and fear God in public and in private.' The sultan kissed the ground, then seated himself upon the high stool reserved for him. The prince of the faithful then said to him: 'He who does not comport himself rightly is not fit to govern others.' The vizier, who was present, repeated these words in Persian and renewed his vows and eulogies. Then the caliph had two sabres brought and handed them solemnly to the sultan, along with two pennants, which he knotted with his own hand. At the conclusion of the interchange, the *imām* al-Mustarshid spoke these words: 'Go, carry that which I have given you, and count yourself among the grateful.'

The ʿAbbasid sovereign evinced great self-assurance, although we may naturally wonder how much of it was a matter of keeping up appearances. He lectured the Turk with nonchalance, certain that the new-found unity of the Seljuks would inevitably threaten his nascent power in the long run, but he nevertheless recognised him as the legitimate sultan. In 1133, however, he dreamt of conquest once again. In June he set out for Mosul at the head of his troops, determined to take the city and to finish off Zangī at the same time. Sultan Masʿūd did not seek to dissuade him. He even suggested that al-Mustarshid reunite Syria and Iraq in a single state under his own authority, an idea that would be taken up often enough in the future. But while putting forward these proposals, the Seljuk also helped Zangī to resist the attacks of the caliph, who besieged Mosul for three months, but in vain.

This setback marked a fatal turn in the fortunes of al-Mustarshid. Abandoned by most of his emirs, he was defeated and captured in June 1135 by Masʿūd, who had him savagely assassinated two months later. The prince of the faithful was found naked in his tent, his ears and nose severed, his body pierced by a score of knife wounds.

As long as Zangī was so totally absorbed in this conflict, he was unable to take a direct interest in Syrian affairs. He would in any case have remained in Iraq until the attempt at ʿAbbasid restoration was definitely crushed had he not received, in January 1135, a desperate appeal from Ismāʿīl, the son of Būri and ruler of Damascus, requesting that he come as quickly as possible to take possession of his city. 'If there is any delay,' wrote Ismāʿīl, 'I shall be compelled to call upon the Franj, and to deliver Damascus and all it contains to them; responsibility for the blood of its inhabitants would then rest with ʿImād al-Dīn Zangī.'

Ismāʿīl, who feared for his life and thought he detected murderers lurking in every nook and cranny of his palace, decided to leave his capital and to seek refuge, under Zangī's protection, in the fortress of Sarkhad south of the city, where he had already moved his wealth and wardrobe.

The reign of the son of Būri had actually begun quite auspiciously. Having come to power at the age of nineteen, he exhibited admirable dynamism; the best illustration of this was his recapture of Baniyās. Granted, he was arrogant and scarcely heeded the advisers of his father, nor those of his grandfather Tughtigin. But people were prepared to attribute this to his youth. On the other hand, Damascenes found it hard to put up with the mounting greed of their master, who regularly imposed new taxes upon them.

It was not until 1134 that the situation began to take a tragic turn, when an old female slave by the name of Ailba, formerly in the service of Tughtigin, tried to assassinate her master. Ismāʿīl, who barely escaped death, insisted on hearing the confession of his assailant personally. 'If I acted as I did,' the slave responded, 'it was to win God's favour by ridding the people of your maleficent existence. You have oppressed the poor and helpless, the artisans, the pedlars and the peasants. You have treated civilians and military men with disrespect.' Ailba was then ordered to list the names of all those who, like herself, desired the death of Ismāʿīl. Traumatised to the point of madness, the son of Būri ordered the arrest of all the people named and had them put to death without further ado. 'Even these unjust executions did not satisfy him,' the chronicler of Damascus relates. 'He suspected his own brother, Sawinj, and inflicted the worst of tortures upon him, locking him in a cell where he finally starved to death. His maleficence and injustice knew no bounds.'

Ismāʿīl was trapped in a vicious circle. Every execution augmented his fear of fresh vengeance, and he ordered yet other death sentences in an effort to protect himself. When he realised that things could not go on much longer, he decided to hand his city over to Zangī and to withdraw to the Sarkhad fortress. Now, for years the people of Damascus had heartily detested the ruler of Aleppo. Their hatred dated back to the end of 1129, when Zangī had written to Būri inviting him to take part in an expedition against the Franj. The lord of Damascus had quickly agreed, and despatched five hundred cavalry commanded by his best officers and accompanied by his own son, the unfortunate Sawinj. After greeting them respectfully, Zangī had disarmed and imprisoned them all, informing Būri that if he ever dared oppose him, the lives of the hostages would be in danger. It was not until two years later that Sawinj was released.

In 1135 the Damascenes still remembered this betrayal, and when the city's dignitaries got wind of Ismāʿīl's designs, they resolved to oppose them by any means necessary. Meetings of the emirs, notables and principal slaves were held; they all wanted to save both their lives and their city. A group of conspirators decided to explain the situation to Ismāʿīl's mother, the princess Zumurrud, 'Emerald'.

> She was horrified at what she heard [the chronicler of Damascus reports]. She summoned her son and upbraided him severely. Her desire to do good, her profound religious sentiments, and her intelligence then led her to conceive a way to extirpate the evil at its roots and to redress the situation of Damascus and its inhabitants. She pored over the affair just as a man of good sense and experience would have done, examining things lucidly. She could find no remedy for the maleficence of her son except to dispose of him and thus to put an end to the mounting disorder for which he was responsible.

The execution of her plan was not long in coming.

> The princess now thought of nothing else but this project. She waited for a time when her son would be alone, without slaves or squires, and ordered his servants to cut him down mercilessly. She herself showed neither compassion nor sorrow. She then had the corpse carried somewhere in the palace where it was sure to be discovered. Everyone rejoiced at the fall of Ismāʿīl. They thanked God, praising and offering prayers for the princess.

Did Zumurrud have her own son killed to prevent him from handing Damascus over to Zangī? It is doubtful, for three years later the princess would marry this same Zangī, and would actually implore him to occupy her city. Nor would she have acted to avenge Sawinj, who was the son of another of Būri's wives. Probably then, we must accept the explanation offered by Ibn al-Athīr: Zumurrud was the mistress of Ismāʿīl's chief adviser, and when she learned that her son planned to kill her lover, and perhaps to punish her as well, she decided to take action.

Whatever her real motives, the princess robbed her future husband of an easy conquest, for on 30 January 1135, the day Ismāʿīl was assassinated, Zangī was already on his way to Damascus. A week later, when his army crossed the Euphrates, Zumurrud installed Maḥmūd, another of her sons, on the throne, and the populace prepared to resist Zangī actively. The *atabeg*, unaware of the death of Ismāʿīl, sent representatives to Damascus to examine the modalities of capitulation.

They were politely received, of course, but were not told of the latest developments. Furious, Zangī refused to turn back. He set up camp north-east of the city and instructed his scouts to find out where and how he could attack. But he soon realised that the defenders were determined to fight to the bitter end. They were led by one Muʿīn al-Dīn ʿUnar, a wily and stubborn Turkish officer and old comrade-in-arms of Tughtigin who was to be a thorn in Zangī's side more than once in years to come. After several skirmishes, the *atabeg* decided to seek a compromise. As a face-saving gesture, the leader of the besieged city paid him homage and recognised his suzerainty, which remained, however, purely nominal.

The *atabeg* left Damascus in the middle of March. To raise the morale of his troops, who had found this useless campaign trying, he immediately led them north and, with stunning alacrity, seized four Frankish strongholds, among them the infamous Maʿarra. In spite of these exploits, his prestige was tarnished. Not until two years later was he able, through a striking action, to bury the memory of his setback at Damascus. Paradoxically, Muʿīn al-Dīn ʿUnar was to be, unwittingly, the man who offered Zangī the opportunity to redeem himself.

VII

An Emir Among Barbarians

In June 1137 Zangī arrived, with an impressive array of siege machinery, in the vineyards surrounding Homs, the principal city of central Syria and traditionally an object of contention between Aleppo and Damascus. At the time, the Damascenes controlled it; indeed, the governor of the city was none other than old Muʿīn al-Dīn ʿUnar. When he saw the catapults and mangonels being set up by his enemy, Muʿīn al-Dīn realised that he would be unable to resist for long. He arranged to send word to the Franj that he planned to capitulate. The knights of Tripoli, who had no desire to see Zangī establish a base a mere two days' march from their city, set out to meet him. ʿUnar's stratagem met with complete success: fearing that he might be forced to fight on two fronts, the *atabeg* concluded a hasty truce with his old enemy and turned against the Franj. He decided to lay siege to their most powerful fortress in the region, Bārin. The uneasy knights of Tripoli called upon King Fulk of Jerusalem to come to their rescue, and he hastened to join them with his army. Thus it was that the first important battle between Zangī and the Franj took place before the walls of Bārin, in a cultivated, terraced valley. It is perhaps surprising that this was the first such engagement, for the *atabeg* had been ruler of Aleppo for more than nine years.

The battle was brief but decisive. Within a few hours the Occidentals, exhausted by their long forced march, were crushed by overwhelming numbers and were cut to pieces. Only the king and a few members of his entourage managed to take refuge in the fortress. Fulk had just enough time to send a message to Jerusalem appealing for reinforcements when, as Ibn al-Athīr relates, 'Zangī cut off all communications, allowing no news to filter through; the besieged no longer knew what was happening in their country, so strict was the control of the routes.'

Such a blockade would have had no effect whatever on the Arabs. For centuries they had used carrier pigeons to convey messages from town to town. Every army on the march carried pigeons that had been raised in various Muslim cities and strongholds. They had been trained always to return to their nests of origin. It was therefore enough to scribble a message, roll it up, attach it to a pigeon's leg, and release the bird, which would then fly, much faster than the swiftest charger, to announce victory, defeat or the death of a prince, to call for assistance or to encourage resistance among a beleaguered garrison. As the Arab mobilisation against the Franj became better organised, a regular pigeon-post service was established between Damascus, Cairo, Aleppo and other cities, the state even paying salaries to the people in charge of raising and training these birds.

In fact, it was during their stay in the Orient that the Franj were initiated into the art of raising and training carrier pigeons, which would later become something of a fad in their home countries. At the time of the siege of Bārin, however, they knew nothing of this means of communication, whereas Zangī was able to take advantage of it. The *atabeg* began by stepping up the pressure on the besieged, but then, after bitter negotiations, he offered them advantageous terms of surrender: they would hand over the fortress and pay 50,000 dinars; in exchange, he would let them leave in peace. Fulk and his men surrendered and fled at a gallop, delighted to have got off so lightly. 'Shortly after leaving Bārin, they encountered the bulk of the reinforcements that were coming to their aid, and they regretted their decision, but it was too late. This had happened', according to Ibn al-Athīr, 'only because the Franj had been completely cut off from the outside world.'

Zangī was especially pleased with his resolution of the Bārin affair, for he had just received some particularly alarming news: the Byzantine emperor John II Comnenus, who had succeeded his father Alexius in 1118, was en route to northern Syria with tens of thousands of men. As soon as Fulk departed Bārin, the *atabeg* leapt on his mount and rushed to Aleppo. This city, a special target of the Rūm in the past, was seething. In anticipation of an attack, the citizens had begun to empty the trenches around the city walls. (In peacetime people

Poet with musicians and singers. The Sunni caliph of Baghdad, twenty-two-year-old al-Mustaẓhir Billah, was sensitive, refined and had a taste for the arts. Chiefly interested in architecture, he also composed love poems: 'When I stretch out my hand to bid my beloved adieu, the ardour of my passion melts ice'

A souk with (from left to right) a jeweller, a herbalist, a butcher and a baker. The souk proved to be fertile ground for the spreading and dissemination of news: 'Seated in the shadows of the creeping vines, the merchants of raw silk, gilded brocades, damask linen and inlaid furniture passed the word from one booth to the next'

صفت صورت ج

بنی شیبه بذ نام از جایگاه

بذ و در دو سالار و الا منش

دو سالار و از هر دو ازیکسه

Franj foot soldiers wearing helmets and mail armour, carrying swords (stone relief from Konya, twelfth century). *Below,* the Umayyad mosque at Damascus, where emir Mawdūd was struck twice by a dagger and killed in October 1113

The murder of Niẓām al-Mulk in 1092 by members of Ḥasan's secretive sect, the *ḥashīshīn*, or 'Assassins'

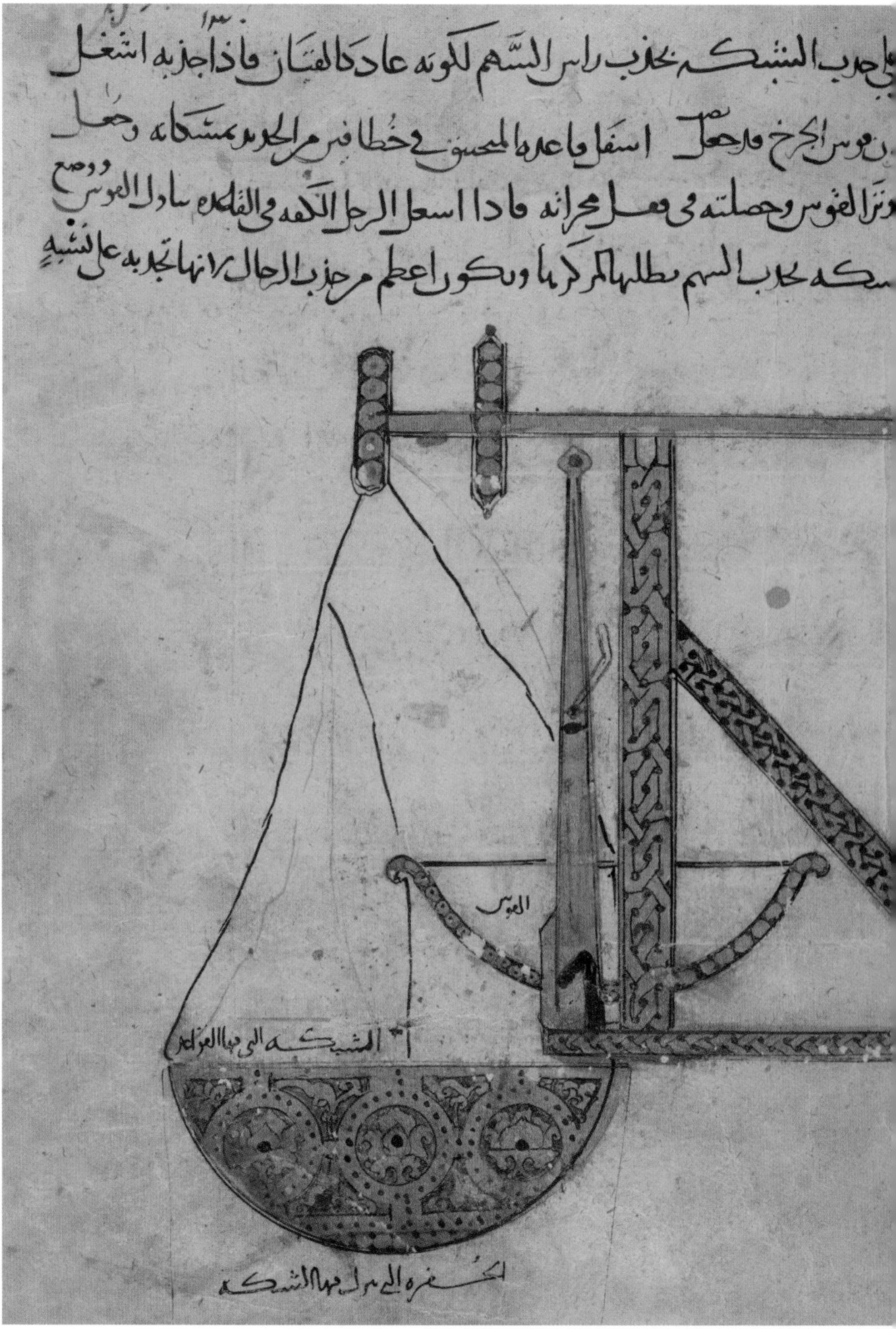

Mangonel from *Tabṣirah fī al-hurūb* ('Treatise on Armoury') written for Saladin. In 1139, Zangī surrounded Baalbek, the last town held by the Damascenes, with fourteen mangonels and proceeded relentlessly to pound the city

بعد ان يضع الحجر في الكفة ويعلق حلقتها في الخطاف الموضوع في راس السهم
الكفة بخطاف من الحديد جعل في اسفلها في حلقة تثبت في قاعدة تمسك ...
وترة مع الحبال التي ترفع الشبكة في خطاف مثبت في الحبال فاذا اطلق الحبا[ل]
السلة في مجراها ورمى عنها ثم تعود في ساعته الى الكفة فعلقها على ما يقوم في
واحد والرجال تحلف حبلها وهذه صورة ذلك

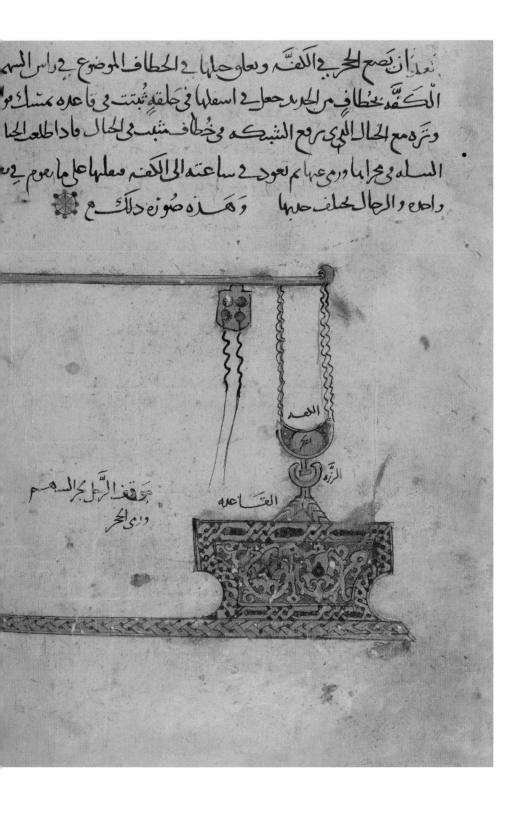

Greek physicists Marinus, Andromachus and Andromachus the Younger, from the *Kitāb al-Diryāq* ('Book of Antidotes'). In contrast to primitive Western medicine, Arab physicians were greatly advanced, though they acknowledged their original debt to the Greeks had the bad habit of dumping their rubbish in them.) But emissaries of the *basileus* soon arrived to reassure Zangī: their objective was not Aleppo but Antioch, the Frankish city to which the Rūm had always laid claim. Indeed the *atabeg* soon learned, not without satisfaction, that Antioch was already under siege, being bombarded with catapults. Leaving the Christians to their own disputes, Zangī turned back to besiege Homs, where ʿUnar continued to hold out against him.

Rūm and Franj, however, reconciled their differences more quickly than expected. To placate the *basileus*, the Occidentals promised to restore Antioch to Constantinople, while in return John Comnenus promised to deliver several Muslim cities of Syria to them. A new war of conquest was launched in March 1138. The emperor's lieutenants were two Frankish commanders, Joscelin II, the new count of Edessa, and a knight by the name of Raymond, who had just taken charge of the principality of Antioch by marrying Constance, the eight-year-old daughter of Bohemond II and Alix.

In April the allies laid siege to Shayzar, bringing eighteen catapults and mangonels into the battle. The old emir Sultan Ibn Munqidh, who had been governor of the city even before the start of the Frankish invasion, scarcely seemed capable of resisting the joint forces of the Rūm and the Franj. According to Ibn al-Athīr, the allies selected Shayzar as their target 'because they hoped that Zangī would not bother to defend with any vigour a city that did not belong to him'. They did not know the man. The Turk organised and directed the resistance personally. In fact, the battle of Shayzar was an occasion for him to display his admirable qualities as a man of state more clearly than ever.

In just a few weeks he turned the entire Middle East upside down. After despatching messengers to Anatolia, where they convinced the successors of Danishmend to attack Byzantine territory, he sent agitators to Baghdad to organise a riot similar to that which Ibn al-Khashāb had fomented in 1111, thus forcing Sultan Masʿūd to send troops to Shayzar. He then wrote to all the emirs of Syria and Jazīra calling upon them, with appropriate accompanying threats, to commit all their forces to driving back this new invasion. The army of the *atabeg* himself, far less numerous than that of the enemy, avoided any frontal attack and instead started to harass the enemy. Meanwhile Zangī initiated an intense correspondence with the *basileus* and the Frankish commanders. He 'informed' the emperor – and this was in fact true – that his allies feared him and were impatiently awaiting his departure from Syria. He then sent messages to the Franj, in particular to Joscelin of Edessa and Raymond of Antioch: 'Do you not understand', he asked them, 'that if the Rūm occupied a single stronghold in Syria, they would soon seize all your cities?' He despatched numerous agents, most of them Christians of Syria, to mingle among the rank-and-file Byzantines and Franj. Their task was to spread demoralising rumours about the approach of gigantic armies coming to the rescue from Persia, Iraq and Anatolia.

This propaganda had its effect, especially among the Franj. While the *basileus*, wearing his golden helmet, personally directed the firing of the catapults, the lords of Edessa and Antioch sat in their tents and played interminable games of dice. This pastime, popular back in pharaonic Egypt, was equally widespread throughout East and West in the twelfth century. The Arabs called it *al-zahr*, a word the Franj adopted to designate not the game itself, but chance (*hasard*).

It was a resounding victory for Zangī. The *atabeg* now appeared as a saviour throughout the Arab world, where the alliance of the Rūm and the Franj had caused great dread. Naturally, he was now determined to use his prestige to seek a quick solution to a number of problems that had been gnawing at him, in the first place the question of Homs. At the end of May, as soon as the battle of Shayzar ended, Zangī reached a curious agreement with Damascus. He would marry the princess Zumurrud and receive the city of Homs as a dowry. Three months later, the mother who had murdered her own son arrived with an entourage to join formally with her new husband. Guests at the ceremony included representatives of the sultan and of the caliphs of Baghdad and Cairo, and even ambassadors sent by the Rūm, who, having experienced Zangī's displeasure, had decided to maintain more friendly relations with him.

Now that he had become master of Mosul, Aleppo and all of central Syria, the *atabeg* set himself the objective of taking Damascus too, with the aid of his new wife. He hoped that she would be able to convince her son Maḥmūd to hand over his capital without a fight. The princess hesitated, stalled. Once he found that he could not rely on her, Zangī abandoned her. But in July 1139, while in Ḥarrān, he received an urgent message from Zumurrud: Maḥmūd had just been assassinated, stabbed to death in his bed by three of his slaves. The princess begged her husband to march on Damascus without delay to take the city and punish her son's murderers. The *atabeg* set out immediately. Although not indifferent to the tears of his wife, he mainly believed that the death of Maḥmūd could be used finally to unite all Syria under his authority.

That was to reckon without the immortal ʿUnar, who had returned to Damascus after the cession of Homs and had taken personal charge of the city's affairs upon the death of Maḥmūd. Expecting an offensive by Zangī, Muʿīn al-Dīn quickly worked out a secret plan to deal with it. For the moment, however, he left the plan in abeyance and saw to the city's defence.

Zangī did not march directly on the city he coveted. He began by attacking the ancient Roman town of Baalbek, the only agglomeration of any importance still held by the Damascenes. His intention was to encircle the Syrian metropolis and simultaneously to demoralise its defenders. In August he set up fourteen mangonels around Baalbek, which he then pounded relentlessly, hoping that he would be able to take the city in just a few days and then begin the siege of Damascus before summer was out. Baalbek itself capitulated with little resistance, but the defenders of the citadel, built with stones taken from an ancient temple of the Phoenician god Baal, held out for two long months. Zangī became so irritated that, when the garrison finally surrendered at the end of October after being assured that their lives would be spared, he ordered the crucifixion of thirty-seven fighters and had the commander burned alive. This act of savagery, meant to convince the Damascenes that any resistance would amount to suicide, had just the opposite effect. Solidly united behind ʿUnar, the population of the Syrian metropolis was more determined than ever to fight to the end. In any case, it would soon be winter, and Zangī could not contemplate any serious attack before spring. ʿUnar would use these few months of respite to perfect his secret plan.

In April 1140, as the *atabeg* stepped up his pressure and prepared for a general attack, ʿUnar decided that the time had come to implement his plan: he would ask the army of the Franj, under the command of King Fulk, to come to the rescue of Damascus. This was not to be a one-off operation, but the inauguration of a proper treaty of alliance that would last beyond the death of Zangī.

Indeed, back in 1138, ʿUnar had sent his friend the chronicler Usāmah Ibn Munqidh to Jerusalem to explore the possibility of Franco-Damascene collaboration against the master of Aleppo. Well received by the Franj, Usāmah had worked out the principles of an accord. Once embassies were established, the chronicler returned to the holy city at the beginning of 1140, carrying detailed proposals with him: the Frankish army would force Zangī to withdraw from the vicinity of Damascus; the forces of the two states would unite in the event of any fresh danger; Muʿīn al-Dīn would pay 20,000 dinars to defray military expenses; finally, a joint expedition would be mounted, under ʿUnar's command, to occupy the fortress of Baniyās, which had recently fallen into the hands of one of Zangī's vassals, and to restore it to the king of Jerusalem. As a demonstration of good faith, the Damascenes would send the Franj hostages selected from the families of major city dignitaries.

In practice, all this amounted to living under a Frankish protectorate, but the population of the Syrian metropolis was resigned to it. Frightened by the *atabeg*'s brutal methods, they unanimously approved the treaty negotiated by ʿUnar, whose policy proved undeniably effective. Fearing that he would be caught in a pincer movement, Zangī withdrew to Baalbek, which he entrusted as a fiefdom to a reliable man, Ayyūb, father of Saladin. He then headed north with his army, promising Ayyūb that he would soon return to avenge this setback. After the departure of the *atabeg*, ʿUnar occupied Baniyās and handed it over to the Franj, in accordance with the terms of the treaty. He then made an official visit to the kingdom of Jerusalem.

Usāmah, who had become the leading Damascene specialist on Frankish affairs, went with him. Fortunately for us, this emir-chronicler did more than simply participate in diplomatic negotiations. He had an inquisitive mind and was a keen observer who left us unforgettable testimony about mores and daily life during the time of the Franj.

> When I was visiting Jerusalem, I used to go to al-Aqṣā mosque, where my Templar friends were staying. Along one side of the building was a small oratory in which the Franj had set up a church. The Templars placed this spot at my disposal that I might say my prayers. One day I entered, said *Allāhu akbar*, and was about to begin my prayer, when a man, a Franj, threw himself upon me, grabbed me, and turned me towards the east, saying, 'Thus do we pray.' The Templars rushed forward and led him away. I then set myself to prayer once more, but this same man, seizing upon a moment of inattention, threw himself upon me yet again, turned my face to the east, and repeated once more, 'Thus do we pray.' Once again the Templars intervened, led him away, and apologised to me, saying, 'He is a foreigner. He has just arrived from the land of the Franj and he has never seen anyone pray without turning to face east.' I answered that I had prayed enough and left, stunned by the behaviour of this demon who had been so enraged at seeing me pray while facing the direction of Mecca.

If the emir Usāmah did not hesitate to call the Templars 'my friends', it was because he believed that their barbarian mores were gradually being refined by contact with the Orient. 'Among the Franj,' he explains, 'we find some people who have come to settle among us and who have cultivated the society of the Muslims. They are far superior to those who have freshly joined them in the territories they now occupy.' He considered the incident in al-Aqṣā mosque 'an instance of the vulgarity of the Franj'. And he mentioned others as well, gathered during his frequent visits to the kingdom of Jerusalem.

> I happened to be in Tiberias one day when the Franj were celebrating one of their holidays. The knights had come out of the city to engage in a jousting tournament. They brought with them two decrepit old women whom they stood at one end of the field; at the other end was a pig, hung suspended over a rock. The knights then organised a foot-race between the two old women. Each one advanced, escorted by a group

of knights who obstructed her path. The old women stumbled, fell, and picked themselves up at almost every step, amid loud bursts of laughter from the spectators. Finally, one of the old women, the first to finish, took the pig as the prize for her victory.

An emir as well-educated and refined as Usāmah was unable to appreciate this burlesque Gallic humour. But his condescending pout shrivelled into a grimace of outright disgust when he witnessed what the Franj called justice.

> In Nablus [he relates] I had the opportunity to witness a curious spectacle. Two men had to meet each other in individual combat. The cause of the fight was this: some brigands among the Muslims had invaded a neighbouring village, and a farmer was suspected of having acted as their guide. He ran away, but was soon forced to return, for King Fulk had imprisoned his children. 'Treat me fairly', the farmer had asked him, 'and allow me to compete against my accuser.' The king then told the lord who had been granted this village as a fiefdom, 'Bring the man's adversary here.' The lord had selected a smith who worked in the village, telling him, 'It is you who will fight this duel.' The possessor of the fiefdom wanted to make sure that none of his peasants would be killed, for fear that his crops would suffer. I looked at this smith. He was a strong young man, but was constantly asking for something to drink, whether he was walking or sitting. As for the accused, he was a courageous old man who stood snapping his fingers in a gesture of defiance. The viscount, governor of Nablus, approached, gave each man a lance and shield, and had the spectators form a circle around them.
>
> The struggle was joined. The old man forced the smith back, pressed him towards the crowd, and then returned to the centre of the arena. There was an exchange of blows so violent that the rivals seemed to form a single column of blood. The fight dragged on, despite the exhortations of the viscount, who was anxious to hasten its conclusion. 'Faster,' he shouted at them. The old man was finally exhausted, and the smith, taking advantage of his experience in handling the hammer, dealt him a blow that knocked the old man down and caused him to lose his lance. He then leapt upon him and tried to dig his fingers into his eyes, but he

> could not manage it, for there was too much blood. The smith then rose and finished off his opponent with a thrust of his lance. A rope was immediately wound around the neck of the corpse, which was dragged to a gallows and hanged. In this example you may see what justice is among the Franj!

The emir's indignation was quite genuine, for justice was a serious business among the Arabs in the twelfth century. The judges, or *qāḍīs*, were highly respected men who were obliged to adhere to a meticulous procedure fixed by the Koran, before rendering their verdict: first came indictment, then plea, then testimony. The 'judgement of God' to which the Occidentals often resorted seemed a macabre farce to the Arabs. The duel described by the chronicler was only one of the forms of trial by ordeal. The test of fire was another. There was also the water torture, which Usāmah described with horror.

> A large cask had been set up and filled with water. The young man who was the object of suspicion was pinioned, suspended from a rope by his shoulder-blades, and plunged into the cask. If he was innocent, they said, he would sink into the water, and they would pull him out by the rope. If he was guilty, it would be impossible for him to sink into the water. When he was thrown into the cask, the unfortunate man made every effort to descend to the bottom, but he could not manage it, and thus had to submit to the rigours of their law, may God's curse be upon them! He was then blinded by a red-hot silver awl.

The Syrian emir's opinion of the 'barbarians' was hardly modified when he discussed their science. In the twelfth century the Franj lagged far behind the Arabs in all scientific and technical fields. But it was in medicine that the gap between the developed East and the primitive West was greatest. Usāmah observed the difference.

> One day [he relates] the Frankish governor of Munaytra, in the Lebanese mountains, wrote to my uncle the sultan, emir of Shayzar, asking him to send a physician to treat several urgent cases. My uncle selected one of our Christian doctors, a man named Thābit. He was gone for just a few

days, and then returned home. We were all very curious to know how he had been able to cure the patients so quickly, and we besieged him with questions. Thābit answered: 'They brought before me a knight who had an abscess on his leg and a woman suffering from consumption. I made a plaster for the knight, and the swelling opened and improved. For the woman I prescribed a diet to revive her constitution.' But a Frankish doctor then arrived and objected, 'This man does not know how to care for them.' And, addressing the knight, he asked him, 'Which do you prefer, to live with one leg or die with two?' When the patient answered that he preferred to live with just one leg, the physician ordered, 'Bring me a strong knight with a well-sharpened battleaxe.' The knight and the axe soon arrived. The Frankish doctor placed the man's leg on a chopping block, telling the new arrival, 'Strike a sharp blow to cut cleanly.' Before my very eyes, the man struck an initial blow, but then, since the leg was still attached, he struck a second time. The marrow of the leg spurted out and the wounded man died that very instant. As for the woman, the Frankish doctor examined her and said, 'She has a demon in her head who has fallen in love with her. Cut her hair.' They cut her hair. The woman then began to eat their food again, with its garlic and mustard, which aggravated the consumption. Their doctor affirmed, 'The devil himself must have entered her head.' Then, grasping a razor, he cut an incision in the shape of a cross, exposed the bone of the skull, and rubbed it with salt. The woman died on the spot. I then asked, 'Have you any further need of me?' They said no, and I returned home, having learned much that I had never known about the medicine of the Franj.

Scandalised as he was by the ignorance of the Occidentals, Usāmah was even more deeply shocked by their morals: 'The Franj', he wrote, 'have no sense of honour. If one of them is walking in the street with his wife and encounters another man, that man will take his wife's hand and draw her aside and speak to her, while the husband stands waiting for them to finish their conversation. If it lasts too long, he will leave her with her interlocutor and go off!' The emir was troubled: 'Imagine this contradiction! These people possess neither jealousy nor honour, whereas they are so courageous. Courage, however, comes only from one's sense of honour and from contempt for that which is evil!'

The more he learned of their ways, the more wretched did Usāmah consider the Occidentals to be. He admired nothing about them except their martial qualities. One may thus readily understand that when one of the 'friends' he had made among them, a knight in King Fulk's army, proposed to take Usāmah's young son to Europe to initiate him in the rules of chivalry, the emir politely declined the invitation, muttering under his breath that he would prefer that his son go 'to prison rather than to the land of the Franj'. Fraternisation with these foreigners had its limits. Besides, the famous collaboration between Damascus and Jerusalem, which had afforded Usāmah the unexpected opportunity to get to know the Occidentals better, soon appeared as a brief interlude. A spectacular event would now rekindle all-out war against the occupier: on Saturday 23 September 1144 the city of Edessa, capital of the oldest of the four Frankish states of the Middle East, fell into the hands of the *atabeg* ʿImād al-Dīn Zangī.

If the fall of Jerusalem in July 1099 marked the climax of the Frankish invasion, and the fall of Tyre in July 1124 the completion of the phase of occupation, the reconquest of Edessa has gone down in history as the capstan of the Arab riposte to the invaders and the beginning of the long march to victory.

No one expected that the occupation would be challenged in such a striking manner. Admittedly, Edessa was no more than an outpost of the Frankish presence, but its counts had succeeded in thoroughly integrating themselves into local politics. The last Western ruler of this majority-Armenian city was Joscelin II, a short, bearded man with a prominent nose, protruding eyes and a malformed body, a man who had never been known for his courage or wisdom. But he was not detested by his subjects, primarily because his mother was Armenian, and conditions in his realm did not seem at all critical. He and his neighbours indulged in routine raids which usually ended in truces.

But the situation changed dramatically in that autumn of 1144. A clever military manoeuvre by Zangī put an end to a half century of

Frankish domination in this part of the Middle East, as he scored a victory that rocked powerful and humble alike, from Persia to the far-off country of the 'Almān', and served as a prelude to a fresh invasion led by the greatest kings of the Franj.

The most stirring account of the conquest of Edessa was bequeathed to us by an eyewitness, the Syrian bishop Abu'l-Faraj Basil, who was directly involved in the events. His attitude during the battle graphically illustrates the tragedy of the Oriental Christian communities to which he belonged. Since his city was under attack, Abu'l-Faraj actively participated in its defence; but at the same time, his sympathies were more with the Muslim army than with his Western 'protectors', whom he did not hold in high esteem.

> Count Joscelin [he relates] had gone pillaging along the banks of the Euphrates. Zangī found out. On 30 November he arrived at the walls of Edessa. His troops were as numerous as the stars in the skies. All the fields around the city were filled with them. Tents were erected everywhere, and the *atabeg* pitched his own to the north of the city, facing the Gate of Hours, on a hill overlooking the Church of the Confessors.

Even though it lay in a valley, Edessa was a difficult city to take, for its powerful triangular walls were solidly anchored in the hills ringing the town. But, as Abu'l-Faraj explains, 'Joscelin had not left any troops behind. He had only shoemakers, weavers, silk merchants, tailors and priests.' It was therefore the Frankish bishop who took charge of the defence of the city, with the help of an Armenian prelate and the chronicler himself, who, however, favoured reaching some accommodation with the *atabeg*.

> Zangī [he writes] constantly sent peace proposals to the besieged, telling them, 'O, unfortunate people! You can see that all hope is lost. What do you want? What can you still expect? Have pity on yourselves, your women, your homes! Act now, that your city may not be devastated and emptied of its inhabitants!' But there was no commander in the city capable of imposing his will. Zangī was answered with stupid rodomontade and insult.

When he saw that sappers were tunnelling under the ramparts, Abu'l-Faraj suggested writing a letter to Zangī proposing a truce, and the Frankish bishop agreed. 'The letter was written and read to the people, but a madman, a silk merchant, reached out, grabbed the letter, and tore it up.' Nevertheless, Zangī reiterated: 'If you desire a truce for several days, we will accord you one, to see whether you will receive any aid. If you do not, surrender and survive!'

But no help arrived. Although Joscelin had been alerted to the offensive against his capital, he did not dare match forces with the *atabeg*. He preferred to camp at Tel Bāshir, expecting that troops from Antioch or Jerusalem would come to his aid.

> The Turks had now dismantled the foundations of the northern wall, and in their place had erected great quantities of wood, joists and beams. They filled the interstices with naphtha, animal fat and sulphur, so fire would spread more easily and the wall would collapse. Then, on Zangī's orders, the fire was started. The heralds of his camp gave the call to prepare for battle, telling the soldiers to rush in through the breach as soon as the wall collapsed, promising to allow them to pillage the city at will for three days. The fire caught in the naphtha and sulphur, and soon the wood and melted fat were in flames. The northerly wind was blowing the smoke towards the defenders. In spite of its great solidity, the wall tottered, then collapsed. After losing many troops passing through the breach, the Turks penetrated the city and began massacring people indiscriminately. About six thousand inhabitants perished on that day. Women, children and young people fled to the upper citadel to escape the massacre. They found the gate barred – the fault of the bishop of the Franj, who had told the guards, 'Do not open the gate unless you see my face!' Groups of people climbed up in succession, trampling one another. It was a lamentable and horrifying spectacle: about five thousand people, perhaps more, died atrociously, twisted, suffocating, pressed together into a single, compact mass.

But Zangī intervened personally to halt the killing, and then despatched his top lieutenant to see Abu'l-Faraj.

> 'Venerable Abu'l-Faraj, we want you to swear to us, on the cross and the New Testament, that you and your community will remain loyal. You know very well that this city was a thriving metropolis during the two hundred years that the Arabs governed it. Today, the Franj have occupied it for just fifty years, and already they have ruined it. Our master ʿImād al-Dīn Zangī is prepared to treat you well. Live in peace, be secure under his authority, and pray for his life!'

Abu'l-Faraj continued:

> In fact the Syrians and Armenians were brought out of the citadel, and they all returned to their homes safe and sound. Everything was taken from the Franj, however: gold, silver, holy vases, chalices, patens, ornamented crucifixes and great quantities of jewels. The priests, nobles and notables were taken aside, stripped of their robes, and led away in chains to Aleppo. Of the rest, the artisans were identified, and Zangī kept them as prisoners, setting each to work at his craft. All the other Franj, about a hundred men, were executed.

When news of the reconquest of Edessa spread, the Arab world was gripped with enthusiasm. The most ambitious projects were attributed to Zangī. The refugees from Palestine and the many coastal cities in the *atabeg*'s entourage had already begun to speak of the reconquest of Jerusalem, an objective that would soon become the rallying cry for resistance to the Franj.

The caliph lost no time in heaping prestigious titles upon the hero of the moment: *al-malik al-manṣūr*, 'victorious king'; *zaynat al-Islām*, 'ornament of Islam'; *nāṣir amīr al-muʾmīn*, 'protector of the prince of the faithful'. Like all leaders of the time, Zangī proudly strung these various titles together, as symbols of his power. In a subtly satirical note, Ibn al-Qalānisi asks readers of his chronicle to excuse him for writing merely 'sultan', 'emir' or '*atabeg* such and such', without appending the full lists of titles. For, he explains, there had been such a proliferation of honorific titles since the tenth century that his text would have become unreadable had he tried to list them all. Discreetly lamenting the epoch of the first caliphs, who were content with the title 'prince of the faithful', superb in its simplicity, the Damascene chronicler cites a few examples to illustrate his point, Zangī himself among them. Ibn al-Qalānisi recalls that every time he mentions Zangī he ought, strictly speaking, to say:

> The emir, the general, the great, the just, the aid of God, the triumphant, the unique, the pillar of religion, the cornerstone of Islam, ornament of Islam, protector of God's creatures, associate of the dynasty, auxiliary of doctrine, grandeur of the nation, honour of kings, supporter of sultans, victor over the infidels, rebels and atheists, commander of the Muslim armies, the victorious king, the king of princes, the sun of the deserving, emir of the two Iraqs and of Syria, conqueror of Iran, Bahlawan, Jihan Alp Inassaj Kotlogh Toghrulbeg *atabeg* Abū Saʿid Zangī Ibn Aq Sunqur, protector of the prince of the faithful.

Whatever their pompous character, at which the Damascene chronicler smiles irreverently, these titles nevertheless reflected the primordial place Zangī now held in the Arab world. The Franj trembled at the very mention of his name. Their disarray was all the greater in that King Fulk had died shortly before the fall of Edessa, leaving two children who were both minors. His wife, who assured the continuity of the crown, quickly sent emissaries to the land of the Franj to bring news of the disaster that had just befallen his people. 'In all their territories', Ibn al-Qalānisi writes, 'calls were issued for people to assemble for an assault on the land of Islam.'

As if to confirm the fears of the Occidentals, Zangī returned to Syria after his victory, giving rise to rumours that he was preparing a broad offensive against the major cities held by the Franj. At first, these projects were greeted with enthusiasm in the cities of Syria. But gradually the Damascenes began to wonder about the *atabeg*'s real intentions, for he had settled in Baalbek, just as he had done in 1139, and was busy building siege machinery. Was it not perhaps Damascus itself that he intended to attack, using the *jihād* as a pretext?

We will never know, for in January 1146, just as his preparations for a spring offensive seemed complete, Zangī found himself compelled to turn north again. His spies had informed him that a plot to massacre the Turkish garrison had been hatched by Joscelin of Edessa and some of his Armenian friends who had remained in the city. The *atabeg* took the situation in hand immediately upon his return to the conquered city, executing the supporters of the former count. Then, in an effort to strengthen the anti-Franj party within the population, he moved in three hundred Jewish families of whose indefectible support he was certain.

This alert, however, convinced Zangī that it would be better to renounce any attempt to extend his domain, temporarily at least, and to concentrate on consolidating it instead. In particular, an Arab emir who controlled the powerful fortress of Jābar, situated on the Euphrates along the main route from Aleppo to Mosul, had refused to recognise the *atabeg*'s authority. Since this insubordination could easily threaten communications between Zangī's two capitals, he laid siege to Jābar in June 1146. He hoped to take it in a few days, but the enterprise proved more difficult than expected. Three long months passed, and the resistance of the besieged forces failed to weaken.

One night in September the *atabeg* fell asleep after imbibing a great quantity of alcohol. Suddenly he was awakened by a noise in his tent. When he opened his eyes, he saw one of his eunuchs, a man of Frankish origin named Yarankash, drinking wine from his own goblet. This infuriated the *atabeg,* who swore he would punish the eunuch severely the following day. Fearing the wrath of his master, Yarankash waited for him to fall asleep again, and then riddled his body with dagger-strokes and fled to Jābar, where gifts were lavished upon him.

Zangī did not die immediately. As he lay half-conscious, one of his close aides entered his tent. Ibn al-Athīr reports his testimony:

> When he saw me, the *atabeg* thought that I had come to finish him off, and with a gesture of his finger, he asked for the *coup de grâce.* Choked with emotion, I fell to my knees and said to him, 'Master, who did this to you?' But he was unable to answer, and gave up his soul, may God have mercy on him!

Zangī's tragic death, coming so soon after his triumph, made a deep impression on his contemporaries. Ibn al-Qalānisi commented on the event in verse:

> The morning found him sprawled upon his bed, lying where
> his eunuch had slaughtered him,
> And yet he slumbered amidst a proud army, ringed by his
> braves with their swords.
> He perished, neither riches nor power of use to him,
> His treasures now the prey of others, by his sons and
> adversaries dismembered.
> At his death did his enemies ride forth, grasping the swords
> they dared not brandish while he lived.

Indeed, when Zangī died there was a mad dash for the spoils. His soldiers, so well-disciplined only a short time ago, now became a horde of uncontrollable plunderers. His treasury, his arsenal, even his personal effects, disappeared in the twinkling of an eye. Then his army began to break up. One after another, the emirs assembled their men and hurried off to occupy some fortress, or to await the sequel of events from some more secure position.

When Muʿīn al-Dīn ʿUnar learned of the death of his adversary, he immediately led his troops out of Damascus and seized Baalbek, re-establishing his suzerainty over all of central Syria in a few weeks. Raymond of Antioch, reviving what seemed a forgotten tradition, launched a raid under the very walls of Aleppo. Joscelin was plotting to retake Edessa.

The saga of the powerful state founded by Zangī seemed over. In reality, it had only just begun.

Part Four

VICTORY (1146–87)

May God grant victory to Islam and not to Maḥmūd. Who is this dog Maḥmūd to merit victory?

NŪR AL-DĪN MAHMŪD
Unifier of the Arab East
(1117–74)

VIII

Nūr al-Dīn, the Saint-King

Only one man remained unruffled amidst the confusion that reigned in Zangī's camp. He was twenty-nine years old, a tall man with dark skin, clean-shaven but for a goatee, his forehead broad, his expression gentle and serene. He approached the still-warm body of the *atabeg* and, trembling, took his hand and removed his signet ring, symbol of power, slipping it onto his own finger. His name was Nūr al-Dīn, Zangī's second son.

'I have read the biographies of the sovereigns of old, and other than among the first caliphs I have found no man as virtuous and just as Nūr al-Dīn.' Ibn al-Athīr virtually worshipped this prince, and with good reason. For although Zangī's son had inherited his father's qualities of austerity, courage and statesmanship, he had none of the defects that made the *atabeg* so odious to some of his contemporaries. Where Zangī struck fright with his truculence and complete lack of scruples, Nūr al-Dīn, from his very first appearance on the scene, managed to cultivate the image of a pious, reserved and just man, one who kept his word and was thoroughly devoted to the *jihād* against the enemies of Islam.

Even more important – and herein lay his genius – he was able to weld these virtues into a formidable political weapon. As far back as the middle of the twelfth century, he understood the invaluable role of psychological mobilisation, and he therefore built a genuine propaganda apparatus. Several hundred men of letters, religious figures for the most part, were entrusted with the mission of winning the active sympathy of the people and of thereby forcing the leaders of the Arab world to flock to his banner. Ibn al-Athīr reports the complaint of an emir of Jazīra who was 'invited' by the son of Zangī to participate in a campaign against the Franj.

> If I do not rush to Nūr al-Dīn's aid [the emir said] he will strip me of my domain, for he has already written to the devotees and ascetics to request the aid of their prayers and to encourage them to incite the Muslims to *jihād*. At this very moment, each of these men sits with his disciples and companions reading Nūr al-Dīn's letters, weeping and cursing me. If I am to avoid anathema, I must accede to his request.

Nūr al-Dīn supervised his corps of propagandists personally. He would commission poems, letters and books, and always took care that they were released at the time when they would produce the desired effect. The principles he preached were simple: a single religion, Sunni Islam, which meant a determined struggle against all the various 'heresies'; a single state that would encircle the Franj on all fronts; a single objective, *jihād*, to reconquer the occupied territories and above all to liberate Jerusalem. During his twenty-eight-year reign, Nūr al-Dīn would call upon various *ʿulamāʾ* to write treatises hailing the merits of al-Quds, the holy city, and public readings were organised in the mosques and schools.

On these occasions, no one ever omitted to eulogise the supreme *mujāhid*, the irreproachable Muslim Nūr al-Dīn. But this cult of the personality was unusually effective and clever in that it was based, paradoxically, on the humility and austerity of the son of Zangī.

According to Ibn al-Athīr:

> Nūr al-Dīn's wife once complained that she did not have enough money to provide adequately for his needs. He had assigned her three shops which he owned in Homs; these generated about 20 dinars a year. When she found that this was not enough, he retorted: 'I have nothing else. With all the money I command, I am but the treasurer of the Muslims, and I have no intention of betraying them, nor of casting myself into the fires of hell on your account.'

Such words, very widely broadcast, proved especially embarrassing to the princes of the region, who lived in luxury and squeezed their subjects to wring every last pittance out of them. In fact, Nūr al-

Dīn's propaganda laid heavy emphasis on the taxes he abolished in the lands subject to his authority.

If he embarrassed his adversaries, the son of Zangī was often no less exacting with his own emirs. As time went on, he became increasingly strict about religious precepts. Not content with forswearing alcohol himself, he forbade his army to partake in it, or to have any truck with 'the tambourine, the flute and other objects displeasing to God', as Kamāl al-Dīn, the chronicler of Aleppo, explains, adding: 'Nūr al-Dīn abandoned luxurious garments and instead covered himself with rough cloth.' The Turkish officers, who were accustomed to heavy drinking and sumptuous adornments, were not always comfortable with this master who smiled so rarely and whose favourite company seemed to be turbaned *ʿulamāʾ*.

Even less reassuring to the emirs was the son of Zangī's tendency to dispense with his title, Nūr al-Dīn ('light of religion'), in favour of his first name, Maḥmūd. 'O God,' he would pray before battle, 'grant victory to Islam and not to Maḥmūd. Who is this dog Maḥmūd to merit victory?' Such manifestations of humility won him the sympathy of the weak and pious, but the powerful considered them simply hypocritical. It appears, however, that he was sincere in his convictions, although his public image was undoubtedly confected in part. In any event, he obtained results: it was Nūr al-Dīn who turned the Arab world into a force capable of crushing the Franj, and it was his lieutenant Saladin who reaped the fruits of victory.

Upon the death of his father, Nūr al-Dīn succeeded in assuming control of Aleppo – not much compared to the enormous domain conquered by the *atabeg*, but the very modesty of his initial realm itself assured the glory of his reign. Zangī had spent most of his life fighting against the caliphs, sultans and various emirates of Iraq and Jazīra. His son would be unencumbered by this exhausting and ungrateful task. Leaving Mosul and its adjoining region to his older brother Sayf al-Dīn, with whom he maintained cordial relations, thereby ensuring that he could count on a powerful friend on his eastern border, Nūr al-Dīn devoted himself to Syrian affairs.

Nevertheless, his position was far from comfortable when he arrived in Aleppo in September 1146, accompanied by his close confidant the Kurdish emir Shīrkūh, uncle of Saladin. Once again the city lived in fear of the knights of Antioch, and at the end of October, even before Nūr al-Dīn had had time to establish his authority beyond the city walls, he was told that Joscelin had succeeded in retaking Edessa, with the aid of part of the Armenian population. Edessa was not just one more city like those that had been lost since the death of Zangī: it was the very symbol of the *atabeg*'s glory, and its fall imperilled the whole future of the dynasty. Nūr al-Dīn reacted swiftly. Riding day and night, abandoning exhausted mounts along the way, he arrived at Edessa before Joscelin had had time to organise a defence. The count, whose courage had not been bolstered by his past ordeals, decided to flee at nightfall. His supporters, who tried to follow him, were caught and massacred by the Aleppan cavalry.

The rapidity with which the insurrection had been crushed brought the son of Zangī fresh prestige of which his nascent regime had great need. Drawing the lesson, Raymond of Antioch became less enterprising. As for ʿUnar, he quickly offered the ruler of Aleppo the hand of his daughter in marriage. 'The marriage contract was drafted in Damascus', Ibn al-Qalānisi explains, 'in the presence of Nūr al-Dīn's envoys. Work on the trousseau began immediately, and as soon as it was ready, the envoys left to return to Aleppo.'

Nūr al-Dīn's position in Syria was apparently secure. But Joscelin's plots, Raymond's raids and the intrigues of the old fox in Damascus would soon seem derisory compared to the fresh danger now looming.

> Reports kept coming in – from Constantinople, from the territory of the Franj, and from neighbouring lands too – that the kings of the Franj were on their way from their countries to attack the land of Islam. They had emptied their own provinces, leaving them devoid of defenders, and had brought with them riches, treasures and immeasurable *matériel*. They numbered, it was said, as many as a million foot soldiers and cavalry, perhaps even more.

Ibn al-Qalānisi was seventy-five when he wrote those lines, and he undoubtedly remembered that he had had to report a similar event, in scarcely different terms, half a century before.

Indeed, from the outset the second Frankish invasion, provoked by the fall of Edessa, seemed a repetition of the first. Countless fighters were unleashed against Asia Minor in the autumn of 1147, and once again they bore on their backs the two strips of cloth sewn into the form of a cross. As they passed Dorylaeum, where the historic defeat of Kilij Arslan had occurred, the latter's son Masʿūd was waiting for them, seeking revenge fifty years on. He laid a series of ambushes and dealt them some particularly deadly blows. 'It was constantly said that their forces were being pared down, so that people began to breathe easier.' But Ibn al-Qalānisi adds that 'after all the losses they suffered, the Franj were still said to number about a hundred thousand'. Here as elsewhere, the figures should not be taken too literally. Like all his contemporaries, the chronicler of Damascus was no slave to precision, and it would have been impossible for him to verify these estimates in any event. Nevertheless, one should pay tribute in passing to Ibn al-Qalānisi's scruples, for he adds an 'it is said' whenever a figure seems suspect to him. Ibn al-Athīr had no such scruples, but he did take care, when presenting his personal interpretation of some event, to conclude with the words *Allāhu ʿaalim*, or 'God alone knows'.

Whatever the exact numerical strength of the new Frankish invaders, there is no doubt that their forces, added to those of Jerusalem, Antioch and Tripoli, were quite adequate to upset the Arab world, which observed their movements with growing dread. One question arose unflaggingly: which city would they attack first? Logically, they should begin with Edessa. Was it not to avenge its fall that they had come? But they could as well assault Aleppo, striking at the head of the rising power of Nūr al-Dīn. In that event, Edessa would fall almost automatically. In fact, neither was the target. 'After lengthy disputes among their kings,' says Ibn al-Qalānisi, 'they finally agreed among themselves to attack Damascus, and they were so sure of taking it that they made agreements in advance about how the dependencies would be divided up.'

Attack Damascus? The city of Muʿīn al-Dīn ʿUnar, the only Muslim leader to have signed a treaty of alliance with Jerusalem? The Franj could have done the Arab resistance no greater service. With hindsight, however, it appears that the powerful kings commanding these armies of Franj believed that only the conquest of a prestigious city like Damascus would justify their long journey to the East. The Arab chroniclers speak mainly of Conrad, king of the Germans, never making the slightest mention of the presence of Louis VII, king of France, a personality, it is true, of no great distinction. 'As soon as he was informed of the designs of the Franj,' Ibn al-Qalānisi reports, 'the emir Muʿīn al-Dīn began preparations to defeat their maleficence. He fortified all the points at which an attack might be feared, deployed soldiers along the routes, replenished the wells, and destroyed the water sources in the environs of the city.'

On 24 July 1148 the Frankish troops arrived before Damascus, followed by long columns of camels laden with their baggage. The Damascenes poured from their city in their hundreds to confront the invaders. Among them was an aged theologian of Moroccan origin, al-Findalawi.

> Upon seeing him walking ahead, Muʿīn al-Dīn approached him [Ibn al-Athīr reports] greeted him, and said, 'Venerable old man, your advanced age exempts you from fighting. It is we who will defend the Muslims.' He asked him to turn back, but al-Findalawi refused, saying: 'I have sold myself and God has bought me.' Thus did he refer to the words of the Almighty: 'God has bought the persons and property of the faithful, and will grant them paradise in return.' Al-Findalawi marched forward and fought the Franj until he fell under their blows.

Al-Findalawi's martyrdom was soon followed by that of another ascetic, a Palestinian refugee named al-Halhuli. But despite these acts of heroism, the advance of the Franj could not be checked. They spread across the plain of Ghūṭa and pitched their tents, coming close to the city walls at several points. On the night of that very first day of battle the Damascenes, fearing the worst, began erecting barricades in the streets.

The next day, 25 July, 'was a Sunday', Ibn al-Qalānisi reports, 'and the inhabitants began making sorties at dawn. The battle ceased only at nightfall, by which time everyone was exhausted. Each side then returned to its own positions. The army of Damascus spent the night opposite the Franj, and the citizens stayed posted on the walls watching, for they could see the enemy close by.'

On Monday morning the Damascenes took heart, for they saw waves of Turkish, Kurdish and Arab cavalry arriving from the north. ʿUnar had written to all the princes of the region appealing for reinforcements, and they were now beginning to reach the besieged city. It was reported that Nūr al-Dīn would arrive the following day, at the head of the army of Aleppo, and so would his brother Sayf al-Dīn, with that of Mosul. According to Ibn al-Athīr, at their approach Muʿīn al-Dīn 'sent one message to the foreign Franj and another to the Franj of Syria'. He addressed the former in the simplest possible terms: 'The king of the Orient is on his way; if you do not depart, I will hand the city over to him, and you will regret it.' For the others, the 'colons', he used a different language:

> Are you now fool enough to aid these people against us? Have you failed to understand that if they take Damascus, they will seek to deprive you of your own cities? As for me, if I am unable to defend the city, I will deliver it to Sayf al-Dīn, and you know very well that if he takes Damascus, you will no longer be able to hold your positions in Syria.

Muʿīn al-Dīn ʿUnar's manoeuvre met with immediate success. Having reached a secret agreement with the local Franj, who now undertook to convince the king of the Germans to abandon Damascus before the arrival of the reinforcing armies, he sought to assure the success of his diplomatic intrigues by granting attractive bonuses. At the same time, he sent hundreds of snipers into the orchards ringing the city to ambush and harass the Franj. By Monday night the dissension aroused by the wily old Turk began to have its effect. The suddenly demoralised attackers had decided on a tactical retreat to regroup their forces, and they now found themselves harassed by the Damascenes on a completely exposed plain, with no water supply whatever. Within a few hours their position had become so untenable that their kings no longer contemplated seizing the Syrian metropolis, but thought only of saving their troops, and themselves, from annihilation. By Tuesday morning the Frankish armies were already falling back towards Jerusalem, pursued by Muʿīn al-Dīn's men.

There was no doubt about it, the Franj were not what they used to be. Negligence and disunity among military commanders, it seemed, were no longer the unhappy prerogative of the Arabs. The Damascenes found this amazing. Was it possible that this powerful Frankish expedition, which for months had caused the entire Middle East to tremble, was disintegrating after only four days of battle? 'It was thought that they were preparing some trick,' Ibn al-Qalānisi says. But no. The new Frankish invasion really was finished. 'The German Franj', Ibn al-Athīr says, returned to their country, which lies over yonder, beyond Constantinople, and God rid the faithful of this calamity.'

ʿUnar's surprising victory raised his prestige and tended to make people forget his past compromises with the invaders. But Muʿīn al-Dīn was in the last days of his career. He died a year after the battle. 'One day when he had eaten lavishly, as was his habit, he was taken ill. It was learned that he had been struck with dysentery. That', Ibn al-Qalānisi notes, 'is a fearful disease from which few recover.' With ʿUnar's death, power passed to the nominal sovereign of the city, ʿAbaq, a descendant of Tughtigin, a young man of sixteen of scant intelligence who would never stand on his own two feet.

The real winner of the battle of Damascus was undoubtedly Nūr al-Dīn. In June 1149 he succeeded in crushing the army of Raymond, prince of Antioch, whom Shīrkūh, the uncle of Saladin, killed with his own hands. Shīrkūh cut off his head and brought it to his master, who in accordance with custom sent it on to the caliph of Baghdad, in a silver box. Having thus removed any Frankish threat to northern Syria, the son of Zangī was free to devote all his efforts to the realisation of his father's old dream: the conquest of Damascus. Back in 1140 the city had preferred to strike an alliance with the Franj rather than submit to the brutal yoke of Zangī. But things had changed. Muʿīn al-Dīn was dead, and the behaviour of the Occidentals had shaken even their most fervent partisans. Above all, Nūr al-Dīn's reputation was nothing like his father's. His aim was to seduce the proud city of the Umayyads, not violate it.

When he and his troops reached the orchards ringing the city, Nūr al-Dīn proved more concerned to win the sympathy of the population than to prepare an assault. 'Nūr al-Dīn', Ibn al-Qalānisi reports, 'acted benevolently towards the peasants and did not impose his presence upon them. Throughout Damascus and in its dependencies, the people prayed to God on his behalf.' When, shortly after his arrival, abundant rains fell, ending a long drought, the populace credited Nūr al-Dīn with ending their sufferings. 'It was thanks to him', they said, 'and to his justice and exemplary conduct.'

Although the nature of his ambitions was clear enough, the master of Aleppo refused to comport himself as a conqueror.

> I have not pitched camp here in order to make war against you or to lay siege [he wrote to the leaders of Damascus]. Only the many complaints of the Muslims have induced me to act in this way, for the peasants have been despoiled of their goods and separated from their children by the Franj, and they have no one to defend them. Since God has bestowed upon me the power to grant succour to the Muslims and to wage war on the infidels, and since I command great quantities of resources and of men, it would be impermissible for me to neglect the Muslims and fail to take up their defence, especially since I well know that you are unable to protect your provinces and am aware of your degradation, which led you to seek the aid of the Franj and to deliver the goods of your poorest subjects to them, subjects whom you have criminally wronged. This pleases neither God nor any Muslim.

This letter revealed the full subtlety of the strategy of the new ruler of Aleppo, who now put himself forward as the defender of the Damascenes, in particular of the disinherited among them, visibly seeking to arouse them against their rulers. The sharp response of the latter only helped to bring the citizenry ever closer to the son of Zangī. 'All that stands between us now is the sword,' they said. 'The Franj will come to help us defend ourselves.'

Despite the sympathy he had gained among the population, Nūr al-Dīn preferred not to confront the reunited forces of Jerusalem and Damascus, and so agreed to withdraw to the north. But not without having made some gains: his name would now be mentioned in the Friday sermons just after those of the caliph and sultan, and coins were struck in his name, a common manifestation of allegiance by Muslim cities seeking to appease conquerors.

Nūr al-Dīn was encouraged by this partial success. A year later, he returned to the Damascus area with his troops, sending a new letter to ʿAbaq and the other leaders of the city. 'I desire no more than the well-being of the Muslims, *jihād* against the infidels, and the release of the prisoners they are holding. If you come over to my side with the army of Damascus, if we help each other to wage the *jihād*, my wish will be fulfilled.' ʿAbaq's only response was to call upon the Franj once again, now marching under the banner of their young King Baldwin III, son of Fulk. They soon arrived, and camped at the gates of Damascus for several weeks. Their knights were even granted permission to wander through the souks at will, which inevitably aroused tension with the people of the city, who had still not forgotten those who had fallen three years before.

Nūr al-Dīn prudently continued to avoid any confrontation with the coalition partners. He withdrew his troops from the environs of Damascus, waiting for the Franj to return to Jerusalem. For him, the battle was primarily political. Playing the bitterness of the citizens for all it was worth, he sent letter after letter to the Damascene notables and religious leaders denouncing ʿAbaq's treason. He also made contact with many military officers exasperated by ʿAbaq's open collaboration with the Franj. For the son of Zangī, it was important no longer merely to stimulate protests that would embarrass ʿAbaq, but to organise a network of accomplices within the coveted city who could induce Damascus to capitulate. The father of Saladin was entrusted with this delicate mission. By 1153, after some skilful organisation, Ayyūb had indeed succeeded in winning the benevolent neutrality of the urban militia, whose commander was a younger brother of Ibn al-Qalānisi. Several personalities of the army adopted a similar attitude, so that ʿAbaq's isolation grew day by day. In the end, he was left with no more than a small group of emirs who still urged him to hold out. Having decided to get rid of these last hardliners, Nūr al-Dīn arranged for false information to be sent to the ruler of Damascus to the effect that a plot was being hatched within his own entourage. Without bothering to find out whether or not the information was well-founded, ʿAbaq quickly executed or imprisoned several of his collaborators. His isolation was now complete.

One last operation remained. Nūr al-Dīn suddenly began intercepting all convoys of food heading for Damascus. Within two days the price of a sack of grain had risen from half a dinar to 25 dinars, and the populace began to fear starvation. It remained only for the agents of the ruler of Aleppo to convince public opinion that there would have been no shortages had ʿAbaq not chosen to ally with the Franj against his coreligionists of Aleppo.

On 18 April 1154 Nūr al-Dīn returned to the gates of Damascus with his troops. Once again ʿAbaq sent an urgent message to Baldwin. But this time the king of Jerusalem did not have time to react.

On 25 April the final assault was launched on the eastern side of the city.

> There was no one defending the walls [the chronicler of Damascus reports], neither soldier nor citizen, except for a handful of Turks in charge of guarding a tower. One of Nūr al-Dīn's soldiers rushed towards a rampart, at the summit of which stood a Jewish woman, who threw him a rope. With it he scaled the wall, reaching the top of the rampart without anyone's noticing. He was followed by many of his comrades, who unfurled a banner, planted it atop the wall, and began to shout: *ya manṣūr*, 'O, victorious one!' The Damascene troops and the population abandoned any resistance, because of their sympathy for Nūr al-Dīn, for his justice and good reputation. A sapper ran to Bāb al-Sharq, the east gate of the city, and shattered the closing apparatus with his pick. Soldiers rushed through it and fanned out through the main arteries of the city without encountering any opposition. Bāb Tūma, Thomas Gate, was also thrown open to the troops. Finally, King Nūr al-Dīn made his entrance, accompanied by his entourage, to the great joy of the inhabitants and soldiers, all of whom were obsessed by their fear of famine and their terror at being besieged by the Franj infidels.

Generous in victory, Nūr al-Dīn granted ʿAbaq and his close collaborators fiefdoms in the region of Homs and allowed them to flee with all their property.

Nūr al-Dīn had conquered Damascus by persuasion more than by force, with little fighting and no bloodbath. The city which for a quarter of a century had fiercely resisted all those who sought to subjugate it, be they Assassins, Franj or supporters of Zangī, had allowed itself to be seduced by the sweet insistence of a prince who promised to guarantee its security and to respect its independence. Damascus was not to regret its decision, and thanks to Nūr al-Dīn and his successors, the city enjoyed one of the most glorious periods of its history.

The day after his victory, Nūr al-Dīn assembled the *ʿulamāʾ*, *qāḍīs* and merchants and delivered a reassuring speech; he also brought along large stocks of food and abolished a number of taxes affecting the fruit trade, the vegetable souk and the distribution of water. An appropriate decree was drafted and announced from the pulpit the following Friday, after the prayer. The eighty-year-old Ibn al-Qalānisi was still on the scene to share in the joy of his fellow citizens. 'The population applauded,' he reports. 'The citizens, the peasants, the women, the poor – everyone addressed public prayers to God that Nūr al-Dīn be granted long life and that his banners be ever victorious.'

For the first time since the beginning of the Frankish wars, the two great Syrian metropolises, Aleppo and Damascus, were united in a single state, under the authority of a thirty-seven-year-old prince who was determined to prosecute the struggle against the occupier. In fact, all of Muslim Syria was now unified, except for the small emirate of Shayzar, where the Munqidhite dynasty still managed to preserve its autonomy. But not for long, for the history of this tiny state was to be shaken in the sharpest and most unexpected manner imaginable.

In August 1157, as rumours were circulating in Damascus that Nūr al-Dīn was preparing an early campaign against Jerusalem, an earthquake of unusual violence devastated all of Syria, sowing death among Arab and Franj alike. Several towers of the Aleppo city walls collapsed, and the terrified population dispersed into the surrounding countryside. In Ḥarrān the earth split so deeply that the remains of an ancient city were visible through the immense breach. In Tripoli, Beirut, Tyre,

Homs and Maʿarra, there were countless dead; innumerable buildings were destroyed.

But two cities were hit harder than any others by the cataclysm: Hama and Shayzar. It is said that a teacher in Hama, who had left his classroom to satisfy a pressing call of nature in a nearby vacant field, found his school demolished and all his pupils dead upon his return. Dumbfounded, he sat bleakly upon the ruins wondering how he would break the news to the parents, but none of them survived to claim their children.

On that same day in Shayzar, the sovereign of the city, the emir Muḥammad Ibn Sultān, a cousin of Usāmah, was organising a reception in the citadel to celebrate his son's circumcision. All the city's dignitaries were there, along with the members of the ruling family, when the earth suddenly began to tremble. The walls collapsed, decimating the entire assembly. The emirate of the Munqidhites simply ceased to exist. Usāmah, who was then in Damascus, was one of the few members of his family to survive. Deeply moved, he wrote: 'Death did not advance step by step to destroy the people of my race, to annihilate them separately or to strike them down two by two. They all died in the twinkling of an eye, and their palaces became their tombs.' Then he added bitterly: 'The earthquakes struck this indifferent country only to rouse it from its torpor.'

The tragedy of the Munqidhites did indeed inspire their contemporaries to much reflexion about the futility of all things human. More prosaically, the cataclysm offered people the opportunity to conquer or pillage with impunity in desolated cities or fortresses whose walls had crumbled. Shayzar in particular was immediately attacked, by both the Assassins and the Franj, before finally being taken by the army of Aleppo.

In October 1157 Nūr al-Dīn was taken ill as he was travelling from city to city supervising the repair of the walls. The prognosis of the Damascene physician Ibn al-Waqqar, who always travelled with him, was pessimistic. The prince hung between life and death for a year and a half, during which time the Franj occupied several fortresses and carried out a number of raids in the environs of Damascus. But Nūr al-Dīn took advantage of this period of enforced inactivity to ponder his destiny. During the first part of his reign, he had unified Muslim Syria under his aegis and had put an end to the internecine struggles that had weakened it. Now he would have to wage the *jihād* to reconquer the great cities occupied by the Franj. Some of his closest collaborators, especially the Aleppans, suggested that he start with Antioch, but to their great surprise, Nūr al-Dīn opposed this. Historically, he explained, that city belonged to the Rūm. Any attempt to seize it would tempt the Byzantines to interfere directly in Syrian affairs, and that would force the Muslim armies to fight on two fronts. No, he insisted, the Rūm must not be provoked. Instead they would try to recover an important coastal city, or even, God willing, Jerusalem.

Unfortunately for Nūr al-Dīn, events were soon to prove his fears justified. In 1159, as he was barely beginning to recover his health, he learned that a powerful Byzantine army, commanded by the emperor Manuel, son and successor of John Comnenus, had been assembled in northern Syria. Nūr al-Dīn quickly despatched ambassadors to the emperor to extend him a courteous welcome. When he received them, the *basileus*, a wise man of majestic bearing and with a genuine interest in medicine, proclaimed his intention to maintain the most cordial possible relations with their master. If he had come to Syria, he assured them, it was only to teach the rulers of Antioch a lesson. It will be remembered that twenty-two years before, Manuel's father had also come to Syria, supposedly for the same purpose; but that had not prevented him from making an alliance with the Occidentals against the Muslims. Nevertheless, Nūr al-Dīn's ambassadors did not doubt the word of the *basileus*. They knew the rage felt by the Rūm at the mere mention of the name of Reynald of Châtillon, the knight who had presided over Antioch since 1153 – a brutal, arrogant, cynical and contemptible man who would come to symbolise for the Arabs everything evil about the Franj and whom Saladin would swear to kill with his own hands.

Prince Reynald, whom the chroniclers called 'Brins Arnat', arrived in the Middle East in 1147, dominated by the already anachronistic mentality of the first invaders: he thirsted for gold, blood and conquest. Shortly after the death of Raymond of Antioch, he managed to seduce and then marry Raymond's widow, thus becoming the lord of the city. His exactions had soon made him odious not only to his Aleppan neighbours, but also to the Rūm and to his own subjects. In 1156, on the pretext that Manuel had refused to pay him a promised sum, he decided to take revenge by organising a punitive raid on the Byzantine island of Cyprus, and he asked the patriarch of Antioch to finance the expedition. When the prelate expressed reluctance, he was thrown into prison and tortured; his wounds were then coated with honey and he was chained and left exposed to the sun for an entire day, his body ravaged by thousands of insects.

The patriarch, not surprisingly, finally opened his treasury, and the prince, after assembling a flotilla, disembarked on the coast of the Mediterranean island, crushed the small Byzantine garrison with no trouble, and unleashed his men on the island. Cyprus never fully recovered from what was done to it in that spring of 1156. All the island's cultivated fields were systematically ravaged, from north to south; all the livestock was slaughtered; the palace, churches and convents were pillaged, and everything that was not carried off was demolished or burned. Women were raped, old men and children slaughtered; rich men were taken as hostages, poor ones beheaded. Before setting off loaded with booty, Reynald ordered all the Greek priests and monks assembled; he then had their noses cut off before sending them, thus mutilated, to Constantinople.

Manuel would have to respond. But as the scion of the emperors of Rome, he could not do so in some merely typical manner. He had to re-establish his prestige by publicly humiliating the brigand knight of Antioch. As soon as Reynald heard that the imperial army was on its way to Syria, he realised that any resistance would be futile and decided to beg forgiveness. As amply gifted with servility as he was with arrogance, he presented himself in Manuel's camp barefoot, dressed as a beggar, and threw himself before the imperial throne.

Nūr al-Dīn's ambassadors were present at the scene. They watched 'Brins Arnat' lie in the dust at the feet of the *basileus*, who, apparently not even deigning to take note of his presence, calmly continued his conversation with his guests, waiting several minutes before finally casting a glance at his adversary and instructing him, with a condescending gesture, to rise.

Reynald obtained his pardon, and was therefore able to preserve his principality, but his prestige in northern Syria was tarnished for ever. In fact, the following year he was captured by Aleppan soldiers during one of his plundering excursions north of the city, and he spent sixteen years in captivity before reappearing on the scene, once again to play the most execrable of roles.

As for Manuel, his authority was to rise steadily after this expedition. He succeeded in imposing his suzerainty over the Frankish principality of Antioch and the Turkish states of Asia Minor alike, thus regaining for the empire a decisive role in Syrian affairs. This resurgence of Byzantine military power, the last in its history, redrew the map of conflict between the Arabs and the Franj. The permanent threat to his borders now represented by the Rūm prevented Nūr al-Dīn from launching the sweeping reconquest he had desired. But since the power of the son of Zangī also kept in check any expansionist inclinations on the part of the Franj, the situation in Syria was effectively at an impasse.

Then suddenly, as if the pent-up energies of the Arabs and the Franj were seeking some other outlet, the epicentre of war shifted to a new theatre of operations: Egypt.

IX

The Rush for the Nile

'My uncle Shīrkūh turned to me and said, "Yūsuf, pack your things, we're going." When I heard this order, I felt as if my heart had been pierced by a dagger, and I answered, "In God's name, even were I granted the entire kingdom of Egypt, I would not go." '

The man who spoke those words was none other than Saladin, recounting the timid beginnings of the adventure that would some day make him one of history's most prestigious sovereigns. With the admirable sincerity typical of everything he said, Saladin carefully refrained from claiming credit for the Egyptian epic. 'In the end I did go with my uncle,' he added. 'He conquered Egypt, then died. God then placed in my hands power that I had never expected.' In fact, although Saladin emerged as the great beneficiary of the Egyptian expedition, it is true that he did not play the major role in it. Nor did Nūr al-Dīn, even though the land of the Nile was conquered in his name.

The real protagonists of this campaign, which lasted from 1163 to 1169, were three extraordinary personalities: Shāwar, an Egyptian vizier whose demoniacal intrigues plunged the region into blood and iron; Amalric, a Frankish king so obsessed with the idea of conquering Egypt that he invaded the country five times in six years; and Shīrkūh, 'the lion', a Kurdish general who proved to be one of the military geniuses of his time.

When Shāwar seized power in Cairo in December 1162, he assumed a post and responsibility that rewarded its holder with honours and riches. But he was not unaware of the other side of the coin: of the fifteen previous leaders of Egypt, only one had left office alive. All the others had been killed, although the methods varied: they had been hanged, beheaded, stabbed to death, crucified, poisoned, lynched by mobs; one was killed by his adoptive son, another by his own father.

In other words, there is no reason to suppose that this dark-skinned emir with the greying temples would allow his freedom of action to be restricted by any hint of scruples. The moment he acceded to power, he quickly massacred his predecessor (along with his entire family), and appropriated their gold, jewels and palace.

But the wheel of fortune continued to spin. After nine months in power the new vizier was himself overthrown by one of his lieutenants, a man named Ḍirghām. Having been warned in time, Shāwar managed to get out of Egypt alive, and he sought refuge in Syria, where he tried to win Nūr al-Dīn's support for his effort to regain power. Although his guest was intelligent and an effective speaker, at first the son of Zangī lent him but half an ear. Very soon, however, events were to force Nūr al-Dīn to change his attitude.

Jerusalem, it seems, was closely watching the upheavals in Cairo. In February 1162 the Franj had acquired a new king, a man of indomitable ambition: the Arabs called him 'Morri', from the French 'Amaury' (Amalric); he was the second son of Fulk. Visibly influenced by the propaganda of Nūr al-Dīn, this twenty-six-year-old monarch was trying to cultivate the image of a sober, pious man devoted to religious study and concerned about justice. But the resemblance was only apparent. The Frankish king had more audacity than wisdom, and despite his great height and impressive head of hair, he was singularly lacking in majesty. His shoulders were abnormally thin; he was frequently seized by fits of laughter so long and noisy that his own entourage was embarrassed by them; he was also afflicted with a stutter that did not facilitate his contact with others. Amalric was driven by one obsession – the conquest of Egypt – and only his indefatigable pursuit of that dream afforded him a certain stature.

His goal, true enough, seemed tempting. The route to the Nile had been open to the Western knights ever since 1153 when they took Ascalon, the last Fatimid bastion in Palestine. Moreover, since 1160 the successive Egyptian viziers, absorbed in their fights with local rivals, had been paying an annual tribute to the Franj in exchange for their abstaining from any intervention in Egyptian affairs. Just after the fall of Shāwar, Amalric took advantage of the confusion that prevailed in the land of the Nile to invade, on the simple pretext that the necessary sum, 60,000 dinars, had not been paid on time. Crossing the Sinai peninsula along its Mediterranean coast, Amalric laid siege to the town of Bilbays, situated on a branch of the Nile that would run dry in centuries to come. The defenders of the city were both dumbfounded and amused when the Franj began erecting siege machinery around the walls, for it was September, and the river was beginning to swell. The authorities had only to breach a few dykes, and the warriors of the Occident soon found themselves surrounded by water. They barely had time to flee back to Palestine. The first invasion was thus over in short order, but at least it had awakened Aleppo and Damascus to Amalric's intentions.

Nūr al-Dīn hesitated. He had no wish to be drawn into the treacherous swamps of Cairene intrigues – in particular since, as a fervent Sunni, he was openly contemptuous of the Shiʿi caliphate of the Fatimids. On the other hand, he had no wish to see Egypt, with its great riches, swept into the camp of the Franj, for that would make them the greatest power in the Orient. In view of the prevailing anarchy, however, it was unlikely that Cairo would withstand Amalric's determination for long. Shāwar, of course, spared no effort in lecturing his host about the potential benefits of an expedition to the land of the Nile. To placate him, Shāwar promised that if Nūr al-Dīn helped him to regain his throne, he would pay all the expenses of the expedition, recognise the suzerainty of the master of Aleppo and Damascus, and hand over one-third of state receipts every year. Above all, Nūr al-Dīn had to reckon with his confidant Shīrkūh, who had been completely won over to the idea of an armed intervention. In fact, he was so enthusiastic about it that the son of Zangī finally authorised him to take personal charge of organising an expeditionary corps.

It would be difficult to imagine two people so closely united and yet so different as Nūr al-Dīn and Shīrkūh. With age, the son of Zangī had become increasingly majestic, sober, dignified and reserved, while Saladin's uncle was a short, obese, one-eyed officer who was constantly flushed by excesses of food and drink. When he lost his temper he would howl like a madman, and from time to time he would lose his head completely, going so far as to kill his opponent. But not everyone was displeased by his unsavoury character. His soldiers adored this commander who lived among them, sharing their mess and their jokes. In the many battles in which he had taken part in Syria, Shīrkūh had emerged as a genuine leader of men, gifted with great physical courage. The Egyptian campaign, however, would reveal his remarkable qualities as a strategist, for from the outset the odds were dead against the enterprise. It was relatively easy for the Franj to get to the land of the Nile. The only obstacle impeding their path was the semi-desert expanse of the Sinai peninsula. But if they took along several hundred water-filled goatskins, carried by camels, the knights would have enough water to reach the gates of Bilbays in three days. Things were less easy for Shīrkūh. To travel from Syria to Egypt, he had to cross Palestine, and thus expose himself to attacks by the Franj.

The departure for Cairo of the Syrian expeditionary corps in April 1164 therefore required elaborate staging. While Nūr al-Dīn's army launched a diversionary attack to lure Amalric and his knights to northern Palestine, Shīrkūh, accompanied by Shāwar and about ten thousand cavalry, headed east. They followed the course of the Jordan river on its east bank, passing through what is now Jordan, and then, at the southern tip of the Dead Sea, they turned west, forded the river, and set out at full gallop towards Sinai. There they continued their advance, keeping away from the coastal route so as to avoid detection. On 24 April they seized Bilbays, Egypt's easternmost port, and by 1 May they were camped at the walls of Cairo. Taken unawares, the vizier Ḍirghām had no time to organise any resistance. Abandoned by everyone, he was killed trying to escape, and his body was thrown to the dogs in the street. Shāwar was officially reinvested in his post by the Fatimid caliph al-ʿĀḍid, a thirteen-year-old adolescent.

Shīrkūh's blitz was a model of military efficiency. Saladin's uncle was more than a little proud at having conquered Egypt in so short a time, practically without suffering any losses, and of thus having outwitted Morri. But barely had he reassumed power when Shāwar did an astonishing volte-face. Breaking his promises to Nūr al-Dīn, he ordered Shīrkūh to leave Egypt forthwith. Saladin's uncle, flabbergasted by such ingratitude and raging with anger, sent word to his former ally that he was determined to stay regardless.

Shāwar had no real confidence in his own army, and when he saw

Shīrkūh's determination, he despatched an ambassador to Jerusalem to seek Amalric's aid against the Syrian expeditionary corps. The Frankish king needed no convincing. He had been looking for an excuse to intervene in Egypt, and for what better pretext could he ask than a call for help from the ruler of Cairo himself? In July 1164 the Frankish army set out for Sinai for the second time. Shīrkūh immediately decided to withdraw from the environs of Cairo, where he had been camped since May, and to dig in at Bilbays. There he repulsed the attacks of his enemies week after week, but his position seemed ultimately hopeless. Far removed from his bases and surrounded by the Franj and their new ally Shāwar, the Kurdish general could not expect to hold out for long.

> When Nūr al-Dīn saw how the situation in Bilbays was developing [Ibn al-Athīr wrote several years later] he decided to launch a great offensive against the Franj in an effort to force them to leave Egypt. He wrote to all the Muslim emirs asking them to participate in the *jihād*, and he marched off to attack the powerful fortress of Ḥārim, near Antioch. All the Franj who had remained in Syria united to confront him – among them were Prince Bohemond, lord of Antioch, and the count of Tripoli. The Franj were crushed in this battle. Ten thousand of them were killed, and all their commanders, among them the prince and the count, were captured.

Once victory was won, Nūr al-Dīn had the cross-embossed banners and blond scalps of some of the Franj killed in the battle brought to him. Then, placing them all in a sack, he entrusted the bundle to one of his most reliable men, telling him: 'Go immediately to Bilbays, find a way to get inside, and give these trophies to Shīrkūh. Tell him that God has granted us victory. Let him exhibit them on the ramparts, and the sight will strike fear among the infidels.'

News of the Ḥārim victory did indeed change things in the battle for Egypt. The morale of the besieged soared, but more importantly, the Franj were forced to return to Palestine. The capture of young Bohemond III – Reynald's successor at the head of the principality of Antioch, whom Amalric had appointed to oversee the affairs of the kingdom of Jerusalem during his absence – and the massacre of his men forced the king to seek a compromise with Shīrkūh. After several exchanges, the two men agreed to leave Egypt simultaneously. At the end of October 1164 Morri returned to Palestine by the coastal route, while the Kurdish general took less than two weeks to get back to Damascus, following the same itinerary as before.

Shīrkūh was far from unhappy at having left Bilbays unharmed and with his head held high, but the real winner of the six months of campaigning was undoubtedly Shāwar. He had used Shīrkūh to regain power, and then used Amalric to neutralise the Kurdish general. Then both had departed, leaving him master of all Egypt. Shāwar would now spend more than two years consolidating his position.

But not without some uneasiness at the turn events had taken. He knew that Shīrkūh would never forgive his betrayal. Indeed, news constantly reached him from Syria suggesting that the Kurdish general was harassing Nūr al-Dīn, asking his permission to undertake a fresh Egyptian campaign. The son of Zangī, however, was reluctant. He was not dissatisfied with the status quo. The important thing was to keep the Franj away from the Nile. As always, though, it was not easy to disengage from the web. Fearing another lightning expedition by Shīrkūh, Shāwar took the precaution of concluding a treaty of mutual assistance with Amalric. This convinced Nūr al-Dīn to authorise his lieutenant to organise a fresh expeditionary corps, just in case the Franj moved to intervene in Egypt. Shīrkūh selected the best elements of the army, among them his nephew Yūsuf. These preparations in turn alarmed the Egyptian vizier, who insisted that Amalric send troops. Thus it was that during the early days of 1167 the race for the Nile began again. The Frankish king and the Kurdish general arrived in the coveted country at about the same time, each by his usual route.

Shāwar and the Franj assembled their allied forces before Cairo, there to await Shīrkūh. But the latter preferred to determine the modalities of the rendezvous himself. Continuing his long march from Aleppo, he skirted the Egyptian capital to the south, sent his troops across the Nile on small boats, and then turned them north again, without even stopping to rest. Shāwar and Amalric, who expected

Shīrkūh to arrive from the east, suddenly saw him surge up from the opposite direction. Worse yet, his camp on the west side of Cairo, near the pyramids of Giza, was separated from his enemies by the formidable natural obstacle of the great river. From this solidly entrenched camp, he sent a message to the vizier: 'The Frankish enemy is at our mercy,' he wrote, 'cut off from their bases. Let us unite our forces and exterminate him. The time is ripe; the opportunity may not arise again.' But Shāwar was not content simply to reject this offer. He had the messenger executed and brought Shīrkūh's letter to Amalric to prove his loyalty.

Despite this gesture, the Franj still distrusted their ally, who, they were sure, would betray them the moment he had no further need of them. They believed that the time had come to take advantage of Shīrkūh's threatening proximity to establish their authority in Egypt once and for all. Amalric asked that an official alliance between Cairo and Jerusalem be signed.

Two knights who knew Arabic – not unusual among the Franj of the Middle East – repaired to the residence of the young caliph al-ʿĀḍid. In an obvious effort to make an impression, Shāwar led them to a superb, richly decorated palace, which they walked through quickly, ringed by a phalanx of armed guards. Then the cortège crossed a vaulted hallway that seemed interminable, impervious to the light of day, and finally came to the threshold of an enormous sculptured gate leading first to a vestibule and then to another gate. After passing through many ornamented chambers, Shāwar and his guests emerged into a courtyard paved with marble and ringed by gilded colonnades, in the centre of which stood a fountain boasting gold and silver pipes. All around were brightly coloured birds from the four corners of Africa. Here the escort guards introduced them to eunuchs who lived on intimate terms with the caliph. Once again they passed through a succession of salons, then a garden stocked with tame deer, lions, bears and panthers. Then, finally, they reached the palace of al-ʿĀḍid.

Barely had they entered an enormous room, whose back wall was a silk curtain encrusted with gold, rubies and emeralds, when Shāwar bowed three times and laid his sword on the floor. Only then did the curtain rise, and the caliph approached, his body draped in silk and his face veiled. The vizier went to him, sat at his feet, and explained the proposed alliance with the Franj. After listening in silence, al-ʿĀḍid, who was then only sixteen, endorsed Shāwar's policy. Shāwar was about to rise when the two Franj asked the prince of the faithful to swear that he would remain loyal to the alliance. The dignitaries surrounding al-ʿĀḍid were visibly scandalised by this demand. The caliph himself seemed shocked, and the vizier hastily intervened. The accord with Jerusalem, he explained to his sovereign, was a matter of life and death for Egypt. He implored the caliph to consider the request of the Franj not as a manifestation of disrespect but only as symptomatic of their ignorance of Oriental customs.

Smiling against his better judgement, al-ʿĀḍid extended his silk-gloved hand and swore to respect the alliance. But one of the Frankish emissaries interrupted. 'An oath', he said, 'must be taken bare-handed, for the glove could be a sign of future betrayal.' The hall was scandalised a second time. The dignitaries whispered among themselves that the caliph had been insulted, and there was talk of punishing the insolent Franj. But after a fresh intervention by Shāwar, the caliph, preserving his calm, removed his glove, extended his bare hand, and repeated word for word the oath dictated to him by Morri's representatives.

As soon as this singular interview had been concluded, the Egyptians and Franj met to elaborate a plan to cross the Nile and decimate Shīrkūh's army, which was then heading south. An enemy detachment, commanded by Amalric, was hard on his heels. Saladin's uncle wanted to create the impression that he was on the run. He was well aware that his major handicap was that he was cut off from his bases, and he therefore sought to put the pursuing army in the same position. When he was more than a week's march from Cairo, he ordered his troops to halt and, in an impassioned harangue, told them that the hour of victory was at hand.

The confrontation actually came on 18 March 1167, near the town of al-Babayn, on the west bank of the Nile. The two armies, exhausted by their interminable race, threw themselves desperately into the fray, eager to get it over with once and for all. Shīrkūh had assigned command of the centre to Saladin, ordering him to retreat as soon as the enemy charged. Amalric and his knights rushed towards him banners unfurled, and when Saladin pretended to flee, they pursued him ardently without realising that the right and left flanks of the Syrian army had already moved in to cut off any possible retreat. Losses among the Frankish knights were heavy, but Amalric managed to escape. He returned to Cairo, where the bulk of his troops remained, firmly resolved to seek vengeance at the earliest opportunity. He and Shāwar were already collaborating on preparations to lead a powerful army back south to Upper Egypt when some barely credible news arrived: Shīrkūh had seized Alexandria, Egypt's largest city, situated in the far north of the country, on the Mediterranean coast.

What had happened was that immediately after his victory at al-Babayn, the unpredictable Kurdish general, without waiting even a single day and before his enemies had time to recover their wits, had crossed the entire length of Egypt at dizzying speed, from south to north, and had entered Alexandria in triumph. The population of the great Mediterranean port, hostile to the alliance with the Franj, greeted the Syrians as liberators.

Shāwar and Amalric, forced to keep pace with the hellish rhythm at which Shīrkūh was waging this war, decided to lay siege to Alexandria. Food was so scarce in the city that within a month the populace, faced with the threat of famine, began to regret having welcomed the Syrian expeditionary corps. When a Frankish fleet arrived and moored alongside the port, the situation seemed hopeless. Nevertheless, Shīrkūh refused to admit defeat. He turned over command of the troops in the city to Saladin, and then, assembling a few hundred of his best cavalry, organised a daring nocturnal sortie. He passed through the enemy lines at full speed and drove his troops, riding day and night . . . back to Upper Egypt!

Meanwhile, the blockade of Alexandria was being steadily tightened. Famine was now compounded by epidemic, and by daily catapult attacks. The command was a weighty responsibility for the twenty-nine-year-old Saladin. But the diversion organised by his uncle worked. Shīrkūh was not unaware that Morri was anxious to wind up this campaign and get back to his kingdom, which was under constant harassment by Nūr al-Dīn. By opening a second front in the south instead of allowing himself to be bottled up in Alexandria, the Kurdish general threatened to prolong the conflict indefinitely. He even fomented an uprising against Shāwar in Upper Egypt, convincing many armed peasants to join him. Once he had enough troops, he moved towards Cairo and sent Amalric a cleverly worded message. We are both wasting time here, he said in substance. If the king would think things through patiently, he would understand that driving me out of this country would be in no one's interest but Shāwar's. Amalric was convinced, and agreement was soon reached: the siege of Alexandria was lifted, and Saladin left the city to the salutes of a guard of honour. In August 1167 the two armies both left Egypt, just as they had three years earlier, returning to their respective countries. Nūr al-Dīn, satisfied at having retrieved the best of his army, was now fed up with these futile Egyptian adventures.

And yet, as if decreed by fate, the race for the Nile broke out yet again the following year. When he had left Cairo, Amalric felt it prudent to leave a detachment of knights behind – just to make sure that his alliance with the Fatimids was properly observed. One of their major duties was to oversee the city gates and to protect the Frankish functionaries assigned to collect the annual tribute of 100,000 dinars that Shāwar had promised to pay the kingdom of Jerusalem. Inevitably, the heavy tax burden, combined with the prolonged presence of this foreign force, aroused resentment among the citizenry.

Public opinion steadily mounted against the occupiers. It was suggested *sotto voce,* even within the caliph's own entourage, that an alliance with Nūr al-Dīn would be a lesser evil. Behind Shāwar's back, messages began to flow to and fro between Cairo and Aleppo. The son of Zangī, in no hurry to intervene, simply observed the reactions of the king of Jerusalem.

The Frankish knights and functionaries stationed in the Egyptian capital, well aware of the growing hostility, were frightened. They sent messages to Amalric begging him to come to their aid. At first the monarch hesitated. The wise choice would have been to withdraw his garrison from Cairo and be content with a neutral and inoffensive Egypt as his neighbour. But he was temperamentally inclined to the leap in the dark. In October 1168, encouraged by the arrival in the Middle East of a large number of Occidental knights eager to 'crush the Saracen', he decided to throw his army against Egypt for the fourth time.

This new campaign began with a slaughter as horrible as it was gratuitous. The Occidentals seized Bilbays and, without the slightest provocation, massacred the inhabitants: men, women and children, Muslims and Christians of the Coptic church. As Ibn al-Athīr said quite correctly, 'if the Franj had acted differently in Bilbays, they could have taken Cairo with the greatest of ease, for the city's notables were prepared to surrender it. But when they heard of the massacres perpetrated in Bilbays, people decided to resist regardless.' As the invaders approached, Shāwar ordered that the old city of Cairo be put to the torch. Twenty thousand jugs of naphtha were poured onto market stalls, houses, palaces and mosques. The inhabitants were evacuated to the new city, founded by the Fatimids in the tenth century, which comprised mainly palaces, administrative offices and barracks, as well as the religious university of al-Azhar. The fire raged for fifty-four days.

In the meantime, the vizier tried to keep open the lines of communication to Amalric, in an effort to convince him to abandon this foolhardy enterprise. Shāwar hoped to be able to achieve this without any fresh intervention by Shīrkūh. But his faction in Cairo was losing strength. In particular, the caliph al-ʿĀḍid had taken the initiative of despatching a letter to Nūr al-Dīn asking him to rush to Egypt's aid. In an effort to move the son of Zangī, the Fatimid sovereign enclosed some locks of hair with his missive. 'These', he explained, 'are locks of hair from my wives. They beseech you to come and rescue them from the outrages of the Franj.'

Nūr al-Dīn's reaction to this anxious message has been preserved thanks to particularly valuable testimony from Saladin himself, who is quoted by Ibn al-Athīr:

> When the appeals from al-ʿĀḍid arrived, Nūr al-Dīn summoned me and told me what was happening. Then he said: 'Go and see your uncle Shīrkūh in Homs and urge him to come at once, for there must be no delay.' I left Aleppo, and a mile from the city I encountered my uncle,

who was already on his way. Nūr al-Dīn ordered him to prepare to leave for Egypt.

The Kurdish general then asked his nephew to accompany him, but Saladin demurred.

> I answered that I was not prepared to forget the sufferings endured in Alexandria. My uncle then said to Nūr al-Dīn: 'It is absolutely necessary that Yūsuf go with me.' And Nūr al-Dīn thus repeated his orders. I tried to explain the state of financial embarrassment in which I found myself. He ordered that money be given to me and I had to go, like a man being led off to his death.

This time there was no confrontation between Shīrkūh and Amalric. Impressed by the determination of the Cairenes, who were prepared to destroy their city rather than surrender it to him, and fearing that he could be attacked from behind by the Syrian army, the Frankish king withdrew to Palestine on 2 January 1169. Six days later the Kurdish general arrived in Cairo, to be hailed as a saviour by the population and the Fatimid dignitaries alike. Shāwar himself even seemed elated. But no one was taken in. Although he had fought against the Franj during past weeks, he was still considered their friend, and he had to pay for it. On 18 January he was lured into an ambush, sequestered in a tent, and then killed by Saladin himself, with the written approval of the caliph. That same day, Shīrkūh replaced him as vizier. But when he donned his brocade silk and went to his predecessor's residence to move in, he found the place empty – there was not even a cushion to sit on. Everything had been stolen as soon as the death of Shāwar was announced.

It had taken the Kurdish general three campaigns to become the real ruler of Egypt. But he was not to savour his pleasure for long. On 23 March, just two months after his triumph, he was taken ill after an excessively sumptuous meal. He was seized by an atrocious sensation of suffocation and died within a few minutes. His death marked the end of an era, but also the beginning of another, one whose repercussions would be infinitely greater. 'Upon the death of Shīrkūh,' Ibn al-Athīr reports, 'the advisers of the caliph al-ʿĀḍid suggested that he name Yūsuf the new vizier, because he was the youngest, and seemingly the most inexperienced and weakest, of the emirs of the army.'

Saladin was indeed summoned to the sovereign's palace, where he was given the title *al-malik al-nāṣir*, 'the victorious king', as well as the distinctive accoutrements of the vizier: a white turban stitched in gold, a robe with a scarlet-lined tunic, a jewel-encrusted sword, a chestnut mare with a saddle and bridle adorned with engraved gold and encrusted pearls, and many other precious objects. Leaving the palace accompanied by a great cortège, he headed for his official residence.

Yūsuf managed to establish his authority within a few weeks. He discharged the Fatimid functionaries whose loyalty seemed doubtful, replacing them with his own close collaborators; a revolt among the Egyptian troops was severely crushed. Finally, in October 1169, he repelled an absurd Frankish invasion, again led by Amalric, who had arrived in Egypt for the fifth and last time in the hope of capturing the port of Damietta, in the Nile delta. Manuel Comnenus, uneasy that one of Nūr al-Dīn's lieutenants now stood at the head of the Fatimid state, had accorded the Franj the support of the Byzantine fleet. But in vain. The Rūm did not have enough supplies, and their allies declined to furnish any additional assistance. Within several weeks, Saladin was able to open talks with them and persuade them to bring the ill-conceived venture to an end.

By the end of 1169 Yūsuf was the unchallenged master of Egypt. In Jerusalem, Morri set his hopes on forging an alliance with Shīrkūh's nephew against the main enemy of the Franj, Nūr al-Dīn. The king's optimism may appear misguided, but it was not wholly without foundation. Saladin soon began to distance himself from his master. He continually assured Nūr al-Dīn of his loyalty and submission, of course, but real authority over Egypt could not be exercised from Damascus or Aleppo.

Relations between the two men finally became dramatically tense. Despite his solid power base in Cairo, Yūsuf never dared to confront his elder directly. Whenever the son of Zangī invited him to a face-to-face meeting, Yūsuf would find some pretext to avoid it, not for fear of falling into a trap, but because he was afraid that he would weaken if he found himself in the presence of his master.

The first serious crisis came during the summer of 1171, when Nūr al-Dīn demanded that the young vizier abolish the Fatimid caliphate. As a Sunni Muslim, the master of Syria could not allow one of his dependencies to remain under the spiritual authority of a 'heretical' dynasty. He sent several messages to this effect to Saladin, who was nevertheless reluctant to act. He was afraid of offending the sentiments of the population, which was mainly Shiʿi, and of alienating the Fatimid dignitaries. Moreover, he was not unaware that he owed the legitimacy of his rule to his investiture by the caliph al-ʿĀḍid. He feared that by dethroning the caliph he would lose whatever formal sanction he had for his power in Egypt, in which case he would be reduced to the status of a mere representative of Nūr al-Dīn. In any case, he considered the son of Zangī's insistence on the matter as an attempt to tighten his own political grip on Egypt, rather than an act of religious zeal. At the beginning of August, the master of Syria's demands that the Shiʿi caliphate be abolished became an imperious order.

His back to the wall, Saladin prepared himself to deal with possible hostile reactions from the population, and even drafted a public proclamation announcing the removal of the caliph. But he still hesitated to publish it. Although he was only twenty, al-ʿĀḍid was seriously ill, and Saladin, who was bound to him by close ties of friendship, could not bring himself to betray his confidence. Then without warning, on Friday 10 September 1171, a citizen of Mosul visiting Cairo entered a mosque, climbed the pulpit ahead of the preacher, and said the prayer in the name of the ʿAbbasid caliph. Curiously, there was no reaction, either at the time or in the following days. Was this man an agent sent by Nūr al-Dīn to embarrass Saladin? Possibly. In any event, after this incident, the vizier could no longer postpone his decision, whatever his reluctance. The order was given that from the following Friday, there was to be no further mention of the Fatimids in the prayers. Al-ʿĀḍid was then on his deathbed, half conscious, and Yūsuf forbade anyone to tell him the news. 'If he recovers', Saladin said, 'then there will be plenty of time for him to find out. If not, let him die untormented.' As it happened, al-ʿĀḍid expired a short time later, never having learned of the unhappy fate of his dynasty.

As might well be expected, the fall of the Shiʿi caliphate after two centuries of often glorious rule was a source of great grief to the Assassins sect, which ever since the days of Ḥasan Ibn al-Ṣabbāḥ had hoped that the Fatimids would shake off their lethargy and usher in a new golden age of Shiʿism. The adherents of the sect were so devastated when they saw this dream vanish for ever that their commander in Syria, Rashīd al-Dīn Sinān, known as 'the old man of the mountain', sent a message to Amalric announcing that he and all his supporters were prepared to convert to Christianity. At the time the Assassins held several fortresses and villages in central Syria, where they lived relatively peaceful lives, seemingly having renounced the spectacular operations of bygone years. Although Rashīd al-Dīn still commanded well-trained groups of killers and devoted preachers, many of the sect's members had become law-abiding peasants, often even compelled to pay a regular tribute to the Order of the Templars.

By promising to convert, the 'old man' hoped, among other things, that his flock would be exempted from the tribute, which only non-Christians had to pay. The Templars, who did not take their financial interests lightly, observed these contacts between Amalric and the Assassins with some disquiet. When it seemed that an agreement was at hand, they decided to block it. One day in 1173, as several envoys of Rashīd al-Dīn were returning from an audience with the king, the Templars laid an ambush and massacred them. There would be no further talk of conversion by the Assassins.

Quite apart from this episode, the abolition of the Fatimid caliphate had another consequence as important as it was unexpected: it invested Saladin with a political dimension he had hitherto lacked. Obviously, Nūr al-Dīn had not foreseen any such result. The elimination of the caliph, instead of reducing Yūsuf to the rank of a mere representative of the master of Syria, made him the effective sovereign of Egypt and the legitimate custodian of the fabulous treasures amassed by the defunct dynasty. Relations between the two men would now grow steadily more embittered.

Soon after these events, Saladin led a daring expedition against the Frankish fortress of Shawbak, east of Jerusalem. As the garrison was about to capitulate, Saladin learned that Nūr al-Dīn had just arrived with his own troops to participate in the operation. Without a moment's delay, Saladin ordered his men to break camp and to return to Cairo at a forced march. The pretext, explained in a letter to the son of Zangī, was that turmoil had supposedly broken out in Egypt, forcing a precipitate departure.

But Nūr al-Dīn was not deceived. Accusing Saladin of disloyalty and treason, he swore that he would personally travel to the land of the Nile to take matters in hand. The uneasy young vizier assembled his closest collaborators, among them his father Ayyūb, and asked them what attitude they thought he should take if Nūr al-Dīn carried out his threat. When some of the emirs declared that they were ready to take up arms against the son of Zangī, and Saladin himself seemed to share their view, Ayyūb intervened, trembling with rage. Speaking to Yūsuf as though he were a mere factotum, he said:

> I am your father, and if there is anyone here who loves you and wishes you well, it is I. But know this: if Nūr al-Dīn came, nothing could ever prevent me from bowing before him and kissing the ground at his feet. If he ordered me to lop off your head with my sabre, I would do it. For this land is his. You shall write this to him: I have learned that you wanted to lead an expedition to Egypt, but there is no need for you to do so. This country belongs to you, and you need only send me a charger or camel and I will come to you a humble and submissive man.

When the meeting was over, Ayyūb gave his young son another lecture, this time in private: 'In God's name, if Nūr al-Dīn tried to take so much as an inch of your territory, I would fight to the death against him. But why allow yourself to appear overtly ambitious? Time is on your side. Let Providence act.' Convinced, Yūsuf sent the message his father had suggested to Syria, and Nūr al-Dīn, now reassured, called off his punitive expedition at the last minute. But Saladin had learned something from this emergency, and shortly afterwards he sent one of his brothers, Tūrān-Shāh, to Yemen, his mission being to conquer this mountainous land in south-west Arabia to prepare a refuge for the Ayyūb family just in case the son of Zangī again considered taking control of Egypt. And Yemen was in fact occupied without much difficulty, 'in the name of King Nūr al-Dīn'.

In July 1173, less than two years after the missed rendezvous of Shawbak, a similar incident occurred. Saladin was leading an expedition east of the Jordan, and Nūr al-Dīn assembled his troops and set out to meet him. But once again the vizier was terrified at having to face his master directly, and hurriedly headed back to Egypt, claiming that his father was dying. In fact, Ayyūb had just fallen into a coma after an accident in which he had been thrown from his horse. But Nūr al-Dīn was unwilling to accept this new excuse. And when Ayyūb died in August, he realised that there was no longer anyone in Cairo in whom he had complete confidence. He therefore decided that the time had come to take personal charge of Egyptian affairs.

'Nūr al-Dīn began preparations to invade Egypt and wrench it away from Ṣalāḥ al-Dīn Yūsuf, for he had noted that the latter was shirking the fight against the Franj, for fear of having to unite with him.' Our chronicler here, Ibn al-Athīr, who was fourteen when these events occurred, takes a clear position in support of the son of Zangī. 'Yūsuf preferred to see the Franj on his borders rather than be the direct neighbour of Nūr al-Dīn. The latter therefore wrote to Mosul and elsewhere asking that he be sent troops. But as he was preparing to march to Egypt with his soldiers, God whispered to him the command that cannot be shunned.' The ruler of Syria fell gravely ill, afflicted, it seems, by a very painful angina. His doctors prescribed bleeding, but he refused: 'One does not bleed a man sixty years old,' he said. Other treatments were tried, but nothing worked. On 15 May 1174 it was announced in Damascus that Nūr al-Dīn Maḥmūd, the saint-king, the *mujāhid* who had united Muslim Syria and enabled the Arab world to prepare for the decisive struggle against the occupier, had died. That night, all the mosques were filled with people who had gathered to recite verses of the Koran in his memory. In time, Saladin would come to be seen as Nūr al-Dīn's continuator rather than his rival, despite their conflict during these latter years.

For the moment, however, resentment was the dominant emotion among the relatives and close associates of the deceased, and they feared that Yūsuf would take advantage of the general confusion to attack Syria. In an effort to gain time, they did not notify Cairo of the news. But Saladin, who had friends everywhere, sent a finely worded message to Damascus by carrier pigeon: 'News has come to us from the accursed enemy regarding the master Nūr al-Dīn. If, God forbid, it should be true, we must above all ensure that no division takes hold in our hearts and that no minds are gripped by unreason, for only the enemy would profit.'

In spite of these conciliatory words, fierce hostility would be aroused by the rise of Saladin.

X

The Tears of Saladin

'You go too far, Yūsuf; you overstep all limits. You are but a servant of Nūr al-Dīn, and now you seek to grasp power for yourself alone? But make no mistake, for we who have raised you out of nothingness shall be able to return you to it!'

Some years later, this warning delivered to Saladin by the dignitaries of Aleppo would seem absurd. But in 1174, when the new master of Cairo was just beginning to emerge as the principal figure of the Arab East, his merits were not yet evident for all to see. In Nūr al-Dīn's entourage, both while he lived and just after his death, no one even spoke the name of Yūsuf any more. Words like 'the upstart', 'the ingrate', 'the disloyal', or, most often, 'the insolent' were used instead.

Saladin himself generally shunned insolence; but his luck was surely insolent. And it was just this that annoyed his adversaries. For this thirty-six-year-old Kurdish officer had never been an ambitious man, and those who knew him from the beginning felt sure that he would have been quite content to be no more than an emir among others had fate not propelled him, willy-nilly, to the forefront of the scene.

He had accompanied his uncle to Egypt somewhat reluctantly and his role in the conquest had been minimal. Nevertheless, just because of his self-effacement, he was drawn to the summit of power. He himself had not dared to proclaim the downfall of the Fatimids, but when he was forced to do so, he found himself heir to the richest of Muslim dynasties. And when Nūr al-Dīn resolved to put him in his place, Yūsuf had no need even to resist: his master suddenly died, leaving as his successor an eleven-year-old adolescent, al-Ṣāliḥ.

On 11 July 1174, less than two months later, Amalric also died, the victim of dysentery, just when he was preparing yet another invasion of Egypt, this time with the support of a powerful Sicilian fleet. He bequeathed the kingdom of Jerusalem to his son Baldwin IV, a young man of thirteen afflicted by the most terrible of maledictions: leprosy. Throughout the Orient, there was but a single monarch who could stand in the way of the irresistible rise of Saladin, and that was Manuel, emperor of the Rūm, who indeed dreamed of some day becoming the suzerain of Syria and who intended to invade Egypt in conjunction with the Franj. But then in September 1176, as if to complete the series of gifts fate bestowed upon Saladin, the powerful Byzantine army, which had checked Nūr al-Dīn for nearly fifteen years, was crushed by Kilij Arslan II, the grandson of the first Kilij Arslan, in the battle of Myriokephalon. Manuel died soon afterwards, condemning the Christian empire in the East to sink into anarchy.

Can one blame Saladin's panegyrists for detecting the hand of Providence in this succession of unexpected events? Yūsuf himself never claimed credit for his good fortune. He always took care to thank, after God, 'my uncle Shīrkūh' and 'my master Nūr al-Dīn'. It is true that the greatness of Saladin lay also in his modesty.

> One day when Ṣalāḥ al-Dīn was tired and was trying to rest, one of his *mamlūks* came to him and handed him a paper to sign. 'I am exhausted,' said the sultan, 'come back in an hour.' But the man insisted. He fairly stuck the page in Ṣalāḥ al-Dīn's face, saying, 'Let the master sign!' The sultan replied, 'But I have no inkwell here.' He was seated at the entrance to his tent, and the *mamlūk* remarked that there was an inkwell inside. 'There is an inkwell, at the back of the tent,' he cried, which meant, in effect, that he was ordering Ṣalāḥ al-Dīn to go and get the inkwell himself, no less. The sultan turned, saw the inkwell, and said, 'By God, you're right.' He reached back, bracing himself with his left hand, and grasped the inkwell in his right. Then he signed the paper.

This incident, related by Bahāʾ al-Dīn, Saladin's personal secretary and biographer, is a striking illustration of what made him so different from the monarchs of his time, indeed of all times: he was able to remain humble with the humble, even after he had become the most powerful of the powerful. The chroniclers, of course, evoke his courage, his sense of justice, and his zeal for the *jihād*, but through their writings a more touching, more human, image always transpires.

> One day [Bahāʾ al-Dīn relates] in the midst of our campaign against the Franj, Ṣalāḥ al-Dīn summoned his close companions. In his hand was a letter he had just finished reading, and when he tried to speak, he broke down. Seeing him in this state, we were unable to hold back our own tears, even though we did not know what was the matter. Finally, his voice choked with tears, he said, 'Taqi al-Dīn, my nephew, is dead.' Then his warm tears began to flow again, as did ours. When I regained my composure I said to him, 'Let us not forget the campaign in which we are engaged, and let us ask God to forgive us for having abandoned ourselves to this grief.' Ṣalāḥ al-Dīn agreed. 'Yes,' he said, 'may God forgive me! May God forgive me!' He repeated these words several times, and then he added, 'Let no one know what has happened!' Then he had rose water brought to wash his eyes.

The tears of Saladin flowed on other occasions besides the deaths of those closest to him.

> Once [Bahāʾ al-Dīn recalls] when I was riding at the sultan's side against the Franj, an army scout came to us with a sobbing woman beating her breast. 'She came from the Franj camp', the scout explained, 'and wants to see the master. We brought her here.' Ṣalāḥ al-Dīn asked his interpreter to question her. She said: 'Yesterday some Muslim thieves entered my tent and stole my little girl. I cried all night, and our commanders told me: the king of the Muslims is merciful; we will let you go to him and you can ask for your daughter back. Thus have I come, and I place all my hopes in you.' Ṣalāḥ al-Dīn was touched, and tears came to his eyes. He sent someone to the slave market to look for the girl, and less than an hour later a horseman arrived bearing the child on his shoulders. As soon as she saw them, the girl's mother threw herself to the ground and smeared her face with sand. All those present wept with emotion. She looked heavenward and began to mutter incomprehensible words. Thus was her daughter returned to her, and she was escorted back to the camp of the Franj.

Those who knew Saladin say little about his physical appearance: he was small and frail, with a short, neat beard. They prefer to speak of his pensive and somewhat melancholy face, which would suddenly light up with a comforting smile that would put anyone talking to him at ease. He was always affable with visitors, insisting that they stay to eat, treating them with full honours, even if they were infidels, and satisfying all their requests. He could not bear to let someone who had come to him depart disappointed, and there were those who did not hesitate to take advantage of this quality. One day, during a truce with the Franj, the 'Brins', lord of Antioch, arrived unexpectedly at Saladin's tent and asked him to return a district that the sultan had taken four years earlier. And he agreed!

Saladin's generosity sometimes bordered on the irresponsible. 'His treasurers', Bahā' al-Dīn reveals, 'always kept a certain sum hidden away for emergencies, for they knew that if the master learned of the existence of this reserve, he would spend it immediately. In spite of this precaution, when the sultan died the state treasury contained no more than an ingot of Tyre gold and forty-seven dirhams of silver.'

When some of his collaborators chided him for his profligacy, Saladin answered with a nonchalant smile: 'There are people for whom money is no more important than sand.' Indeed, he felt genuine contempt for riches and luxury, and when the fabulous palaces of the Fatimid caliphs fell into his hands, he settled his emirs in them, preferring himself to live in the more modest residence reserved for the viziers.

This was but one of many features that Saladin and Nūr al-Dīn appeared to have in common. In fact, Saladin's adversaries saw him as no more than a pale reflection of his master. In reality, in his contacts with others, especially his soldiers, he behaved far more warmly than his predecessor had. And although he observed the letter of religious precepts, he lacked the slight streak of bigotry that the son of Zangī had manifested on occasion. In general, one may say that Saladin was as demanding of himself as Nūr al-Dīn had been, but more lenient with others, although he was even more merciless than his elder when dealing with those who had insulted Islam, be they 'heretics' or certain of the Franj.

Beyond these differences of personality, Saladin was strongly influenced, especially at the beginning, by the imposing stature of Nūr al-Dīn, of whom he strove to be a worthy successor, relentlessly pursuing the same objectives: to unify the Arab world, and to mobilise the Muslims, both morally, with the aid of a powerful propaganda apparatus, and militarily, in order to reconquer the occupied territories, above all Jerusalem.

In the summer of 1174, as the emirs of Damascus who supported young al-Ṣāliḥ were discussing the best way to hold out against Saladin, even considering an alliance with the Franj, the ruler of Cairo sent them a genuinely challenging letter. In it, judiciously concealing his conflict with Nūr al-Dīn, he unhesitatingly presented himself as the continuator of his suzerain's work and the faithful guardian of his heritage.

> If [he wrote] our late king had detected among you a man as worthy of his confidence as me, would he not have entrusted him with the leadership of Egypt, the most important of his provinces? You may be sure that had Nūr al-Dīn not died so soon, he would have designated me to educate his son and to watch over him. Now, I observe, you are behaving as though you alone served my master and his son, and you are attempting to exclude me. But I shall soon arrive. In honour of the memory of my master, I shall perform deeds that will have their effect, and each of you will be punished for his misconduct.

Here it is difficult to recognise the circumspect man of previous years. It is as if the death of his master had unleashed long-pent-up aggression. It is true that the circumstances were exceptional, for this message had a precise function: it was the declaration of war with which Saladin would begin the conquest of Muslim Syria. When he sent this message in October 1174, the ruler of Cairo was already on his way to Damascus, leading seven hundred cavalry. That was far too few for a siege of the Syrian metropolis, but Yūsuf had carefully calculated the odds. Frightened by the uncharacteristically violent tone of Saladin's missive, al-Ṣāliḥ and his collaborators preferred to retreat to Aleppo. Crossing Franj territory with no difficulty via what could now be called the 'Shīrkūh trail', Saladin arrived at Damascus in late October; supporters of his family quickly threw open the gates and welcomed him.

Encouraged by this victory, won without a single sword-stroke, he continued on his way. He left the Damascus garrison under the command of one of his brothers and headed for central Syria, where he seized Homs and Hama. During this lightning campaign, Ibn al-Athīr tells us 'Ṣalāḥ al-Dīn claimed to be acting in the name of the king al-Ṣāliḥ, son of Nūr al-Dīn. He said that his aim was to defend the country against the Franj.' Still faithful to the Zangī dynasty, the Mosul historian is at least suspicious of Saladin, whom he accuses of duplicity. He was not entirely wrong. Yūsuf, anxious not to act as a usurper, did indeed present himself as the protector of al-Ṣāliḥ. 'In any event,' he said, 'this adolescent cannot govern alone. He needs a tutor, a regent, and no one is better placed than me to perform that function.' He sent al-Ṣāliḥ letter after letter assuring him of his loyalty, ordered prayers to be said for him in the mosques of Cairo and Damascus, and coined money in his name.

The young monarch was wholly unmoved by these gestures. In December 1174, when Saladin laid siege to Aleppo 'to protect King al-Ṣāliḥ from the nefarious influence of his advisers', the son of Nūr al-Dīn assembled the people of the city and delivered a moving speech: 'Behold this unjust and ungrateful man who wishes to take my country from me without regard to God or man! I am an orphan, and I rely upon you to defend me, in memory of my father who so loved you.' Deeply touched, the Aleppans decided to resist 'the outlaw' come what may. Yūsuf, seeking to avoid a direct conflict with al-Ṣāliḥ, lifted the siege. On the other hand, he now decided to proclaim himself 'king of Egypt and Syria', and would thus no longer depend on any suzerain. The chroniclers would also call him 'sultan', but he himself never adopted this title. Saladin later returned several times to the walls of Aleppo, but he could never bring himself to cross swords with the son of Nūr al-Dīn.

Al-Ṣāliḥ's advisers decided to resort to the services of the Assassins in an effort to remove this permanent threat. They made contact with

Rashīd al-Dīn Sinān, who promised to get rid of Yūsuf for them. The 'old man of the mountain' could have asked nothing better than to settle accounts with the gravedigger of the Fatimid dynasty. The first assault came at the beginning of 1175: some Assassins penetrated Saladin's camp as far as his tent, where an emir recognised them and barred their way. He was seriously wounded, but the alarm had been sounded. Guards came running, and after a murderous fight, the Bāṭinis were massacred. This only postponed matters. On 22 May 1176, when Saladin was again campaigning in the region of Aleppo, an Assassin burst into his tent and dealt him a dagger-stroke in the head. Fortunately, the sultan had been on his guard since the previous attack, and had taken the precaution of wearing a headdress of mail under his fez. The would-be killer then went for his victim's neck. But again his blade was checked. Saladin was wearing a long tunic of thick material whose high collar was reinforced with mail. One of the army emirs then arrived, seized the dagger with one hand and with the other struck the Bāṭini, who collapsed. But before Saladin had had time to rise, a second killer leapt upon him, then a third. The guards, however, had meanwhile arrived, and the assailants were massacred. Yūsuf emerged from his tent haggard and reeling, amazed that he had escaped injury.

As soon as he had regained his wits, he decided to mount an attack on the lair of the Assassins in central Syria, where Rashīd al-Dīn Sinān controlled ten or so fortresses. Saladin laid siege to the most formidable of them, Maṣyāf, perched on the summit of a cliff. Exactly what happened in the land of the Assassins that August of 1176 will probably always remain a mystery. One version, that of Ibn al-Athīr, has it that Sinān sent a letter to a maternal uncle of Saladin's, swearing to have all the members of the ruling family killed. Such a threat from the Assassins sect could not be taken lightly, especially after the two attempts to assassinate the sultan. The siege of Maṣyāf was then lifted, according to this account.

A second version of events has come down to us from the Assassins themselves. It is recounted in one of the few surviving writings of the sect, a narrative signed by one of their adherents, a certain Abū Firās, whose story runs as follows. Sinān was away from Maṣyāf when the fortress was besieged. He and two companions posted themselves on a neighbouring hill, from which Sinān observed the development of operations. Saladin then ordered his men to go and capture Sinān. A large detachment surrounded him, but when the soldiers tried to approach, their arms and legs were paralysed by a mysterious force. The 'old man of the mountain' then asked them to inform the sultan that he wanted to meet him personally and in private; the terrified soldiers ran to tell their master what had just happened. Saladin, suspecting that something was amiss, had lime and ashes spread around his tent to detect any footprints, and at nightfall he posted guards with torches to protect him. Suddenly, in the middle of the night, he awoke with a start, and barely glimpsed an unknown figure gliding out of his tent, a figure he believed to be Sinān himself. On the bed the mysterious visitor had left a poisoned cake and a piece of paper on which someone had written: 'You are in our power.' Saladin is then said to have cried out, and his guards came running. They swore they had seen nothing. The next day, Saladin hurriedly lifted the siege and returned to Damascus.

This account is undoubtedly highly embellished, but it is a fact that Saladin reversed his policy towards the Assassins very suddenly. Despite his aversion for heretics of all varieties, he never again tried to threaten the territory of the Bāṭinis. On the contrary, he now sought to conciliate them, thus depriving his enemies, Muslim and Franj alike, of a precious auxiliary. The sultan had decided to make sure that he held all the trumps in the battle for control of Syria. It is true that for all practical purposes victory was his from the time of his conquest of Damascus. But the conflict nevertheless dragged on interminably. The many campaigns that had to be waged – against the Frankish states, against Aleppo, against Mosul, which was also ruled by a descendant of Zangī, and against various other princes of Jazīra and Asia Minor – were exhausting. Apart from all that, Saladin had to return to Cairo regularly to discourage intriguers and conspirators.

The situation began to be resolved only towards the end of 1181, when al-Ṣāliḥ suddenly died, possibly poisoned, at the age of eighteen. Ibn al-Athīr gives an emotional account of his last moments.

> When his condition worsened, the physicians advised him to take a bit of wine. He told them: 'I will not do so without advice from an *ʿālim.*' One of the leading doctors of law was then brought to his bedside and explained that religion authorised the use of wine as a medicine. Al-Ṣāliḥ asked: 'And do you really think that if God has decided to end my life he will change his mind if he sees me drinking wine?' The man of religion had to answer, No. 'Then', the dying man concluded, 'I do not want to meet my creator with a forbidden drink in my stomach.'

Eighteen months later, on 18 June 1183, Saladin solemnly entered Aleppo. Egypt and Syria were now one, not merely in name, as during the reign of Nūr al-Dīn, but in fact, under the uncontested authority of the Ayyubid sovereign. Curiously, the emergence of this powerful Arab state whose pressure mounted daily did not induce the Franj to exhibit greater solidarity among themselves. On the contrary. As the king of Jerusalem, hideously deformed by leprosy, sank into impotence, two rival clans embarked on a power struggle. The first, which favoured coming to some arrangement with Saladin, was led by Raymond, the count of Tripoli. The spokesman for the second, extremist faction was Reynald of Châtillon, the former prince of Antioch.

Very dark, with a hawk-nose, fluent in Arabic, and an attentive reader of Islamic texts, Raymond could have passed for a Syrian emir but for his large stature, which betrayed his Western origins.

> Among the Franj at that time [Ibn al-Athīr tells us] there was no wiser or more courageous man than the lord of Tripoli, Raymond Ibn Raymond al-Sanjīlī, a descendant of Saint-Gilles. But he was very ambitious, and desired to become king. He acted as regent for some time, but was soon deposed. So resentful was he that he wrote to Ṣalāḥ al-Dīn, aligned himself with him, and asked for his help in becoming king of the Franj. Ṣalāḥ al-Dīn was delighted at the request, and quickly freed a number of knights of Tripoli who had been imprisoned among the Muslims.

Saladin paid close attention to this discord. When Raymond's 'Oriental' current seemed in the ascendancy in Jerusalem, he struck a conciliatory note. In 1184 Baldwin IV's leprosy was in its final stages. His arms and legs had grown flaccid, his eyes dim. But he lacked neither courage nor common sense, and he had confidence in the count of Tripoli, who was striving to establish friendly relations with Saladin. The Andalusian traveller Ibn Jubayr, who visited Damascus that year, was surprised to find that in spite of the war, caravans travelled freely between Cairo and Damascus, passing through Franj territory. 'The Christians', he noted, 'make the Muslims pay a tax, which is applied without abuses. The Christian merchants in turn pay duty on their merchandise when they pass through the territory of the Muslims. There is complete understanding between the two sides, and equity is respected. The men of war pursue their war, but the people remain at peace.'

Far from being in any hurry to put an end to this coexistence, Saladin indicated that he was prepared to go even further on the road to peace. In March 1185 the leprous king of Jerusalem died at the age of twenty-four, bequeathing the throne to his nephew Baldwin V, a six-year-old child. The regency went to the count of Tripoli, who, aware that he needed time to consolidate his power, quickly despatched emissaries to Damascus to seek a truce. Although Saladin felt sure that he was now in a position to open the decisive battle with the Occidentals, he nevertheless demonstrated that he was not seeking a confrontation at any price. He agreed to a four-year truce.

But a year later, when the child-king died in August 1186, a struggle broke out for the post of regent.

> The mother of the young monarch [Ibn al-Athīr explains] had fallen in love with a man named Guy, a Franj recently arrived from the West. She married him, and when the child died, she gave the throne to her husband, summoning the patriarch, the priests, the monks, the Hospitallers, the Templars and the barons and informing them that she had transferred power to Guy, to whom she then had them swear allegiance. Raymond refused; he preferred to reach an agreement with Ṣalāḥ al-Dīn.

The Guy in question was King Guy of Lusignan, a handsome, dim-witted man completely devoid of political or military competence and always inclined to agree with the last person to whom he had spoken. In reality, he was no more than a puppet in the hands of the 'hawks', the leader of whom was old 'Brins Arnat', Reynald of Châtillon.

Following his Cypriot adventure and his exactions in northern Syria, Reynald had spent fifteen years in the prisons of Aleppo before being released in 1175 by the son of Nūr al-Dīn. His captivity had only aggravated his defects. More fanatical, greedy and bloodthirsty than ever, Arnat aroused more hatred between the Arabs and Franj than had been caused by decades of war and massacres. After his release he had failed to retake Antioch, where his stepson Bohemond III now held the throne. He therefore settled in the kingdom of Jerusalem, where he quickly married a young widow who presented him as a dowry with various territories lying east of the Jordan river, in particular the powerful fortresses of Karak and Shawbak. Having formed an alliance with the Templars and with many newly arrived knights, he enjoyed mounting influence at the court in Jerusalem, which only Raymond succeeded in counterbalancing for a time. Reynald sought to impose the same policy as that pursued by the first Frankish invaders: to fight relentlessly against the Arabs, to pillage and massacre without restraint, to conquer new territories. He regarded any conciliation, any compromise, as treason. He felt bound by no truce or agreement. In any event, he explained cynically, what was the value of an oath sworn to infidels?

In 1180 an agreement between Damascus and Jerusalem had guaranteed the free circulation of goods and persons in the region. A few months later, a caravan of rich Arab merchants crossing the Syrian desert on its way to Mecca was attacked by Reynald, who confiscated all the merchandise. Saladin complained to Baldwin IV, who dared not punish his vassal. In the autumn of 1182 a more serious incident occurred: Arnat decided to raid Mecca itself. The expedition set out from Eilat, which was then a small Arab fishing village on the Gulf of Aqaba. Some Red Sea pirates guided the Franj along the coast; they attacked Yanbūḥ, the port servicing Medina, and then Rabīgh, not far from Mecca. Along the way Reynald sank a boat carrying Muslim pilgrims to Jidda. 'Everyone was taken by surprise,' Ibn al-Athīr explains, 'for the people of these regions had never seen a

Franj before, whether merchant or warrior.' Drunk with success, the attackers took their time filling their ships with booty. Reynald then returned to his own territory, while his men spent many months plying the Red Sea. Saladin's brother al-ʿĀdil, who was governing Egypt in his brother's absence, armed a fleet and sent it out against the pillagers, who were crushed. Some of them were taken to Mecca, where they were publicly beheaded, 'an exemplary punishment', the Mosul historian concludes, 'for those who had sought to violate the holy places'. News of Reynald's insane escapade spread throughout the Muslim world, where Arnat would henceforth symbolise everything most hideous about the Frankish enemy.

Saladin had responded by staging a few raids against Reynald's territory, but in spite of his anger, the sultan remained magnanimous. In November 1183, for example, he had set up catapults around the citadel of Karak and was bombarding it with huge chunks of rock, when the defenders sent word that a princely marriage was being celebrated inside. Although the bride was Reynald's stepdaughter, Saladin asked the besieged in which pavilion the newly-weds would reside and then ordered his men to spare that sector.

Such gestures, alas, counted for nothing with Arnat. For a while he had been neutralised by the wise Raymond, but with the accession of King Guy in 1186, he was again able to lay down the law. A few weeks later, ignoring the truce that was to have remained in effect for another two and a half years, the prince swooped, like a bird of prey, on a large caravan of Arab pilgrims and merchants who were peacefully making their way to Mecca. He massacred all the armed men and led the rest of the troop into captivity in Karak. When some of them dared to remind Reynald of the truce, he told them defiantly: 'Let your Muḥammad come and deliver you!' When these words were reported to Saladin several weeks later, he swore that he would kill Arnat with his own hands.

For the time being, however, the sultan sought to temporise. He sent emissaries to Reynald asking that the captives be released and their property restored, in accordance with the terms of the truce. When the prince refused to receive them, the emissaries went to Jerusalem, where they were greeted by Guy. He professed to be shocked

The supreme masterpiece of Islamic metalwork, the Baptistère de St Louis, depicts Occidental characters in an Oriental manner, clearly showing the influence of the Franj

كرانبايه ايوان دخت وبلادرا ارزايے داشت وهرد وشرع خدمت وبندكى بجاى وردند و درمعز كش ازنظامے

ازبراهمه كه خواها با بران غط تعبير كرده بودند وبران قرارداده ملك مشاله داد تا ايشا نزانكال كردند بعضى ابر

داركشيدند وبعضى رابشمشير بكذ اينذند وكيار يدون جكيم رأس زكرد وبواهب خطير مستظهر ومستغنى كردايند

ومشاله داد تا بران جال را بذوبود دكفت جفاينان وسزاى غادراق ايذجكيم روى بازدشاه

A Sultan dispenses justice. Usāmah, disgusted by what the Franj called justice – the barbaric 'trial by ordeal' – preferred the Arab form, whereby *qāḍīs* would 'adhere to a meticulous procedure fixed by the Koran'

When Zangī captured Edessa in 1144, artisans were identified and set to work, and other Franj executed, but the 'priests, nobles and notables were taken aside, stripped of their robes and led away in chains to Aleppo'

Following Shirkuh's dazzling march across Egypt, the Franj decided to lay siege to Alexandria and, as the blockade tightened, the city fell victim to famine and epidemic. *Below,* coin struck for the defender of Alexandria, Saladin, who finally became established as the ruler of Syria and Egypt in 1183

A crossbow from *Tabṣirah fī al-hurūb* ('Treatise on Armoury'), a work commissioned by Saladin to provide a discussion of tactics and weaponry

The Prophet Muḥammad rises to heaven astride the steed Buraq, delivered to him by the archangel Jabril (Gabriel). Saladin argued that Jerusalem was as holy a city to Muslims as to the Franj, and even more so, as it was the place where the Prophet made this 'miraculous nocturnal journey'

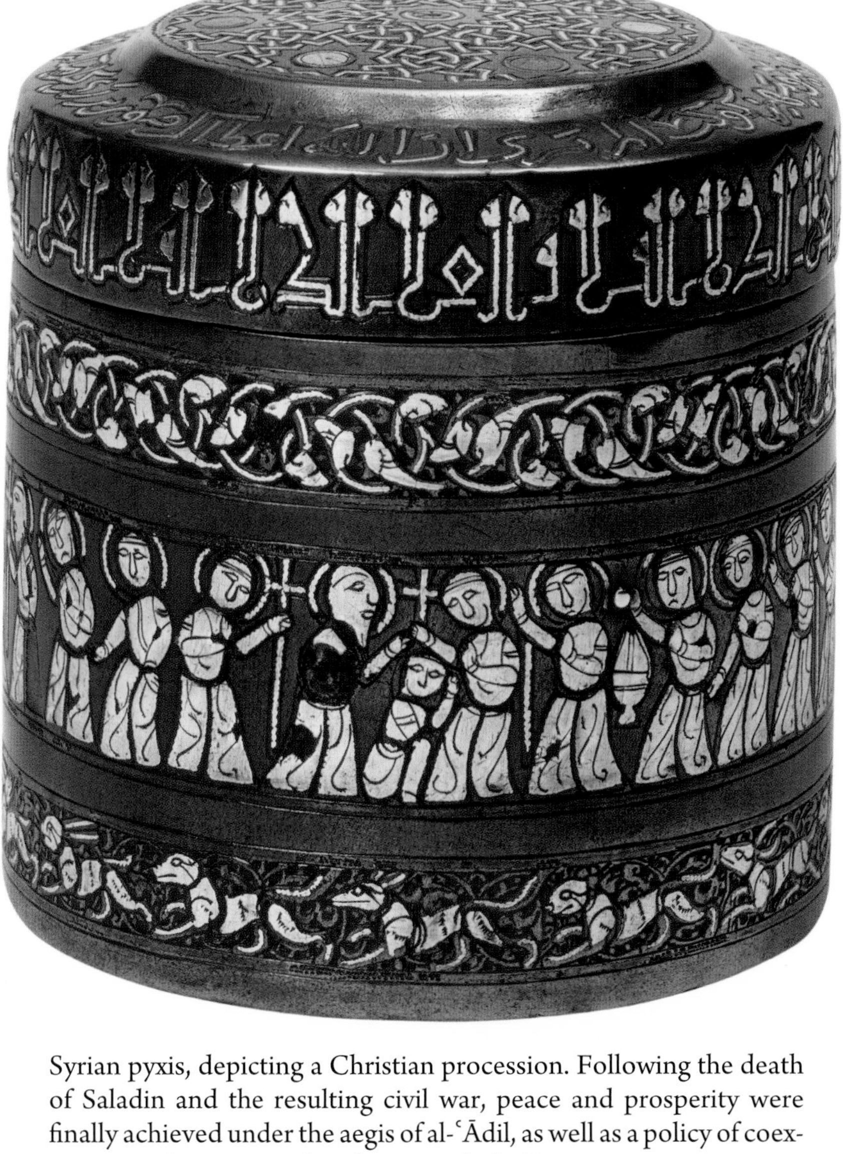

Syrian pyxis, depicting a Christian procession. Following the death of Saladin and the resulting civil war, peace and prosperity were finally achieved under the aegis of al-ʿĀdil, as well as a policy of coexistence and commercial exchange with the Franj

The Mongol horde at Baghdad. In 1258 the grandson of Genghis Khan, Hülegü, destroyed Baghdad after a few weeks of bitter fighting, burning the neighbourhoods and massacring nearly 80,000 men, women and children. It marked the tragic end of the ʿAbbasid caliphate at the behaviour of his vassal but dared not risk a conflict with him. The ambassadors insisted: would the hostages of Prince Arnat continue to rot in the dungeons of Karak, in violation of all the agreements and oaths? The inept Guy washed his hands of the matter.

The truce was broken. Although Saladin was prepared to have honoured it for its full duration, he was not apprehensive at the resumption of hostilities. He despatched messengers to the emirs of Egypt, Syria, Jazīra and elsewhere announcing that the Franj had treacherously flouted their commitments, and he called upon his allies and vassals to unite all the forces at their command to take part in the *jihād* against the occupier. Thousands of cavalry and foot soldiers converged on Damascus from all the lands of Islam. The city was inundated by a sea of waving banners, small camel-skin tents in which soldiers took shelter from the sun and rain, and vast royal pavilions of richly coloured fabric adorned with calligraphic verses from the Koran or poems.

While this mobilisation proceeded, the Franj remained mired in their internecine quarrels. King Guy thought it a propitious moment to dispose of his rival Raymond, whom he accused of complicity with the Muslims. The army of Jerusalem prepared for an attack on Tiberias, a small city of Galilee belonging to the wife of the count of Tripoli. Alerted, the count went to see Saladin and proposed an alliance. Saladin accepted immediately and sent a detachment of troops to reinforce the Tiberias garrison. The Jerusalem army withdrew.

On 30 April 1187, as successive waves of Arab, Turkish and Kurdish fighters continued to converge on Damascus, Saladin sent a messenger to Tiberias asking Raymond, in accordance with the agreement, to allow his scouts to make a reconnaissance tour of the coast of Lake Galilee. The count was embarrassed, but could not refuse. His only demands were that the Muslim soldiers be out of his territory by nightfall and that they promise not to attack his subjects or their property. To avoid any incidents, he warned all the surrounding localities that the Muslim troops would be passing through, and he asked the inhabitants to stay at home.

At dawn the next day, Friday 1 May, seven thousand cavalry under the command of one of Saladin's lieutenants passed before the walls of Tiberias. That same night, as they retraced their steps on their return passage, they respected the count's demands to the letter: they attacked neither village nor chateau, looted neither gold nor cattle, yet their passage was not without incident. By chance, the grand masters of the Templars and the Hospitallers happened to have been in one of the area's fortresses the evening before, when Raymond's messenger arrived to announce that a Muslim detachment would be passing through. The monk-soldiers pricked up their ears. They had no pact with the Saracens. Hastily gathering a few hundred knights and foot soldiers, they decided to assault the Muslim cavalry near the village of Saffurīya, north of Nazareth. But the Franj were decimated in a matter of minutes. Only the grand master of the Templars managed to escape.

> Frightened by this defeat [Ibn al-Athīr relates] the Franj sent their patriarch, priests and monks, together with a large number of knights, to Raymond. They remonstrated bitterly with him about his alliance with Ṣalāḥ al-Dīn, saying: 'You must surely have converted to Islam, otherwise you could never tolerate what has just happened. You would not have allowed Muslims to cross your territory, to massacre Templars and Hospitallers, to carry off prisoners, without doing anything to stop it!' The count's own soldiers, those of Tripoli and Tiberias, also chided him, and the patriarch threatened to excommunicate him and to annul his marriage. Raymond was unnerved by this pressure. He begged their pardon and repented. They forgave him, there was a reconciliation, and they asked him to place his troops at the disposal of the king and to join the battle against the Muslims. The count left with them. The Franj reassembled their troops, cavalry and foot soldiers, near Acre, and then they marched, shuffling along, towards the village of Saffurīya.

In the Muslim camp, the debacle of these universally feared and detested military-religious orders gave a foretaste of victory. Emirs and soldiers alike would henceforth hasten to cross swords with the Franj. In June Saladin assembled all his troops midway between Damascus and Tiberias: twelve thousand cavalry paraded before him, not to mention the foot soldiers and auxiliary volunteers. From the saddle of his charger, the sultan shouted the order of the day, soon re-echoed by thousands of excited voices: 'Victory over God's enemy!'

Saladin calmly analysed the situation for his general staff: 'The opportunity now before us may well never arise again. In my view, the Muslim army must confront all the infidels in an organised battle. We must throw ourselves resolutely into the *jihād* before our troops disperse.' The sultan wanted to prevent his vassals and allies returning home with their troops before the final victory was won, for the fighting season ended in the autumn. The Franj, however, were extremely cautious warriors. Would they not seek to avoid the battle once they saw how numerous and well-organised the Muslim forces were?

Saladin decided to lay a trap for them, praying to God that they would step into it. He headed for Tiberias, occupied the city in a single day, ordered many fires to be set, and laid siege to the citadel, which was occupied by the countess, wife of Raymond, and a handful of defenders. The Muslim army was quite capable of crushing all resistance, but the sultan restrained his men. The pressure had to be stepped up little by little. He pretended to prepare for the final assault while awaiting the enemy's reaction.

> When the Franj learned that Ṣalāḥ al-Dīn had occupied and set fire to Tiberias [Ibn al-Athīr relates] they met in council. Some proposed marching against the Muslims to fight them and prevent them from seizing the citadel. But Raymond intervened: 'Tiberias belongs to me,' he said, 'and it is my own wife who is besieged. But I would be ready to allow the citadel to be taken and to let my wife be captured if I could be sure that Saladin's offensive would stop there; for, in God's name, I have seen many a Muslim army in the past, but none as numerous or as powerful as the one Saladin commands today. Let us therefore avoid a confrontation with him. We can always retake Tiberias later, and ransom our prisoners.' But Prince Arnat, lord of Karak, said to him, 'You are trying to frighten us with this talk of the strength of the Muslim forces simply because you like them and prefer their friendship. Otherwise you would not proffer such words. If you tell me that they are

numerous, I answer: the fire is not daunted by the quantity of wood to burn.' The count then said: 'I am one of you. I will do as you wish, fight at your side, but you will see what will happen.'

Once again, the most extremist arguments had triumphed among the Franj.

Everything was ready for the battle. The army of Saladin was deployed in a fertile plain covered with fruit trees. Behind it was the fresh water of Lake Tiberias, fed by the Jordan river, while further on, towards the north-east, the majestic outline of the Golan Heights could be seen. Near the Muslim camp was a hill with two peaks, called 'the horns of Ḥiṭṭīn', after the village perched on its slopes.

On 3 July the Frankish army, about twelve thousand strong, began to move. In normal times, it did not take long to travel from Saffurīya to Tiberias: it was four hours' march at most, but in summer this stretch of Palestinian land was arid. There were no sources of water and no wells, and the riverbeds were dry. Nevertheless, as they left Saffurīya in the early morning, the Franj were confident that by afternoon they would be able to slake their thirst at the lakeside. Saladin, however, had laid his trap carefully. Throughout the day his cavalry harassed the enemy, attacking from behind, from in front, and then on both flanks, pouring clouds of arrows down upon them relentlessly. Some losses were inflicted on the Occidentals in this way, but more important, they were forced to slow their advance.

Shortly before nightfall, the Franj reached a promontory from which they could overlook the entire area. Just below them lay the small village of Ḥiṭṭīn, a few earth-coloured houses, while the waters of Lake Tiberias glimmered at the bottom of the valley. Between the Franj and the lake, in the verdant plain stretching along the riverbank, was the army of Saladin. If they were to drink, they would need the sultan's permission.

Saladin smiled. He knew that the Franj were exhausted, dying of thirst, that they had neither the strength nor the time to cut themselves a passage to the lake before dark, and that they would therefore have to spend the night without a drop to drink. Would they really be able to fight in these conditions? That night, Saladin divided his time between prayers and meetings with his general staff. At the same time, he ordered several of his emirs to slip behind the enemy in order to cut off any possible retreat, while making sure that all his men were in position and understood their orders.

The next day, 4 July 1187, at first light of dawn, the Franj, now surrounded and crazy with thirst, desperately tried to move down the hill to reach the lake. Their foot soldiers, more sorely tested than the knights by the previous day's exhausting march, rushed ahead blindly, bearing their battleaxes and maces like a burden. Wave upon wave of them were crushed as they encountered a solid wall of swords and lances. The survivors were pressed back up the hill in disarray, where they intermingled with the knights, now certain of their own defeat. No line of defence could be held. Yet they continued to fight with the courage born of despair. At the head of a handful of close collaborators, Raymond tried to cut a pathway through the Muslim lines. Saladin's lieutenants recognised him and allowed him to escape. He rode all the way back to Tripoli.

> After the count's departure, the Franj were on the point of capitulating [Ibn al-Athīr writes]. The Muslims had set fire to the dry grass, and the wind was blowing the smoke into the eyes of the knights. Assailed by thirst, flames and smoke, by the summer heat and the fires of combat, the Franj were unable to go on. But they believed that they could avoid death only by confronting it. They launched attacks so violent that the Muslims were about to give way. Nevertheless, with each assault the Franj suffered heavy losses and their numbers diminished. The Muslims gained possession of the True Cross. For the Franj, this was the heaviest of losses, for it was on this cross, they claim, that the Messiah, peace be upon him, was crucified.

According to Islam, Christ was crucified only in appearance, for God loved the son of Mary too much to allow such an odious torture to be inflicted upon him.

In spite of this loss, the last of the Franj survivors, nearly 150 of their best knights, continued to fight bravely, digging in on the high ground above the village of Ḥiṭṭīn, where they pitched their tents and organised resistance. But the Muslims pressed them from all sides, and finally only the king's tent remained standing. What happened next was recounted by the son of Saladin himself, al-Malik al-Afḍal, who was seventeen at the time.

> I was at my father's side during the battle of Ḥiṭṭīn, the first I had ever seen. When the king of the Franj found himself on the hill, he and his men launched a fierce attack that drove our own troops back to the place where my father was standing. I looked at him. He was saddened; he frowned and pulled nervously at his beard. Then he advanced, shouting 'Satan must not win!' The Muslims again assaulted the hill. When I saw the Franj retreat under the pressure of our troops, I screamed with joy, 'We have won!' But the Franj attacked again with all their might, and once again our troops found themselves grouped around my father. Now he urged them into the attack once more, and they forced the enemy to retreat up the hill. Again I screamed, 'We have beaten them!' But my father turned to me and said, 'Silence! We will have crushed them only when that tent on the hill has fallen!' Before he had time to finish his sentence, the king's tent collapsed. The sultan then dismounted, bowed down and thanked God, weeping for joy.

In the midst of the cries of joy Saladin rose, mounted his charger, and headed for his tent. The leading prisoners were brought before him, notably King Guy and Prince Arnat. The writer ʿImād al-Dīn al-Asfahāni, one of the sultan's advisers, was present at the scene.

> Ṣalāḥ al-Dīn [he wrote] invited the king to sit beside him, and when Arnat entered in his turn, he seated him next to his king and reminded him of his misdeeds: 'How many times have you sworn an oath and then violated it? How many times have you signed agreements that you have never respected?' Arnat answered through an interpreter: 'Kings have always acted thus. I did nothing more.' During this time, Guy was gasping with thirst, his head dangling as though he were drunk, his face betraying great fright. Ṣalāḥ al-Dīn spoke reassuring words to him, had cold water brought, and offered it to him. The king drank, then handed what remained to Arnat, who slaked his thirst in turn. The sultan then

said to Guy: 'You did not ask my permission before giving him water. I am therefore not obliged to grant him mercy.'

Indeed, according to Arab tradition, a prisoner who is offered food or drink must be spared, an engagement Saladin could not have respected in the case of a man he had sworn to kill with his own hands. ʿImād al-Dīn continues:

> After pronouncing these words, the sultan smiled, mounted his horse, and rode off, leaving his captives in terror. He supervised the return of the troops, then came back to his tent. He ordered Arnat brought there, advanced towards him, sword in hand, and struck him between the neck and shoulder-blade. When Arnat fell, he cut off his head and dragged the body by its feet to the king, who began to tremble. Seeing him thus upset, the sultan said to him in a reassuring tone: 'This man was killed only because of his maleficence and his perfidy.'

Although the king and most of the prisoners were spared, the Templars and Hospitallers suffered the same fate as Reynald of Châtillon.

Even before that memorable day had ended, Saladin assembled his chief emirs and congratulated them on their victory, which, he said, had restored the honour so long scorned by the invaders. The Franj, he believed, no longer had an army, and it was necessary to seize upon this opportunity without delay to recover all the lands unjustly occupied. The next day, a Sunday, he therefore attacked the Tiberias citadel, where the wife of Raymond, knowing that further resistance would have been futile, surrendered. Saladin, of course, allowed the defenders to leave unmolested, with all their property.

The following Tuesday the victorious army marched on the port of Acre, which capitulated without resistance. The city had acquired considerable economic importance during these past years, for trade with the West was channelled through it. The sultan tried to convince the many Italian merchants to remain, promising that they would enjoy all the necessary protection. But they preferred to depart for the neighbouring port of Tyre. Although he regretted their decision, the sultan did not try to stop them. He even allowed them to take away all their riches and offered them an escort to protect them from brigands.

Saladin saw no point in his roaming the countryside at the head of such a powerful army, so he ordered his emirs to reduce the various strongholds of the Franj in Palestine. The Frankish settlements of Galilee and Samaria surrendered one after the other, sometimes in a few hours, sometimes over several days. The inhabitants of Nablus, Haifa and Nazareth headed for Tyre or Jerusalem. The only serious engagement occurred in Jaffa, where an army from Egypt, commanded by Saladin's brother al-ʿĀdil, met with fierce resistance. When he finally managed to take the city, al-ʿĀdil reduced the entire population to slavery. Ibn al-Athīr says that he himself bought a young Frankish woman from Jaffa at a slave market in Aleppo.

> She had a one-year-old child. One day, as she was carrying the child in her arms, she fell and scratched her face. She burst into tears. I tried to console her, telling her that the wound was not serious and that there was no reason to shed bitter tears over such a trifle. She answered, 'That is not why I am crying; it is because of the misfortune that has befallen us. I had six brothers, and all were killed. I don't know what has become of my husband and sisters.' Of all the Franj of the littoral [the Arab historian explains] only the people of Jaffa suffered such a fate.

Indeed, everywhere else the reconquest was nearly bloodless. After his short stay in Acre, Saladin headed north. He passed Tyre, deciding not to waste time at its powerful walls, and set out in a triumphant march along the coast. On 29 July, after seventy-seven years of occupation, Saida capitulated without a fight, followed a few days later by Beirut and Jubayl. The Muslim troops were now quite close to the county of Tripoli, but Saladin, feeling that he no longer had anything to fear from that quarter, turned south, and again paused before Tyre, wondering whether or not he should lay siege to it. 'After some hesitation,' Bahāʾ al-Dīn tells us, 'the sultan decided not to do so. His troops were widely scattered, and exhausted by this overlong campaign. And Tyre was too well defended, for all the Franj of the coast were now gathered there. He therefore preferred to attack Ascalon, which was easier to take.'

Saladin would later come to regret this decision bitterly. For the moment, however, his triumphal march continued. On 4 September Ascalon capitulated, followed by Gaza, which was held by the Templars. At the same time, Saladin despatched several of his army's emirs to the environs of Jerusalem, where they seized a number of positions, including Bethlehem. The sultan now had but one desire: to crown his victorious campaign, and his career, with the reconquest of the holy city.

Would he be able to duplicate the feat of the caliph ʿUmar, and enter this venerated city without destruction or bloodshed? He sent a message to the inhabitants of Jerusalem inviting them to hold talks on the future of the city. A delegation of notables came to meet him in Ascalon. The victor's proposal was reasonable: the city would be handed over to him without combat; those inhabitants who desired to leave could do so, taking their property with them; the Christian places of worship would be respected; in the future, those who wished to visit the city as pilgrims would not be molested. But to the sultan's great surprise, the Franj responded as arrogantly as they had during the time of their ascendancy. Deliver Jerusalem, the town where Jesus had died? Out of the question! The city was theirs and they would defend it come what may.

Swearing that he would now take Jerusalem only by the sword, Saladin ordered his troops, dispersed in the four corners of Syria, to assemble around the holy city. All the emirs came at the run. What Muslim would not wish to be able to say to his creator on Judgement Day: I fought for Jerusalem. Or better still: I died a martyr for Jerusalem. An astrologer had once predicted that Saladin would lose an eye if he entered the holy city, to which Saladin had replied: 'To take it I am ready to lose both eyes!'

Inside the besieged city, the defence was under the command of Balian of Ibelin, the ruler of Ramlah, 'a lord', according to Ibn al-Athīr, 'who held a rank among the Franj more or less equal to that of king'. He had managed to escape from Ḥiṭṭīn shortly before the defeat of his troops, and had taken refuge in Tyre. During the summer he had asked Saladin for permission to go and fetch his wife from Jerusalem, promising that he would not bear arms and that he would spend only a single night in the holy city. Once there, however, they begged him to stay, for no one else had sufficient authority to direct the resistance. Balian, who was a man of honour, felt that he could not agree to defend Jerusalem and its people without betraying his agreement with the sultan. He therefore turned to Saladin himself to ask what he should do. The magnanimous sultan released him from his commitment. If duty required that he remain in the holy city and bear arms, so be it! And since Balian was now too busy organising the defence of Jerusalem to look after his wife, the sultan supplied an escort to lead her back to Tyre!

Saladin would never refuse a request from a man of honour, even the fiercest of his enemies. In this particular case, however, the risk was minimal. Despite his bravery, Balian could not seriously resist the Muslim army. Though the ramparts were solid and the Frankish population deeply attached to their capital, the defenders were limited to a handful of knights and a few hundred townsmen with no military experience. Moreover, the Orthodox and Jacobite Oriental Christians of Jerusalem were favourable to Saladin – especially the clergy, for they had been treated with unrelenting disdain by the Latin prelates. One of the sultan's chief advisers was an Orthodox priest by the name of Yūsuf Batit. It was he who took charge of contacts with the Franj, as well as with the Oriental Christian communities. Shortly before the siege began, the Orthodox clerics promised Batit that they would throw open the gates of the city if the Occidentals held out too long.

As it happened, the resistance of the Franj was courageous but short-lived, and conducted with few illusions. The encirclement of Jerusalem began on 20 September. Six days later Saladin, who had established his camp on the Mount of Olives, asked his troops to intensify their pressure in preparation for the final assault. On 29 September sappers managed to open a breach in the northern part of the wall, very close to the place where the Occidentals had achieved their own breach back in 1099. When he saw that there was no longer any point in continuing the fight, Balian asked for safe conduct and presented himself before the sultan.

Saladin was intractable. Had he not offered the inhabitants the best possible terms on which to capitulate well before the battle? Now was not the time for negotiations, for he had sworn to take the city by the sword, just as the Franj had done. He could be released from his oath only if Jerusalem threw open its gates and surrendered to him completely and unconditionally.

> Balian insisted on obtaining a promise from Saladin to spare his life [Ibn al-Athīr reports] but Ṣalāḥ al-Dīn would promise nothing. Balian tried to soften his heart, but in vain. He then addressed him in these terms: 'O sultan, be aware that this city holds a mass of people so great that God alone knows their number. They now hesitate to continue the fight, because they hope that you will spare their lives as you have spared so many others, because they love life and hate death. But if we see that death is inevitable, then, by God, we will kill our own women and children and burn all that we possess. We will not leave you a single dinar of booty, not a single dirham, not a single man or woman to lead into captivity. Then we shall destroy the sacred rock, al-Aqṣā mosque and many other sites; we will kill the five thousand Muslim prisoners we now hold, and will exterminate the mounts and all the beasts. In the end, we will come outside the city, and we will fight against you as one fights for one's life. Not one of us will die without having killed several of you!'

Although he was not impressed by the threats, Saladin was moved by the man's fervour. In order not to appear to soften too easily, he turned to his advisers and asked them if he could not be released from his pledge to take the city by the sword – simply in order to avoid the destruction of the holy places of Islam. Their response was affirmative, but since they were aware of their master's incorrigible generosity, they insisted that he obtain financial compensation from the Franj before he allowed them to leave, for the long campaign had emptied the state treasury. The infidels, the advisers explained, were virtual prisoners. To purchase their freedom, each should pay a ransom: 10 dinars for each man, 5 for a woman and 1 for a child. Balian accepted the principle, but he pleaded for the poor, who, he said, would be unable to pay such a sum. Could not seven thousand of them be released in exchange for 30,000 dinars? Once again, the request was granted, despite furious protests from the treasurers. Satisfied, Balian ordered his men to lay down their arms.

So it was that on Friday 2 October 1187, or 27 Rajab 583 by the Muslim calendar, the very day on which Muslims celebrate the Prophet's nocturnal journey to Jerusalem, Saladin solemnly entered the holy city. His emirs and soldiers had strict orders: no Christian, whether Frankish or Oriental, was to be touched. And indeed, there was neither massacre nor plunder. Some fanatics demanded that the Church of the Holy Sepulchre be destroyed in retaliation for the excesses committed by the Franj, but Saladin silenced them. On the contrary, he strengthened the guard at the Christian places of worship and announced that the Franj themselves would be allowed to come on pilgrimage whenever they liked. The Frankish cross attached to the Dome of the Rock mosque was removed, of course. And al-Aqṣā mosque, which had been turned into a church, became a Muslim place of worship again, after its walls had been sprinkled with rose water.

Most of the Franj remained in the city as Saladin, surrounded by a mass of companions, went from sanctuary to sanctuary weeping, praying and prostrating himself. The rich made sure to sell their houses, businesses or furniture before going into exile, the buyers generally being Orthodox or Jacobite Christians who planned to stay on. Other property was later sold to Jewish families settled in the holy city by Saladin.

As for Balian, he sought to raise the money needed to buy back the freedom of the poorest citizens. In itself, the ransom was not excessive, although for a prince it regularly ran to several tens of thousands of dinars, sometimes even 100,000 or more. But for ordinary people, something like 20 dinars per family represented a year or two's income. Thousands of unfortunates had gathered at the gates of the city to beg for coins. Al-ʿĀdil, who was as sensitive as his brother, asked Saladin's permission to free a thousand poor prisoners without payment of any ransom. When he heard this, the Frankish patriarch asked the same for seven hundred others, and Balian for another five hundred. They were all freed. Then, on his own initiative, the sultan announced that all old people would be allowed to leave without paying anything and that imprisoned men with young children would also be released. When it came to Frankish widows and orphans, he not only exempted them from any payment, but also offered them gifts before allowing them to leave.

Saladin's treasurers despaired. If the least fortunate were to be set free for nothing, they argued, at least the ransom for the rich should be raised. The anger of these worthy servants of the state knew no bounds when the patriarch of Jerusalem drove out of the city accompanied by numerous chariots filled with gold, carpets and all sorts of the most precious goods. ʿImād al-Dīn al-Asfahāni was scandalised:

> I said to the sultan: 'This patriarch is carrying off riches worth at least 200,000 dinars. We gave them permission to take their personal property with them, but not the treasures of the churches and convents. You must not let them do it!' But Ṣalāḥ al-Dīn answered: 'We must apply the letter of the accords we have signed, so that no one will be able to accuse the believers of having violated their treaties. On the contrary, Christians everywhere will remember the kindness we have bestowed upon them.'

The patriarch paid his 10 dinars just like everyone else, and was even provided with an escort to make sure that he reached Tyre without incident.

Saladin had conquered Jerusalem not to amass gold, and still less to seek vengeance. His prime objective, as he himself explained, was to do his duty before his God and his faith. His victory was to have liberated the holy city from the yoke of the invaders – without a bloodbath, destruction or hatred. His reward was to be able to bow down and pray in places where no Muslim would have been able to pray had it not been for him. On Friday 9 October, a week after the victory, an official ceremony was organised in al-Aqṣā mosque. Many religious leaders competed for the honour of delivering the sermon on this memorable occasion. In the end, it was the *qāḍī* of Damascus Muḥī al-Dīn Ibn al-Zaki, the successor of Abū Ṣaʿad al-Ḥarawi, who was designated by the sultan to mount the pulpit, garbed in a superb black robe. Although his voice was clear and powerful, a slight tremor betrayed his emotion as he spoke: 'Glory to God who has bestowed this victory upon Islam and who has returned this city to the fold after a century of perdition! Honour to this army, which He has chosen to complete the reconquest! And may salvation be upon you, Ṣalāḥ al-Dīn Yūsuf, son of Ayyūb, you who have restored the spurned dignity of this nation!'

Part Five

REPRIEVE (1187–1244)

When the master of Egypt decided to hand Jerusalem over to the Franj, a great storm of indignation swept all the lands of Islam.

SIBṬ IBN AL-JAWZI
Arab chronicler (1186–1256)

XI

The Impossible Encounter

Although venerated as a hero after the reconquest of Jerusalem, Saladin was nevertheless subjected to criticism – although amicable on the part of his close collaborators, from his opponents it became increasingly severe.

> Ṣalāḥ al-Dīn [writes Ibn al-Athīr] never evinced real firmness in his decisions. He would lay siege to a city, but if the defenders resisted for some time, he would give up and abandon the siege. Now, a monarch must never act in this way, even if destiny smiles upon him. It is often preferable to fail while remaining firm than to succeed while subsequently squandering the fruits of one's success. Nothing illustrates the truth of this observation better than the behaviour of Ṣalāḥ al-Dīn at Tyre. It is his fault alone that the Muslims suffered a setback before the walls of that city.

Although he stopped short of any systematic hostility, the Mosul historian, who was still loyal to the Zangī dynasty, was always somewhat reserved in his evaluation of Saladin. Ibn al-Athīr shared the general elation that swept the Arab world after Ḥiṭṭīn and Jerusalem. But that did not prevent him from taking note, without the slightest complacency, of the mistakes made by the hero of these events. In the case of Tyre, the historian's criticism seems perfectly justified.

> Every time he seized a Frankish city or stronghold such as Acre, Ascalon or Jerusalem, Ṣalāḥ al-Dīn allowed the enemy soldiers and knights to seek refuge in Tyre, a city that had thus become virtually impregnable. The Franj of the littoral sent messages to the others overseas, and the latter promised to come to their rescue. Ought we not to say that in a sense it was Ṣalāḥ al-Dīn himself who organised the defence of Tyre against his own army?

Of course, there is no reproaching the sultan for the magnanimity with which he treated the vanquished. In the eyes of history, his repugnance for needless bloodshed, his strict respect for his commitments, and the touching nobility of his acts of compassion are as valuable as his conquests. Nevertheless, it is incontestable that he made a serious political and military error. He knew that by taking Jerusalem he was issuing a challenge to the West, and that the West would respond. In these conditions, to permit tens of thousands of Franj to entrench themselves in Tyre, the most powerful stronghold of the Levantine coast, was to offer an ideal beachhead for a fresh invasion. This was especially so since in the absence of King Guy, who was still a captive, the knights had found a particularly tenacious leader in the person of the man the Arab chroniclers would call al-Markish, the marquis Conrad of Montferrat, who had recently arrived from Europe.

Although he was not unaware of the danger, Saladin nevertheless underestimated it. In November 1187, a few weeks after the conquest of the holy city, he laid siege to Tyre. But he did so without great determination. This ancient Phoenician city could not have been taken without massive assistance from the Egyptian fleet. Saladin was well aware of this, yet he appeared before its ramparts supported by no more than ten vessels, five of which were burned by the defenders in a daring raid. The other ships then withdrew to Beirut. Once deprived of its fleet, the Muslim army could attack Tyre only across the narrow ridge connecting the city to the mainland. In these conditions a siege could easily drag on for months, especially since the Franj, effectively mobilised by al-Markish, seemed ready to fight to the bitter end. Most of his emirs, exhausted by this endless campaign, advised Saladin to call off the siege. Had he offered them enough gold, the sultan could probably have convinced some of them to remain. But soldiers were expensive in winter, and the state coffers were empty. He himself was weary. He therefore demobilised half his troops; then, lifting the siege, he headed north, where many cities and fortresses could be reconquered without great effort.

For the Muslim army, it was yet another triumphant march: Latakia, Ṭarṭūs, Baghras, Safid, Kawkab – the list of conquests was long. In fact, it is easier to name the towns the Franj retained: Tyre, Tripoli, Antioch and its port, and three isolated fortresses. But the most perceptive of Saladin's entourage were not deceived. What was the use of piling up conquests if there was no guarantee that a fresh invasion could be effectively discouraged? The sultan himself seemed to view any new trial of strength with equanimity. 'If the Franj come from beyond the seas, they will suffer the fate of those who have preceded them here,' he exclaimed when a Sicilian fleet appeared off the coast of Latakia. In July 1188 he even released Guy, after eliciting a solemn promise that he would never again take up arms against the Muslims.

This last generous gesture was to cost him dear. In August 1189 the Frankish king broke his word and laid siege to the port of Acre. Guy's forces were modest at first, but ships were soon arriving daily, pouring successive waves of Western fighters onto the beach.

> After the fall of Jerusalem [Ibn al-Athīr reports] the Franj dressed in black, and they journeyed beyond the seas to seek aid and succour in all their lands, especially Rome the Great. To incite people to vengeance, they carried with them a painting of the Messiah, peace be upon him, bloodied by an Arab who was striking him. They would say: 'Look, here is the Messiah and here is Muḥammad, the Prophet of the Muslims, beating him to death!' The Franj were moved and gathered together, women included; those who could not come along would pay the expenses of those who went to fight in their place. One of the enemy prisoners told me that he was an only son and that his mother had sold her house to buy his equipment for him. The religious and psychological motivation of the Franj was so strong that they were prepared to surmount all difficulties to achieve their ends.

From the first days of September, Guy's troops began to receive wave after wave of reinforcements. Thus began the battle of Acre, one of the longest and most gruelling of all the Frankish wars. Acre is built on a peninsula shaped like a protruding nose: to the south is the port, to the west the sea; to the north and east two solid city walls form a right angle. The city was doubly encircled. Around the ramparts, firmly held by the Muslim garrison, the Franj formed an ever thicker semicircle, but they had to deal with Saladin's army at their rear. At first, Saladin tried to trap the enemy in a pincer movement, hoping to decimate them. But he soon realised that this would be impossible, for although the Muslim army won several successive victories, the Franj immediately compensated for their losses. Every sunrise saw fresh batches of fighters arrive, from Tyre or from beyond the seas.

In October 1189, as the battle of Acre raged, Saladin received a message from Aleppo informing him that the 'king of the Almān', the emperor Frederick Barbarossa, was approaching Constantinople, en route to Syria, with two hundred, perhaps two hundred and sixty, thousand men. The sultan was deeply worried, or so we are told by the faithful Bahā᾽ al-Dīn, who was with Saladin at the time.

> In view of the extreme gravity of the situation, he felt it necessary to call all Muslims to *jihād* and to inform the caliph of the development of the situation. He therefore sent me to visit the rulers of Sinjar, Jazīra, Mosul and Irbil, to implore them to come with their soldiers to participate in the *jihād*. I was then to go to Baghdad to urge the prince of the faithful to react. This I did.

In an effort to rouse the caliph from his lethargy, Saladin sent him a letter saying that 'the pope who resides in Rome has ordered the Frankish peoples to march on Jerusalem'. At the same time, Saladin sent messages to leaders in the Maghreb and in Muslim Spain inviting them to come to the aid of their brothers, 'since the Franj of the West have acted in concert with those of the East'. Throughout the Arab world, the enthusiasm originally aroused by the reconquest was giving way to fear. It was being whispered that the vengeance of the Franj would be terrible, that there would be a new bloodbath, that the holy city would be lost once more, that Syria and Egypt would both fall into the hands of the invaders. Once again, however, luck, or Providence, intervened on Saladin's behalf.

After crossing Asia Minor in triumph, in the spring of 1190 the German emperor arrived at Konya, the capital of the successors of Kilij Arslan. Frederick soon forced the gates open and then sent emissaries to Antioch to announce his imminent arrival. The Armenians of southern Anatolia were alarmed at the news. Their clergy despatched a messenger to Saladin begging him to protect them against this new Frankish invasion. In the event, no intervention by the sultan would be necessary. On 10 June, a stifling dog-day afternoon, Frederick Barbarossa went for a swim in a little stream at the foot of the Taurus mountains. Somehow, probably as the result of a heart attack, he drowned – 'in a place', Ibn al-Athīr explains, 'where the water was barely hip-deep. His army dispersed, and thus did God spare the Muslims the maleficence of the Germans, who constitute a particularly numerous and tenacious species of Franj.'

The German danger was thus miraculously removed, but it had paralysed Saladin for several months, preventing him from joining the decisive battle against the troops besieging Acre. The situation at the Palestinian port was now at an impasse. Although the sultan had received sufficient reinforcements to hold his position against any counter-attack, the Franj could no longer be dislodged. Gradually, a modus vivendi was established. Between skirmishes, knights and emirs would invite one another to banquets and would chat together quite calmly, sometimes even playing games, as Bahā' al-Dīn relates.

> One day, the men of the two camps, tired of fighting, decided to organise a battle between children. Two boys came out of the city to match themselves against two young infidels. In the heat of the struggle, one of the Muslim boys leapt upon his rival, threw him to the ground, and seized him by the throat. When they saw that he was threatening to kill him, the Franj approached and said: 'Stop! He has become your prisoner, forsooth, and we shall buy him back from you.' The boy took 2 dinars and let the other go.

Despite the carnival atmosphere, the belligerents were hardly living in enviable conditions. There were many dead and wounded, epidemics were raging, and it was not easy to get supplies in winter. It was the position of the Acre garrison that was of greatest concern to Saladin. As more and more vessels arrived from the West, the sea blockade grew ever tighter. On two occasions, an Egyptian fleet comprising several dozen ships had managed to cut a path to the port, but their losses had been heavy, and the sultan soon had to resort to trickery to resupply the besieged soldiers. In June 1190 he armed an enormous ship in Beirut, filling it with grain, cheese, onions and sheep.

> A group of Muslims boarded the ship [Bahā᾽ al-Dīn explains]. They were dressed like Franj; they had also shaved their beards, sewn crosses to the mast, and positioned pigs prominently on the deck. Then they approached the city, slipping alongside the enemy vessels. When they were stopped the Franj said, 'You seem to be heading for Acre.' Our soldiers, feigning astonishment, asked, 'Haven't you taken the city?' The Franj, who thought they were dealing with their own congeners, replied, 'No, we have not yet taken it.' 'Well then,' our soldiers replied, 'we will moor near the camp, but there is another ship behind us. You had better alert them so that they do not sail into the city.' The Beirutis had indeed noticed that there was a Frankish ship behind them. The enemy sailors headed towards it immediately, while our brothers unfurled all sails for a rush to the port of Acre, where they were greeted with cries of joy, for hunger was stalking the city.

But such stratagems could not be repeated too often. If Saladin's army could not loosen the vice, Acre would eventually capitulate. As the months dragged on, the chances of a Muslim victory, of a new Ḥiṭṭīn, seemed increasingly remote. The influx of Occidental fighters, far from waning, was still on the rise. In April 1191 the king of France, Philip Augustus, disembarked with his troops in the environs of Acre; he was followed, at the beginning of June, by Richard the Lionheart.

> This king of England (Malik al-Inkitar) [Bahā᾽ al-Dīn tells us] was courageous, energetic and daring in combat. Although of lower rank than the king of France, he was richer and more renowned as a warrior. On his way east he had seized Cyprus, and when he appeared before Acre, accompanied by twenty-five galleys loaded with men and equipment for war, the Franj let out cries of joy and lit great fires to celebrate

his arrival. As for the Muslims, their hearts were filled with fear and apprehension.

The thirty-three-year-old red-headed giant who wore the English crown was the prototype of the belligerent and flighty knight whose noble ideals did little to conceal his baffling brutality and complete lack of scruples. While no Occidental was impervious to his charm and undeniable charisma, Richard himself was in turn fascinated by Saladin, whom he sought to meet immediately upon his arrival. Despatching a messenger to al-ʿĀdil, he asked him to arrange an interview with his brother. The sultan answered without a moment's hesitation: 'Kings meet together only after the conclusion of an accord, for it is unthinkable for them to wage war once they know one another and have broken bread together.' He nevertheless authorised his brother to meet Richard, provided each would be accompanied by his own soldiers. Contacts continued, but without much result. 'In fact,' Bahāʾ al-Dīn explains, 'the intention of the Franj in sending messengers to us was primarily to probe our strong and weak points. Our aim in receiving them was exactly the same.' Although Richard was sincere in his desire to meet the conqueror of Jerusalem, he had decidedly not come to the Middle East to negotiate with him.

While these exchanges continued, the English king was actively preparing for the final assault on Acre. The city was now completely cut off from the outside world, and racked by famine as well. Only a few elite swimmers could still reach it, at the risk of their lives. Bahāʾ al-Dīn relates the adventure of one of these commandos.

> It was one of the most curious and exemplary episodes of this long battle. There was a Muslim swimmer by the name of ʿIsā who used to dive under enemy ships at night and come up on the other side, where the besieged soldiers awaited him. He usually carried money and messages for the garrison, these being attached to his belt. One night, when he had dived down carrying three sacks containing 1,000 dinars and several letters, he was caught and killed. We found out very quickly that some misfortune had befallen him, for ʿIsā regularly informed us of his

> safe arrival by releasing a pigeon in our direction. That night we received no signal. A few days later, some inhabitants of Acre happened to be walking along the water's edge and saw a body washed up on the shore. As they approached it, they recognised ʿIsā the swimmer; the gold and the wax with which the letters were sealed were still attached to his belt. Who has ever heard of a man fulfilling his mission in death as faithfully as though he were alive?

The heroism of some of the Arab fighters was not enough. The position of the Acre garrison was fast becoming critical. By the beginning of the summer of 1191 the appeals of the besieged had become cries of despair: 'We are at the end of our tether, and no longer have any choice but to capitulate. If nothing has been done for us by tomorrow, we will request that our lives be spared and we will hand over the city.' Saladin gave way to depression. Having lost any illusion that the besieged city could be saved, he wept bitter tears. His closest collaborators feared for his health, and the doctors prescribed potions to soothe him. He asked heralds to move through the camp announcing that a massive attack would be launched to lift the siege of Acre. But his emirs refused to obey his orders. 'Why endanger the Muslim army uselessly?' they retorted. There were now so many Franj, and they were so solidly entrenched, that any offensive would have been suicidal.

On 11 July 1191, after a siege lasting two years, cross-embossed banners suddenly appeared on the ramparts of Acre.

> The Franj let out an immense cry of joy, while in our camp everyone was stunned. The soldiers wept and lamented. As for the sultan, he was like a mother who has just lost her child. I went to see him to do my best to console him. I told him that now we had to think of the future of Jerusalem and the coastal cities, and to do something about the fate of the Muslims captured in Acre.

Overcoming his grief, Saladin sent a messenger to Richard to discuss conditions for the release of the prisoners. But the Englishman was pressed for time. Determined to take advantage of his success to launch a sweeping offensive, he had no intention of bothering about captives, any more than had the sultan four years earlier, when the Frankish cities were falling into his hands one after another. The only difference was that when Saladin wanted to avoid being burdened with prisoners, he released them, whereas Richard preferred to have them killed. Two thousand and seven hundred soldiers of the Acre garrison were assembled before the city walls, along with nearly three hundred women and children of their families. Roped together so that they formed one enormous mass of flesh, they were delivered to the Frankish fighters, who fell upon them viciously with their sabres, with lances, and even with stones, until all the wails had been stilled.

After this expeditious resolution of the problem, Richard led his troops out of Acre. He headed south along the coast, his fleet following closely behind, while Saladin took a parallel route further inland. There were many clashes between the two armies, but none was decisive. The sultan now realised that he could not prevent the invaders from regaining control of the Palestinian coast, much less destroy their army. His ambition was simply to contain them, to bar their route to Jerusalem whatever the cost, for the loss of that city would be a terrible blow to Islam. It was the darkest moment of his career. Profoundly shaken, he nevertheless strove to sustain the morale of his troops and collaborators. To the latter, he acknowledged that he had suffered a serious setback – but, he explained, he and his people were there to stay, whereas the Frankish kings were only indulging in an expedition that would have to end sooner or later. Had not the king of France left Palestine in August, after spending a hundred days in the Orient? Had not the king of England often repeated that he yearned to return to his far-off kingdom?

Richard had moreover made many diplomatic overtures. In September 1191, just after his troops had scored a number of successes, in particular in the Arsūf coastal plain north of Jaffa, he prevailed upon al-ʿĀdil to come to a rapid agreement.

> Men of ours and of yours have died [he told him in a message] the country is in ruins, and events have entirely escaped anyone's control. Do you not believe that it is enough? As far as we are concerned, there

are only three subjects of discord: Jerusalem, the True Cross and territory.

As for Jerusalem, it is our place of worship, and we will never agree to renounce it, even if we have to fight to the last man. As territory, all we want is that the land west of the Jordan be ceded to us. As for the Cross, for you it is merely a piece of wood, whereas for us its value is inestimable. Let the sultan give it to us, and let us put an end to this exhausting struggle.

Al-ʿĀdil immediately carried the message to his brother, who consulted his chief collaborators before dictating his response:

The city is as holy to us as it is to you; it is even more important for us, because it was there that our Prophet made his miraculous nocturnal journey, and it is there that our community will be reunited on judgement day. It is therefore out of the question for us to abandon it. The Muslims would never accept it. As for territory, this land has always been ours, and your occupation is only transitory. You were able to settle in it because of the weakness of the Muslims who then peopled it, but so long as there is war, we will not allow you to enjoy your possessions. As for the Cross, it is a great trump in our hands, and we will surrender it only in return for some important concession on behalf of Islam.

The apparent firmness of these two messages was deceptive. Although each side was presenting maximal demands, the path of compromise was not entirely barred. A mere three days after this exchange, Richard sent Saladin's brother a most curious proposition.

Al-ʿĀdil sent for me [Bahāʾ al-Dīn relates] to inform me of the results of his latest contacts. According to the agreement being proposed, al-ʿĀdil would marry the sister of the king of England. She had been married to the ruler of Sicily, who had died. The Englishman therefore brought his sister east with him, and he proposed that al-ʿĀdil marry her. The couple would reside in Jerusalem. The king would consign the lands under his control, from Acre to Ascalon, to his sister, who would become queen of the coast, of the *sāḥil*. The sultan would cede his coastal possessions to his brother, who would become king of the *sāḥil*. The Cross would be entrusted to them jointly, and prisoners would be released on both sides. Once peace was thus concluded, the king of England would return to his country beyond the seas.

Al-ʿĀdil was visibly tempted. He recommended that Bahāʾ do his utmost to convince Saladin. The chronicler promised to try.

Thus did I present myself before the sultan, and repeated to him what I had heard. He immediately told me that he saw no obstacle, but he did not believe that the king of England himself would ever accept such an arrangement. It was, he thought, only a joke, or a trick. Three times I asked him to confirm his approval, and he did so. I then returned to al-ʿĀdil to inform him of the sultan's agreement. He hurriedly sent a message to the enemy camp conveying his response. But the accursed Englishman then told him that his sister had returned home in a terrible rage when she was told about his proposal: she had sworn that she would never give herself to a Muslim!

As Saladin had guessed, Richard had been indulging in a bit of trickery. He had hoped that the sultan would reject his plan out of hand, and that this would greatly displease al-ʿĀdil. By accepting, Saladin instead compelled the Frankish monarch to reveal his double game. Indeed, for several months Richard had been trying to establish special relations with al-ʿĀdil, calling him 'my brother', pandering to his ambition in an effort to use him against Saladin. It was a clever tactic. The sultan, for his part, employed similar methods. Parallel to the negotiations with Richard, he engaged in talks with al-Markish Conrad, the ruler of Tyre, whose relations with the English king were somewhat strained, since Conrad suspected Richard of seeking to deprive him of his possessions. He even went so far as to offer Saladin an alliance against the 'overseas Franj'. Without taking this offer literally, the sultan used it to intensify his diplomatic pressure on Richard, who became so exasperated with the policy of the marquis that he had him assassinated several months later!

His manoeuvre having failed, the king of England asked al-ʿĀdil to organise a meeting with Saladin. But the latter's response was the same as it had been a few months earlier:

> Kings meet only after the conclusion of an accord. In any event, I do not understand your language, and you are ignorant of mine, and we therefore need a translator in whom we both have confidence. Let this man, then, act as a messenger between us. When we arrive at an understanding, we will meet, and friendship will prevail between us.

The negotiations dragged on for another year. Entrenched in Jerusalem, Saladin let the time pass. His peace proposals were simple: each side would keep what it had; the Franj, if they wished, could come unarmed to make their pilgrimages to the holy city, which, however, would remain in Muslim hands. Richard, who yearned to return home, twice tried to force a decision by marching in the direction of Jerusalem, but without attacking it. For months he tried to work off his excess energy by constructing a formidable fortress in Ascalon, which he dreamed of turning into a jumping-off point for a future expedition to Egypt. When the work was done, Saladin demanded that it be dismantled, stone by stone, before the conclusion of peace.

By August 1192 Richard had reached the end of his tether. Seriously ill, abandoned by many knights who rebuked him for not having tried to retake Jerusalem, accused of the murder of Conrad, and urged by his friends to return to England without delay, he could postpone his departure no longer. He virtually begged Saladin to leave him Ascalon, but the response was negative. He then sent another message, repeating his request and explaining that if an acceptable peace agreement had not been arrived at within six days, 'he would be compelled to spend the winter here'. This veiled ultimatum amused Saladin, who, inviting Richard's messenger to be seated, addressed him in these terms:

> You will tell the king that as far as Ascalon is concerned, I shall not give way. As for his plan to spend the winter in this country, I think that it is

> inevitable, for he knows full well that the land that he has seized will be taken from him the moment he departs. Does he really want to spend the winter here, two months distant from his family and his country, while he is still young and strong enough to enjoy the pleasures of life? For my part, I could spend the winter, the summer, and then another winter and another summer here, for I am in my own land, among my children and relatives, who care for me, and I have one army for the summer and another for the winter. I am an old man, who no longer indulges in the pleasures of existence. So I shall wait, until God grants one of us victory.

Apparently impressed by this argument, Richard let it be known during succeeding days that he was prepared to give up Ascalon. At the beginning of September 1192 a five-year peace was signed. The Franj retained the coastal zone from Tyre to Jaffa but recognised Saladin's authority over the rest of the country, including Jerusalem. The Western warriors, who had been granted safe conduct by the sultan, rushed to the holy city to pray at the tomb of Christ. Saladin courteously received the most important of them, even inviting them to share his meals and reassuring them of his firm desire to uphold freedom of worship. But Richard refused to go. He would not enter as a guest a city that he had sworn to storm as a conqueror. A month after the conclusion of peace, he left the East without ever having seen either the holy sepulchre or Saladin.

The sultan had finally emerged victorious in his arduous confrontation with the West. True, the Franj had recovered control of some cities, thus winning a reprieve that was to last nearly a hundred years. But never again would they constitute a force capable of dictating terms to the Arab world. From now on, they would control not genuine states, but mere settlements.

In spite of this success, Saladin felt bruised, even somewhat diminished. He bore scant resemblance to the charismatic hero of Ḥiṭṭīn. His authority over his emirs had been weakened, and his detractors were increasingly virulent. Physically, he was not well. His health had never been excellent, and for years he had had to consult the court physicians regularly, in Damascus as in Cairo. In the Egyptian capital, he was particularly attached to the services of a prestigious Jewish-Arab *ṭabīb* originally from Spain, Mūsa Ibn Maymūn, better known as Maimonides. During these most difficult years of the struggle against the Franj, Saladin had suffered frequent attacks of malaria, which confined him to his bed for days on end. In 1192, however, it was not the ravages of any particular illness that concerned his doctors, but a general weakness, a sort of premature old age evident to anyone who had close dealings with the sultan. Saladin was only in his fifty-fifth year, but he himself seemed to realise that he was nearing the end of his life.

Saladin spent his last days peacefully among his relatives in his favourite city, Damascus. Bahāʾ al-Dīn never left his side, and affectionately jotted down each one of his acts. On Thursday 18 February 1193 Bahāʾ al-Dīn joined the sultan in the garden of his palace in the citadel.

> The sultan was seated in the shade, surrounded by the youngest of his children. He asked who was waiting for him inside. 'Frankish messengers', he was told, 'as well as a group of emirs and notables.' He had the Franj summoned. When they came before him, he was dandling one of his small sons on his knees, the emir Abū Bakr, of whom he was especially fond. When the child looked upon the Franj, with their clean-shaven faces, their cropped hair and their curious clothing, he was frightened and began to cry. The sultan apologised to the Franj and halted the interview without listening to what they wanted to tell him. Then he said to me: 'Have you eaten at all today?' It was his way of inviting someone to a meal. He added: 'Have them bring us something to eat!' We were served rice with *labneh* and other similar light dishes, and he ate. This reassured me, for I had thought that he had lost his appetite completely. For some time he had felt bloated, and could not bring himself to eat. He moved only with great effort, and was always begging people's pardon.

That Thursday Saladin even felt well enough to go on horseback to greet a caravan of pilgrims returning from Mecca. But two days later he could no longer stand. Gradually, he sank into a state of lethargy. Moments of consciousness were becoming increasingly rare. News of his illness had spread throughout the city, and the Damascenes feared that their city would soon drift into anarchy. 'Cloth was withdrawn from the souks for fear of pillage. And every night, when I left the sultan's bedside to return home, people would gather along my way trying to guess, from my expression, whether the inevitable had yet come to pass.'

On the night of 2 March 1193 the sickroom was invaded by women from the palace unable to hold back their tears. Saladin's condition was so serious that his eldest son al-Afḍal asked Bahā' al-Dīn and another of the sultan's close collaborators, the *qāḍī* al-Fāḍil, to spend the night in the citadel. 'That might be imprudent', the *qāḍī* suggested, 'for if the people of the city do not see us leave, they will think the worst, and there could be pillaging.' A shaykh who lived within the citadel was therefore summoned to watch over the patient.

> He read verses of the Koran, and spoke of God and the Beyond, while the sultan lay unconscious. When I returned the following morning, he was already dead. May God have mercy on him! I was told that when the shaykh read the verse that says, 'There is no God but God, on him alone do I rely,' the sultan smiled. His face lit up, and then he gave up his soul.

The moment news of his death became known, many Damascenes headed for the citadel, but guards prevented them from entering. Only great emirs and the principal *ʿulamā'* were permitted to present their condolences to al-Afḍal, the late sultan's eldest son, who was seated in one of the salons of the palace. The poets and orators were told to keep silent. Saladin's youngest children went out into the street and mingled with the sobbing crowd.

> These unbearable scenes [Bahā' al-Dīn recounts] continued until after the midday prayer. They then set about bathing the body and wrapping it in the shroud; all the products used for this purpose had to be borrowed, for the sultan possessed nothing of his own. Although I was invited

to the bathing ceremony, performed by the theologian al-Dawlāhi, I could not bring myself to attend. After the midday prayer, the body was brought out in a coffin wrapped in a cloth. At the appearance of the funeral cortège, cries of lamentation erupted from the crowd. Then group after group came to recite prayers over the remains. The sultan was carried to the gardens of the palace, where he had been cared for during his illness, and was buried in the western pavilion. He was laid to rest at the time of the afternoon prayer. May God sanctify his soul and illuminate his tomb!

XII

The Perfect and the Just

Saladin had the same immediate successor as all the great Muslim leaders of his time: civil war. Barely had he died than his empire was dismembered. One of his sons took Egypt, another Damascus, a third Aleppo. Fortunately, most of his seventeen male children and his only daughter were too young to fight; this limited the fragmentation somewhat. But the sultan had two brothers and several nephews, each of whom wanted his share of the heritage, or all of it if possible. It took nearly nine years of combat – with innumerable alliances, betrayals and assassinations – before the Ayyubid empire once again obeyed a single master: al-ʿĀdil, 'the Just', the skilful negotiator who had almost become Richard the Lionheart's brother-in-law.

Saladin had been somewhat suspicious of his younger brother, who was too fluent a talker, too much the intriguer, too ambitious, and too accommodating to the Occidentals. He had thus entrusted him with a fiefdom of no great importance: the chateaux taken from Reynald of Châtillon along the east bank of the Jordan. From this arid and almost uninhabited territory, Saladin thought, his brother could never claim to lead the empire. But the sultan had reckoned wrong. In July 1196 al-ʿĀdil seized Damascus from al-Afḍal. Saladin's twenty-six-year-old son had proved incapable of governing. Ceding effective power to his vizier, Dīya al-Dīn Ibn al-Athīr (brother of the historian), he abandoned himself to alcohol and the pleasures of the harem. His uncle disposed of him through a plot and exiled him to the neighbouring fortress of Sarkhad, where al-Afḍal, devoured by remorse, swore to forsake his life of dissolution to devote himself instead to prayer and meditation. In November 1198 another of Saladin's sons, al-ʿAzīz, the ruler of Egypt, was killed in a fall from his horse while hunting wolves near the pyramids. Al-Afḍal could no longer resist the temptation to abandon his retreat and succeed his brother, but his uncle had little trouble divesting him of his new possession and sending him back to his life as a recluse. By 1202 al-ʿĀdil, now fifty-seven years old, was the uncontested master of the Ayyubid empire.

Although he lacked the charisma and genius of his illustrious brother, he was a better administrator. Under his aegis the Arab world experienced a period of peace, prosperity and tolerance. After the recovery of Jerusalem and the weakening of Frankish power, the sultan saw no reason for continuing the holy war against the Franj; he therefore adopted a policy of coexistence and commercial exchange with them. He even encouraged several hundred Italian merchants to settle in Egypt. An unprecedented calm prevailed on the Arab–Frankish front for several years.

At first, while the Ayyubids were absorbed in their internal quarrels, the Franj tried to restore some order in their own seriously eroded territory. Before leaving the Middle East, Richard had entrusted the 'kingdom of Jerusalem', whose capital was now Acre, to one of his nephews, 'al-kond Herri', Count Henry of Champagne. As for Guy of Lusignan, whose stock had fallen since his defeat at Ḥiṭṭīn, he was exiled with honour, becoming king of Cyprus, where his dynasty would reign for four centuries. To compensate for the weakness of his state, Henry of Champagne sought to conclude an alliance with the Assassins. He went in person to al-Kahf, one of their fortresses, and there met with their grand master. Sinān, the old man of the mountain, had died not long before, but his successor exercised the same absolute authority over the sect. To prove this to his Frankish visitor, he ordered two adherents to hurl themselves off the ramparts, which they did without a moment's hesitation. It seems that the grand master was even prepared to continue the killing, but Henry begged him to hold off. A treaty of alliance was concluded. To honour their guest, the Assassins enquired whether he did not perhaps have a murder he wanted committed. Henry thanked them, promising to call upon their services should the occasion arise. Ironically, on 10 September 1197, not long after witnessing this scene, Richard's nephew died when he accidentally fell from a window of his palace in Acre.

The weeks following his death saw the only serious conflicts of this period. Some fanatical German pilgrims seized Saida and Beirut before being cut to pieces on the road to Jerusalem, while at the same moment al-ʿĀdil was retaking Jaffa. But on 1 July 1198 a new truce was signed for a period of five years and eight months. Saladin's brother took advantage of the lull to consolidate his power. An astute statesman, he was aware that if he was to ward off a fresh invasion, it would not be enough to reach an understanding with the Franj of the Mediterranean coast: he had to address himself to the West itself. Might it not be opportune to use his good relations with the Italian merchants to convince them no longer to agree to unleash waves of uncontrolled warriors onto the shores of Egypt and Syria?

In 1202 he recommended to his son al-Kāmil, 'the Perfect', who was viceroy of Egypt, that talks be opened with the illustrious republic of Venice, which was then the principal maritime power in the Mediterranean. Since both states understood the language of pragmatism and commercial interests, an accord was rapidly reached. Al-Kāmil guaranteed the Venetians access to the ports of the Nile Delta, such as Alexandria and Damietta, offering them all necessary protection and assistance. In return, the republic of the doges undertook not to support any Western expedition against Egypt. The Italians preferred not to reveal the fact that they had already signed an agreement with a group of Western princes whereby, in exchange for a large sum, they would transport nearly thirty thousand Frankish warriors to Egypt. Skilful negotiators, the Venetians resolved not to violate any of their commitments.

When the knights in question arrived in Venice eager to embark on their voyage, they were warmly greeted by the doge Dandolo. According to Ibn al-Athīr, 'He was a very old, blind man, and when he rode on horseback, he needed a squire to guide his mount.' In spite of his age and infirmity, Dandolo announced that he himself intended to take part in the expedition now being mustered under the banner of the cross. Before departing, however, he demanded that the knights pay the agreed sum. When they requested that payment be deferred, Dandolo replied that he would accept only on condition that the expedition begin by occupying the port of Zadar, which for several years had been Venice's rival in the Adriatic. The knights agreed with some reluctance, for Zadar was a Christian city belonging to the king of Hungary, a faithful servant of Rome. But they had little choice. The doge demanded this small service or the immediate payment of the promised sum. Zadar was therefore attacked and plundered in November 1202.

But the Venetians were aiming for greater things. They now sought to convince the commanders of the expedition to make a detour to Constantinople in order to place on the throne a young prince who favoured the Occidentals. Although it was clear that the doge's ultimate objective was to bring the Mediterranean under the control of his republic, the arguments he advanced were clever indeed. He played upon the knights' distrust of the Greek 'heretics', held out to them the prospect of the immense treasures of Byzantium, and explained to the commanders that control of the city of the Rūm would enable them to launch more effective attacks against the Muslims. In the end, these appeals were convincing. In July 1203 the Venetian fleet arrived at Constantinople.

> The king of the Rūm fled without a fight [Ibn al-Athīr writes] and the Franj placed their young candidate on the throne. But he held power in name only, for the Franj made all the decisions. They imposed very heavy tribute on the people, and when payment proved impossible, they seized all the gold and jewels, even that which was part of the crosses and images of the Messiah, peace be upon him. The Rūm then revolted, killed the young monarch, expelled the Franj from the city, and barricaded the city gates. Since their forces were meagre, they sent a messenger to Süleymān, the son of Kilij Arslan, ruler of Konya, asking that he come to their aid. But he was unable to do so.

The Rūm were in no position to defend themselves. Not only was a good part of their army made up of Frankish mercenaries, but many Venetian agents were acting against them within the walls. In April 1204, after barely a week of fighting, the city was invaded. For three days, it was delivered to pillage and carnage. Icons, statues, books and innumerable works of art – testimony to the Greek and Byzantine civilisations – were stolen or destroyed, and thousands of inhabitants were slaughtered.

> All the Rūm were killed or despoiled [the Mosul historian relates]. Some of their notables, pursued by the Franj, attempted to seek refuge in the great church they call Sophia. A group of priests and monks came out bearing crosses and Bibles, begging the attackers to spare their lives, but the Franj paid no heed to their entreaties. They massacred them all and plundered the church.

It is also reported that a prostitute who had come on the Frankish expedition sat on the patriarch's throne singing lewd songs, while drunken soldiers raped Greek nuns in neighbouring monasteries. As Ibn al-Athīr explains, after the sack of Constantinople, one of the most reprehensible acts of history, a Latin emperor of the Orient was crowned: Baldwin of Flanders. The Rūm, of course, never recognised his authority. Those who had escaped from the imperial palace settled in Nicaea, which became the provisional capital of the Greek empire until the recapture of Byzantium fifty-seven years later.

Far from reinforcing the Frankish settlements in Syria, the demented Constantinople escapade dealt them a severe blow. In fact, many of the knights who had come to seek their fortune in the Orient now felt that Greek territory offered better prospects, for here there were fiefdoms to be taken and riches to be amassed, whereas the narrow coastal strip around Acre, Tripoli and Antioch held little attraction for these adventurers. In the short term, the expedition's detour to Constantinople deprived the Franj of Syria of the reinforcements that might have permitted a fresh operation against Jerusalem, and in 1204 they felt compelled to ask the sultan to renew the truce. Al-ʿĀdil agreed to a six-year extension. Although he was now at the apogee of his power, the brother of Saladin had no intention of throwing himself into any grandiose enterprise of reconquest. He was not in the least disturbed by the presence of the Franj on the coast.

The majority of the Franj of Syria would have liked nothing better than a prolongation of peace, but the others across the sea, especially in Rome, dreamed only of a reprise of hostilities. In 1210 control of the kingdom of Antioch passed, by marriage, to John of Brienne, a sixty-year-old knight recently arrived from the West. Although he agreed to renew the truce for another five years in July 1212, he besieged the pope with messengers urging him to accelerate preparations for a powerful expedition, so that an offensive could be launched as early as the summer of 1217. The first vessels of armed pilgrims reached Acre somewhat later, in September of that year. They were soon followed by hundreds of others. In April 1218 a new Frankish invasion began. Its target was Egypt.

Al-ʿĀdil was surprised, and above all disappointed, by this expedition. Had he not done everything in his power, not only since his accession to the throne but even before, during his negotiations with Richard, to put an end to the state of war? Had he not suffered for years the sarcastic taunts of religious leaders, who accused him of having abandoned the cause of *jihād* out of friendship for these fair-haired men? This seventy-three-year-old man, who was in ill health, had for months refused to lend credence to the reports reaching him. When a band of demented Germans began pillaging some villages in Galilee, he considered it just another instance of the usual misadventure and did not react. He refused to believe that the West would mount a massive invasion after a quarter of a century of peace.

Nevertheless, the reports were becoming increasingly detailed. Tens of thousands of Frankish fighters had gathered before the city of Damietta, which controls access to the principal branch of the Nile. On his father's instructions, al-Kāmil led his troops out to meet them. But he was alarmed by their number, and avoided a confrontation. Cautiously, he established his camp south of the port, so that he could support the garrison without being forced into a set-piece battle. Damietta was one of Egypt's best-defended cities. To the east and south its ramparts were ringed by a narrow band of marshy ground, while to the north and west the Nile assured a permanent link to the hinterland. The town could therefore be effectively encircled only if the enemy was able to establish control of the river. To protect themselves against just that danger, the people of the city had invented an ingenious device consisting of a huge iron chain: one end was affixed to the ramparts of the city, the other to a citadel built on an island near the opposite bank of the river. This chain barred access to the Nile. When the Franj saw that no vessel could pass through unless the chain was detached, they stubbornly assaulted the citadel. For three months their attacks were repelled, until finally they hit upon the idea of trimming two great vessels and making them into a sort of floating tower as high as the citadel. On 25 August 1218 they assaulted the citadel. The chain was broken.

Several days later, when a carrier pigeon brought al-ʿĀdil news of this defeat at Damietta, he was profoundly shaken. It seemed clear that the fall of the citadel would soon lead to the fall of Damietta itself, and no obstacle would then impede the invaders' path to Cairo. A long campaign loomed, one he had neither the strength nor the inclination to contest. Just a few hours later, he succumbed to a heart attack.

The real catastrophe for the Muslims was not the fall of the river citadel but the death of the aged sultan. In purely military terms, al-Kāmil managed to contain the enemy, to inflict severe losses upon him, and to prevent him from completing the encirclement of Damietta. Politically, however, the inevitable debilitating struggle for succession erupted, despite the sultan's many efforts to ensure that his sons would avoid that fate. He had determined the division of his domain before his death: Egypt was to go to al-Kāmil, Damascus and Jerusalem to al-Muʿazam, Jazīra to al-Ashraf, and less important fiefdoms to his younger sons. But it was impossible to satisfy ambitions all around: even if relative harmony prevailed among the brothers, certain conflicts were inevitable. In Cairo many of the emirs took advantage of al-Kāmil's absence to try to place one of his younger brothers on the throne. The coup d'état was on the point of success when the ruler of Egypt was informed about it. Forgetting all about Damietta and the Franj, he broke camp and rushed back to his capital, there to re-establish order and punish the conspirators. The invaders swiftly occupied the positions he had abandoned. Damietta was now surrounded.

Although he had received the support of his brother al-Muʿazam, who rushed from Damascus to Damietta with his army, al-Kāmil was no longer in a position to save the city, and still less to halt the invasion. He therefore made the peace overtures particularly generous. After asking al-Muʿazam to dismantle the fortifications of Jerusalem, al-Kāmil sent word to the Franj assuring them that he was prepared to hand the holy city over to them if they would agree to leave Egypt. But the Franj, who now felt they were in a position of strength, refused to negotiate. In October 1219 al-Kāmil made his offer more explicit: he would deliver not only Jerusalem, but all of Palestine west of the Jordan, with the True Cross thrown in to boot. This time the invaders took the trouble to study the proposals. John of Brienne favoured acceptance, as did all the Franj of Syria. But the final decision was in the hands of a man named Pelagius, a Spanish cardinal and fanatical advocate of holy war, whom the pope had appointed head of the expedition. Never, he said, would he agree to negotiate with Saracens. To make sure that his rejection of peace terms could not be misunderstood, he ordered an immediate assault on Damietta. The garrison, decimated by fighting, famine and a recent epidemic, offered no resistance.

Pelagius had now decided to seize all of Egypt. If he did not march on Cairo immediately, it was because he was awaiting the imminent arrival of the West's most powerful monarch, Frederick II of Hohenstaufen, king of Germany and Sicily, who was in command of a large expedition. Al-Kāmil, who had inevitably got wind of these rumours, prepared for war. His emissaries ranged through the lands of Islam calling upon his brothers, cousins and allies to rush to the aid of Egypt. In addition, west of the delta, not far from Alexandria, he outfitted a fleet; in the summer of 1220 it took the Occidental vessels by surprise off the coast of Cyprus, inflicting a crushing defeat upon them. Once the enemy had thus been deprived of his mastery of the sea, al-Kāmil hurried to make another peace offer, this time promising to sign a thirty-year truce. In vain. Pelagius saw this excessive generosity as proof that the ruler of Cairo was at bay. Had they not just heard that Frederick II had been crowned emperor in Rome and had sworn to leave for Egypt without delay? He was expected by the spring of 1221 at the latest: hundreds of vessels and tens of thousands of soldiers would accompany him. In the meantime, the Frankish army had to sustain a situation of no war, no peace.

In fact, Frederick II was not to arrive until eight years later! Pelagius waited for him patiently until the beginning of the summer of

1221. In July the Frankish army left Damietta, heading resolutely for Cairo. In the Egyptian capital, al-Kāmil's soldiers had to use force to prevent the inhabitants from fleeing. But the sultan seemed confident, for two of his brothers had come to his aid: al-Ashraf, who with his troops from Jazīra had joined him in trying to prevent the invaders reaching Cairo, and al-Muʿazam, who was leading his Syrian army north, boldly interposing his forces between the enemy and Damietta. As for al-Kāmil himself, he was anxiously watching, with barely concealed joy, the gradual swelling of the waters of the Nile, for the level of the river had begun rising without the Occidentals taking any notice. In mid-August the land became so muddy and slippery that the knights had first to halt their advance and then to withdraw their entire army.

Barely had the retreat begun when a group of Egyptian soldiers moved to demolish the dykes. It was 26 August 1221. Within a few hours, as the Muslim troops cut off the exit routes, the entire Frankish army found itself mired in a sea of mud. Two days later, Pelagius, now desperate to save his army from annihilation, sent a messenger to al-Kāmil to seek peace. The Ayyubid sovereign laid down his conditions: the Franj would have to evacuate Damietta and sign an eight-year truce. In return, their army could leave by sea unhindered. Obviously, there was no longer any question of offering them Jerusalem.

In celebrating this victory, as complete as it was unexpected, many Arabs wondered whether al-Kāmil had been serious when he had offered the Franj the holy city. Had it not perhaps been a trick, an attempt to gain time? All would soon become clear.

During the distressing crisis of Damietta, the ruler of Egypt had often wondered about this famous Frederick, 'al-enboror' (the emperor), whose arrival was so eagerly awaited by the Franj. Was he really as powerful as they said? Was he truly determined to wage holy war against the Muslims? As he showered his collaborators with ever more questions and gathered more information from travellers who had been to Sicily, the island kingdom over which Frederick ruled, al-Kāmil's sense of astonishment mounted steadily. In 1225, when he learned that the emperor had just married Yolanda, the daughter of John of Brienne, thereby acquiring the title of king of Jerusalem, he decided to send an embassy headed by a subtle diplomat, the emir Fakhr al-Dīn Ibn al-Shaykh. The latter was amazed when he arrived in Palermo: yes, everything they said about Frederick was true. He spoke and wrote Arabic perfectly, he felt unconcealed admiration for Muslim civilisation, and he had nothing but contempt for the barbarous West, especially for the pope of Rome. His closest collaborators were Arabs, and so were the soldiers of his palace guard; at times of prayer, they bowed down in the direction of Mecca. This man of inquiring mind, who had spent his entire youth in Sicily, then a major centre of Arab sciences, felt that he had little in common with the dull and fanatical Franj. The voice of the muezzin rang out across his kingdom unimpeded.

Fakhr al-Dīn soon became a friend and confidant of Frederick. Through him, close links were forged between the Germanic emperor and the sultan of Cairo. The two monarchs exchanged letters in which they discussed the logic of Aristotle, the immortality of the soul and the genesis of the universe. When al-Kāmil learned of his correspondent's passion for observing animal behaviour, he sent him bears, apes and dromedaries, as well as an elephant, which the emperor entrusted to the Arab caretaker of his private zoo. The sultan was more than a little content to discover an enlightened Western leader who, like himself, understood the futility of these endless religious wars. He therefore unhesitatingly told Frederick of his desire for him to come to the Orient in the near future, adding that he would be happy to see the emperor in possession of Jerusalem.

This outburst of generosity becomes more comprehensible if we remember that at the time the offer was made, the holy city belonged not to al-Kāmil but to his brother al-Muʿazam, with whom the ruler of Cairo had just fallen out. Al-Kāmil felt that the occupation of Palestine by his ally Frederick would create a buffer state protecting him from any undertakings in which al-Muʿazam might indulge. In the long run, a reinvigorated kingdom of Jerusalem could also effectively interpose itself between Egypt and the warrior peoples of Asia, for the threat from that quarter was now looming. A fervent Muslim would never have so coldly contemplated abandoning Jerusalem, but al-Kāmil was quite different from his uncle Saladin. He regarded the question of Jerusalem as primarily political and military; the religious aspect was relevant only to the extent that it influenced public opinion. Frederick, who felt no closer to Christianity than to Islam, took an identical attitude. If he wanted to take possession of the holy city, it was not to commune with his thoughts at the tomb of Christ, but because a success of that kind would strengthen his position in his struggle against the pope, who had just excommunicated him as punishment for having postponed his expedition to the East.

When the emperor disembarked at Acre in September 1228 he was convinced that with al-Kāmil's help he would be able to enter Jerusalem in triumph, thus silencing his enemies. In fact, the ruler of Cairo found himself in an extremely embarrassing position, for recent events had completely redrawn the regional map. Al-Muʿazam had died suddenly in November 1227, bequeathing Damascus to his son al-Nāṣir, a young man lacking in all experience. Al-Kāmil, who could now contemplate seizing Damascus and Palestine himself, was no longer interested in establishing a buffer state between Egypt and Syria. In other words, al-Kāmil was not greatly pleased at the prospect of the arrival of Frederick, who in all friendship would lay claim to Jerusalem and its environs. A man of honour like al-Kāmil could not renege on his promises, but he could try to stall, telling the emperor that the situation had suddenly changed.

Frederick, who had come with a mere three thousand men, thought that the taking of Jerusalem would be no more than a formality. He therefore did not dare attempt a policy of intimidation, but instead sought to cajole al-Kāmil. 'I am your friend,' he wrote to him. 'It was you who urged me to make this trip. The pope and all the kings of the West now know of my mission. If I return empty-handed, I will lose much prestige. For pity's sake, give me Jerusalem, that I may hold my head high!' Al-Kāmil was touched, and so he sent his friend Fakhr al-Dīn to Frederick, bearing gifts and a double-edged reply. 'I too', he wrote, 'must take account of opinion. If I deliver Jerusalem to you, it could lead not only to a condemnation of my actions by the caliph, but also to a religious insurrection that would threaten my throne.'

For each side, it was a matter of saving face. Frederick implored Fakhr al-Dīn to find an honourable way out. The latter, with the sultan's agreement, threw Frederick a lifeline. 'The people would never accept the surrender of Jerusalem, won at such cost by Saladin, without a battle. On the other hand, if agreement on the holy city could avoid bloody warfare . . .' The emperor understood. He smiled, thanked his friend for his advice, and then ordered his small force of troops to prepare for combat. At the end of November 1228, as Frederick marched with great pomp towards the port of Jaffa, al-Kāmil spread the word throughout the country that it was necessary to prepare for a long and bitter war against the powerful sovereign from the West.

A few weeks later, with no battle having been joined, the text of an accord was ready: Frederick obtained Jerusalem and a corridor linking it to the coast, as well as Bethlehem, Nazareth, the environs of Tyre and the powerful fortress of Tibnīn, east of Tyre. In the holy city itself, the Muslims preserved a presence in the Ḥaram al-Sharīf sector, where their principal sanctuaries were clustered. The treaty was signed on 18 February 1229 by Frederick and by the ambassador Fakhr al-Dīn, in the name of the sultan. A month later, the emperor went to Jerusalem, whose Muslim population had been evacuated by al-Kāmil, except for some religious leaders left in charge of the Islamic places of worship. Frederick was received by Shams al-Dīn, the *qāḍī* of Nablus, who gave him the keys to the city and acted as a sort of guide. The *qāḍī* himself related what happened during this visit.

> When the emperor, king of the Franj, came to Jerusalem, I remained with him, as al-Kāmil had requested of me. I entered Ḥaram al-Sharīf with him, where he toured the small mosques. Then we went to al-Aqṣā mosque, whose architecture he admired, as well as the Dome of the Rock. He was fascinated by the beauty of the minbar, and climbed the stairs to the top. When he descended, he took me by the hand and led me back towards al-Aqṣā. There he found a priest who, Bible in hand, was trying to enter the mosque. Furious, the emperor began to browbeat him. 'What brings you to this place? By God, if one of you dares step in here again without permission, I will pluck out his eyes!' The priest departed trembling. That night, I asked the muezzin not to call the

prayer, in order not to inconvenience the emperor. But when I saw him the next day, the emperor asked me, '*Qāḍī*, why didn't the muezzins call the prayer as usual?' I answered: 'It is I who prevented them from doing so, out of respect for Your Majesty.' 'You should not have acted thus,' the emperor said, 'for if I spent this night in Jerusalem, it was above all to hear the muezzin's call in the night.'

During his visit to the Dome of the Rock, Frederick read an inscription saying: SALADIN HAS PURGED THIS HOLY CITY OF MUSHRIKĪN. This term, which literally means 'associationists', or even 'polytheists', was applied to those who associated other divinities to the worship of the one God. In this context it designated Christians, believers in the Trinity. Pretending to be unaware of this, the emperor, with an amused grin, asked his embarrassed hosts who these *mushrikīn* might be. A few minutes later, Frederick noticed a wooden lattice at the entrance to the Dome; he asked what it was for. 'It is to prevent birds from entering this place,' came the answer. Before his flabbergasted guides, Frederick then commented, in an obvious allusion to the Franj, 'And to think that God allowed pigs in!' Sibṭ Ibn al-Jawzi, a Damascene chronicler and brilliant orator who was aged forty-three in 1229, interpreted these remarks as proof that Frederick was neither a Christian nor a Muslim 'but most certainly an atheist'. Basing himself on the testimony of those who had seen the emperor close up in Jerusalem, he added that he 'was covered with red hair, bald and myopic. Had he been a slave, he would not have fetched 200 dirhams.'

Sibṭ's hostility to the emperor reflects the sentiments of the great majority of Arabs. In other circumstances, his friendly attitude to Islam and its civilisation would undoubtedly have been appreciated. But public opinion was scandalised by the terms of the treaty signed by al-Kāmil. 'As soon as the news that the holy city had been ceded to the Franj became known,' says the chronicler, 'the lands of Islam were swept by a veritable storm. Because of the gravity of the event, demonstrations of public mourning were organised.' In Baghdad, Mosul and Aleppo, meetings were held in the mosques to denounce al-Kāmil's betrayal. But it was in Damascus that reaction was most violent. 'King al-Nāṣir asked me to assemble the people in the great mosque of Damascus,' Sibṭ recounts, 'so that I could speak to them of what had happened in Jerusalem. I could not but accept, for my duty to the faith compelled me.'

The chronicler-preacher mounted the steps of the pulpit before a delirious crowd, his head enveloped in a turban of black cloth. 'The new disaster that has befallen us', he began, 'has broken our hearts. Our pilgrims can no longer visit Jerusalem, the verses of the Koran will no longer be recited in its schools. How great is the shame of the Muslims today!' Al-Nāṣir attended the demonstration in person. Open war was declared between him and his uncle al-Kāmil. No sooner had the latter handed Jerusalem over to Frederick than the Egyptian army imposed a tight blockade on Damascus. The struggle against the treason of the ruler of Cairo became the slogan under which the people of the Syrian metropolis were mobilised in firm support of their young sovereign. Sibṭ's eloquence, however, was not enough to save Damascus. Al-Kāmil, with his overwhelming numerical superiority, emerged victorious from the confrontation, forcing the city to capitulate and re-establishing the unity of the Ayyubid empire under his own authority.

In June 1229 al-Nāṣir was forced to abandon his capital. Bitter, but by no means without hope, he settled in the fortress of Karak east of the Jordan, where during the years of truce he would become the symbol of steadfastness in the face of the enemy. Many Damascenes retained their personal attachment to him, and many religious militants, disappointed with the excessively conciliatory policy of the other Ayyubids, kept up hope thanks to this spirited young prince, who incited his peers to continue the *jihād* against the invaders. 'Who but I', he wrote, 'expends all his efforts to protect Islam? Who else fights for the cause of God in all circumstances?' In November 1239, one hundred days after the truce had expired, al-Nāṣir retook Jerusalem in a surprise raid. There was an explosion of joy throughout the Arab world. The poets compared the victor to his great-uncle Saladin, and sung his praises for having thus expunged the outrage of al-Kāmil's betrayal.

His apologists failed to mention that al-Nāṣir had been reconciled with the ruler of Cairo shortly before the latter's death in 1238, probably hoping that the government of Damascus would thereby be restored to him. The poets also omit to point out that the Ayyubid prince did not seek to retain Jerusalem after retaking it. Believing the city indefensible, he quickly destroyed the Tower of David and the other fortifications recently built by the Franj. He then withdrew with his troops to Karak. Fervour, one might say, did not exclude political or military realism. The subsequent behaviour of this hard-line leader is nevertheless intriguing. During the inevitable war of succession that followed the death of al-Kāmil, al-Nāṣir proposed to the Franj that together they form an alliance against his cousins. In 1243 he officially recognised their right to Jerusalem in an effort to pacify the Occidentals, even offering to withdraw the Muslim religious leaders from Ḥaram al-Sharīf. Al-Kāmil had never gone so far in appeasement.

Part Six

EXPULSION (1244–91)

Attacked by Mongols – the Tartars – in the east and by Franj in the west, the Muslims had never been in such a critical position. God alone could still rescue them.

IBN AL-ATHĪR

XIII

The Mongol Scourge

> The events I am about to describe are so horrible that for years I avoided all mention of them. It is not easy to announce that death has fallen upon Islam and the Muslims. Alas! I would have preferred my mother never to have given birth to me, or to have died without witnessing all these evils. If one day you are told that the earth has never known such calamity since God created Adam, do not hesitate to believe it, for such is the strict truth. Nebuchadnezzar's massacre of the children of Israel and the destruction of Jerusalem are generally cited as among the most infamous tragedies of history. But these were as nothing compared to what has happened now. No, probably not until the end of time will a catastrophe of such magnitude be seen again.

Nowhere else in his voluminous *Perfect History* does Ibn al-Athīr adopt such a pathetic tone. Page after page, his sadness, terror and incredulity spring out as if he was superstitiously postponing the moment when he would finally have to speak the name of the scourge: Genghis Khan.

The rise of the Mongol conqueror began shortly after the death of Saladin, but not until another quarter of a century had passed did the Arabs feel the approach of the threat. Genghis Khan first set about uniting the various Turkic and Mongol tribes of central Asia under his authority; he then embarked on what he hoped would be the conquest of the world. His forces moved in three directions: to the east, where the Chinese empire was reduced to vassal status and then annexed; to the north-west, where first Russia and then eastern Europe were devastated; to the west, where Persia was invaded. 'All cities must be razed', Genghis Khan used to say, 'so that the world may once again become a great steppe in which Mongol mothers will suckle free and happy children.' And prestigious cities indeed would be destroyed, their populations decimated: Bukhārā, Samarkand and Herat, among others.

The first Mongol thrust into an Islamic country coincided with the various Frankish invasions of Egypt between 1218 and 1221. At the time the Arab world felt trapped between Scylla and Charybdis. This was undoubtedly part of the explanation for al-Kāmil's conciliatory attitude over the question of Jerusalem. But Genghis Khan finally abandoned any attempt to venture west of Persia. With his death in 1227 at the age of sixty-seven, the pressure of the horsemen of the steppes on the Arab world eased for some years.

In Syria the scourge first made itself felt indirectly. Among the many dynasties crushed by the Mongols on their way was that of the Khwarazmian Turks, who had earlier supplanted the Seljuks from Iraq to India. With the dismantling of this Muslim empire, whose hour of glory had passed, remnants of its army were compelled to flee as far as possible from the terrifying victors. Thus it was that one fine day some ten thousand Khwarazmian horsemen arrived in Syria, pillaging and holding cities hostage and participating as mercenaries in the internal struggles of the Ayyubids. In June 1224, believing themselves strong enough to establish a state of their own, the Khwarazmians attacked Damascus. They plundered the neighbouring villages and sacked the orchards of Ghūṭa. But then, since they were incapable of sustaining a long siege against the city's resistance, they changed their target and suddenly headed for Jerusalem, which they occupied without difficulty on 11 July. Although the Frankish population was largely spared, the city itself was plundered and put to the torch. To the great relief of all the cities of Syria, a fresh attack on Damascus several months later was decimated by a coalition of Ayyubid princes.

This time the Frankish knights would never retake Jerusalem. Frederick, whose diplomatic skill had enabled the Occidentals to keep the flag of the cross flying over the walls of the city for fifteen years, was no longer interested in its fate. Abandoning his Oriental ambitions, he now preferred to maintain more amicable relations with the Cairene leaders. In 1247, when Louis IX of France planned an expedition against Egypt, the emperor sought to dissuade him. Better still, he kept Ayyūb, son of al-Kāmil, regularly informed of the preparations of the French expedition.

Louis arrived in the East in 1248, but he did not immediately head for the Egyptian border, for he felt it would be too risky to undertake a campaign before spring. He therefore settled in Cyprus and spent these months of respite striving to realise the dream that was to haunt the Franj to the end of the thirteenth century and beyond: the conclusion of an alliance with the Mongols that would trap the Arab world in a pincer movement. Emissaries thus shuttled regularly between the camps of the invaders from the East and the invaders from the West. Late in 1248 Louis received a delegation in Cyprus that put forward the tempting possibility that the Mongols might convert to Christianity. Entranced by this prospect, he hastily responded by despatching precious and pious gifts. But Genghis Khan's successors misinterpreted the meaning of this gesture. Treating the king of France as they would a mere vassal, they asked him to send gifts of equivalent value every year. This misunderstanding saved the Arab world from a concerted attack by its two enemies, at least temporarily.

Thus it was that the Occidentals alone launched their assault on Egypt on 5 June 1249, although not before the two monarchs had exchanged thunderous declarations of war, in accordance with the customs of the epoch.

> I have already warned you many times [wrote Louis] but you have paid no heed. Henceforth my decision is made: I will assault your territory, and even were you to swear allegiance to the cross, my mind would not be changed. The armies that obey me cover mountains and plains, they are as numerous as the pebbles of the earth, and they march upon you grasping the swords of fate.

To bolster these threats, the king of France reminded his enemy of a number of successes scored by the Christians against the Muslims in Spain the year before: 'We chased your people before us like herds of oxen. We killed the men, made widows of the women, and captured girls and boys. Was that not a lesson to you?' Ayyūb replied in similar vein: 'Foolish as you are, have you forgotten the lands you occupied which we have reconquered, even quite recently? Have you forgotten the damage we have inflicted upon you?' Apparently aware of the numerical inferiority of his forces, the sultan found an appropriately reassuring quotation from the Koran: 'How often has a small troop vanquished a great, with God's permission, for God is with the good.' This encouraged him to predict to Louis: 'Your defeat is ineluctable. Soon you will bitterly regret the adventure on which you have embarked.'

At the outset of their offensive, however, the Franj scored a decisive success. Damietta, which had resisted the last Frankish expedition so courageously thirty years before, was this time abandoned without a fight. Its fall, which sowed disarray in the Arab world, starkly revealed how weak the legatees of the great Saladin had become. Sultan Ayyūb, who was immobilised by tuberculosis and unable to take personal command of his troops, preferred to adopt the policy of his father al-Kāmil rather than lose Egypt: he proposed to Louis that Damietta be exchanged for Jerusalem. But the king of France refused to deal with a defeated and dying 'infidel'. Ayyūb then decided to resist, and had himself transported by litter-bearers to the city of Manṣūra, 'the victorious', which had been built by al-Kāmil on the very spot at which the previous Frankish invasion had been defeated. Unfortunately, the sultan's health was sinking fast. Racked by fits of coughing so severe that it seemed that they would never end, he fell into a coma on 20 November, just as the Franj, encouraged by the receding waters of the Nile, left Damietta for Manṣūra. Three days later, to the great consternation of his entourage, the sultan died.

How could the army and the people be told that the sultan was dead while the enemy was at the gates of the city and Ayyūb's son Tūrān-Shāh was somewhere in northern Iraq, several weeks' march away? It was then that a providential personality intervened: Shajar al-Durr, or 'Tree of Pearls', a female slave of Armenian origin, beautiful and crafty, who for years had been Ayyūb's favourite wife. Gathering the members of the sultan's family together, she ordered them to keep silent about his death until the prince arrived, and even asked the aged emir Fakhr al-Dīn, Frederick's old friend, to write a letter in the sultan's name summoning the Muslims to *jihād*. According to Ibn

Wāṣil, a Syrian chronicler and one of Fakhr al-Dīn's associates, the king of France soon learned of the death of Ayyūb, which encouraged him to step up the military pressure. In the Egyptian camp, however, the secret was kept long enough to prevent the troops becoming demoralised.

The battle raged around Manṣūra throughout the long winter months. Then on 10 February 1250 the Frankish army, aided by treason, penetrated the city by surprise. Ibn Wāṣil, who was then in Cairo, relates:

> The emir Fakhr al-Dīn was in his bath when they came and told him the news. Flabbergasted, he immediately leapt into the saddle – without armour or coat of mail – and rushed to see what the situation was. He was attacked by a troop of enemy soldiers, who killed him. The king of the Franj entered the city, and even reached the sultan's palace. His soldiers poured through the streets, while the Muslim soldiers and the inhabitants sought salvation in disordered flight. Islam seemed mortally wounded, and the Franj were about to reap the fruit of their victory when the Mamluk Turks arrived. Since the enemy had dispersed through the streets, these horsemen rushed bravely in pursuit. Everywhere the Franj were taken by surprise and massacred with sword or mace. At the start of the day, the pigeons had carried a message to Cairo announcing the attack of the Franj without breathing a word about the outcome of the battle, so we were all waiting anxiously. Throughout the quarters of the city there was sadness until the next day, when new messages told us of the victory of the Turkish lions. The streets of Cairo became a festival.

In subsequent weeks, from his post in the Egyptian capital, the chronicler would observe two sequences of events that were to change the face of the Arab East: on the one hand, the victorious struggle against the last great Frankish invasion; on the other, a revolution unique in history, one that was to raise a caste of officer-slaves to power for nearly three centuries.

After his defeat at Manṣūra, the king of France realised that his military position was becoming untenable. Unable to take the city, and constantly harassed by the Egyptians in a muddy terrain criss-crossed by countless canals, Louis decided to negotiate. At the beginning of March he sent a conciliatory message to Tūrān-Shāh, who had just arrived in Egypt. In it he declared that he was now prepared to accept Ayyūb's proposal to abandon Damietta in exchange for Jerusalem. The new sultan's response was not long in coming: the generous offers made by Ayyūb should have been accepted during Ayyūb's lifetime. Now it was too late. At this point, the most Louis could hope for was to save his army and get out of Egypt alive, for pressure was mounting on all sides. In mid-March several dozen Egyptian galleys inflicted a severe defeat on the Frankish fleet, destroying or capturing nearly a hundred vessels of all sizes and removing any possibility of the invaders' retreating towards Damietta. On 7 April the invading army tried to run the blockade and was assaulted by the Mamluk battalions, swelled by thousands of volunteers. After several hours of fighting, the Franj had their backs to the wall. To halt the massacre of his men, the king of France capitulated and asked that his life be spared. He was led in chains to Manṣūra, where he was locked in the house of an Ayyubid functionary.

Curiously, the new sultan's brilliant victory, far from enhancing his power, brought about his downfall. Tūrān-Shāh was engaged in a dispute with the chief Mamluk officers of his army. The latter believed, not without reason, that Egypt owed its salvation to them, and they therefore demanded a decisive role in the leadership of the country. The sovereign, on the other hand, wanted to take advantage of his newly acquired prestige to place his own supporters in the major posts of responsibility. Three weeks after the victory over the Franj, a group of these Mamluks met together on the initiative of a brilliant forty-year-old Turkish officer named Baybars, a crossbowman, and decided to take action. A revolt broke out on 2 May 1250 at the end of a banquet organised by the monarch. Tūrān-Shāh, wounded in the shoulder by Baybars, was running towards the Nile, hoping to flee by boat, when he was captured by his assailants. He begged them to spare his life, promising to leave Egypt for ever and to renounce any claim to power. But the last of the Ayyubid sultans was finished off mercilessly. An envoy of the caliph even had to intervene before the Mamluks would agree to give their former master a proper burial.

Despite the success of their coup d'état, the slave-officers hesitated to seize the throne directly. The wisest among them racked their brains to find a compromise that would confer a semblance of Ayyubid legitimacy on their nascent power. The formula they devised would go down in history in the Muslim world, as Ibn Wāṣil, an incredulous witness to the singular event, remarked.

> After the assassination of Tūrān-Shāh [he relates] the emirs and *mamlūks* met near the sultan's pavilion and decided that Shajar al-Durr, a wife of Sultan Ayyūb, would be placed in power, becoming queen and sultana. She took charge of the affairs of state, establishing a royal seal in her name inscribed with the formula 'Umm Khalīl' ('mother of Khalīl'), a child of hers who had died at an early age. In all the mosques, the Friday sermon was delivered in the name of Umm Khalīl, sultana of Cairo and of all Egypt. This was unprecedented in the history of Islam.

Shortly after she was placed on the throne, Shajar al-Durr married one of the Mamluk chiefs, Aybeg, and conferred the title of sultan upon him.

The replacement of the Ayyubids by the Mamluks marked a clear hardening of the Muslim world's attitude towards the invaders. The descendants of Saladin had proved more than a little conciliatory towards the Franj, and their declining power was no longer capable of confronting the perils threatening Islam from East and West alike. The Mamluk revolution soon appeared as an enterprise of military, political and religious rectification.

The coup d'état in Cairo did not alter the fate of the king of France. An agreement in principle reached during the time of Tūrān-Shāh stipulated that Louis would be released in return for the withdrawal of all Frankish troops from Egyptian territory, Damietta in particular, and the payment of a ransom of one million dinars. The French sovereign was indeed released several days after the accession to power of Umm Khalīl, but not before being treated to a lecture by the Egyptian negotiators: 'How could a sensible, wise and intelligent man like you embark on a sea voyage to a land peopled by countless Muslims? According to our law, a man who crosses the sea in this way cannot testify in court.' 'And why not?' asked the king. 'Because', came the reply, 'it is assumed that he is not in possession of all his faculties.'

The last Frankish soldier left Egypt before the end of May.

Never again would the Occidentals attempt to invade the land of the Nile. The 'blond peril' would soon be eclipsed by the far more terrifying danger of the descendants of Genghis Khan. The great conqueror's empire had been weakened somewhat by the wars of succession that had flared after his death, and the Muslim East had enjoyed an unexpected respite. By 1251, however, the horsemen of the steppes were united once again, under the authority of three brothers, grandsons of Genghis Khan: Möngke, Kubilay and Hülegü. The first had been designated uncontested sovereign of the empire, whose capital was Karakorum, in Mongolia. The second reigned in Peking. It was the ambition of the third, who had settled in Persia, to conquer the entire Muslim East to the shores of the Mediterranean, perhaps even to the Nile. Hülegü was a complex personality. Initially interested in philosophy and science, a man who sought out the company of men of letters, he was transformed in the course of his campaigns into a savage animal thirsting for blood and destruction. His religious attitudes were no less contradictory. Although strongly influenced by Christianity – his mother, his favourite wife and several of his closest collaborators were members of the Nestorian Church – he never renounced shamanism, the traditional religion of his people. In the territories he governed, notably Persia, he was generally tolerant of Muslims, but once he was gripped by his lust to destroy any political entity capable of opposing him, he waged a war of total destruction against the most prestigious metropolises of Islam.

His first target was Baghdad. At first, Hülegü asked the ʿAbbasid caliph, al-Mustaʿṣim, the thirty-seventh of his dynasty, to recognise Mongol sovereignty as his predecessors had once accepted the rule of the Seljuk Turks. The prince of the faithful, overconfident of his own prestige, sent word to the conqueror that any attack on his capital would mobilise the entire Muslim world, from India to north-west Africa. Not in the least impressed, the grandson of Genghis Khan announced his intention of taking the city by force. Towards the end of 1257 he and, it would appear, hundreds of thousands of cavalry began advancing towards the ʿAbbasid capital. On their way they destroyed the Assassins' sanctuary at Alamūt and sacked its library of inestimable value, thus making it almost impossible for future generations to gain any in-depth knowledge of the doctrine and activities of the sect. When the caliph finally realised the extent of the threat, he decided to negotiate. He proposed that Hülegü's name be pronounced at Friday sermons in the mosques of Baghdad and that he be granted the title of sultan. But it was too late, for by now the Mongol had definitively opted for force. After a few weeks of courageous resistance, the prince of the faithful had no choice but to capitulate. On 10 February 1258 he went to the victor's camp in person and asked if he would promise to spare the lives of all the citizens if they agreed to lay down their arms. But in vain. As soon as they were disarmed, the Muslim fighters were exterminated. Then the Mongol horde fanned out through the prestigious city demolishing buildings, burning neighbourhoods, and mercilessly massacring men, women and children – nearly eighty thousand people in all. Only the Christian community of the city was spared, thanks to the intercession of the khan's wife. The prince of the faithful was himself strangled to death a few days after his defeat. The tragic end of the ʿAbbasid caliphate stunned the Muslim world. It was no longer a matter of a military battle for control of a particular city, or even country: it was now a desperate struggle for the survival of Islam.

In the meantime the Tartars continued their triumphant march towards Syria. In January 1260 Hülegü's army overran Aleppo, which was taken rapidly despite heroic resistance. As in Baghdad, massacres and destruction raged throughout this ancient city, whose crime was merely to have stood up to the conqueror. A few weeks later, the invaders were at the gates of Damascus. The Ayyubid kinglets who still governed the various Syrian cities were naturally unable to stem the tide. Some decided to recognise the suzerainty of the Great Khan, even contemplating the futile dream of forming an alliance with the invaders against the Mamluks of Egypt, enemies of their dynasty. Views were divided among the Christians, Oriental and Frankish alike. The Armenians, in the person of their king, Hethoum, took the side of the Mongols, as did Prince Bohemond of Antioch, Hethoum's brother-in-law. The Franj of Acre, on the other hand, took a neutral position generally favourable to the Muslims. But the prevalent impression in both East and West was that the Mongol campaign was a sort of holy war against Islam, a pendant to the Frankish expeditions. This impression was enhanced by the fact that Hülegü's chief lieutenant in Syria, General Kitbuga, was a Nestorian Christian. When Damascus was taken on 1 March 1260, three Christian princes – Bohemond, Hethoum and Kitbuga – entered the city as conquerors, to the great consternation of the Arabs.

How far would the Tartars go? Some people were convinced that they would go all the way to Mecca, thus dealing the *coup de grâce* to the religion of the Prophet. In any event they would reach Jerusalem, and soon. All Syria was convinced of this. Just after the fall of Damascus, two Mongol detachments quickly seized two Palestinian cities: Nablus in the centre of the country, and Gaza in the south-west. When Gaza, which lies on the edge of Sinai, was overrun in that tragic spring of 1260, it seemed that not even Egypt would escape devastation. Even before his Syrian campaign had ended, Hülegü despatched an ambassador to Cairo to demand the unconditional surrender of the land of the Nile. The emissary was received, spoke his piece, and was then beheaded. The Mamluks were not joking. Their methods bore no resemblance to those of Saladin. These sultan-slaves, who had now been ruling for ten years, reflected the hardening, the intransigence, of an Arab world now under attack from all directions. They fought with all the means at their disposal. No scruples, no magnanimous gestures, no compromises. But with courage and to great effect.

All eyes were now turned in their direction, for they represented the last hope of stemming the advance of the invader. For twelve months, power in Cairo had been in the hands of an officer of Turkish origin named Quṭuz. Shajar al-Durr and her husband Aybeg had governed together for seven years, but had finally killed each other. There have been many conflicting versions of the end of their rule. The one favoured by popular storytellers is a mix of love and jealousy spiced with political ambition. The sultana, it says, was bathing her husband, as was her custom. Taking advantage of this moment of détente and intimacy, she scolded the sultan for having taken a pretty fourteen-year-old girl slave as his concubine. 'Do I no longer please you?' she murmured, to soften his heart. But Aybeg answered sharply: 'She is young, while you are not.' Shajar al-Durr trembled with rage at these words. She rubbed soap in her husband's eyes, while whispering conciliatory words to allay any suspicion, and then suddenly seized a dagger and stabbed him in the side. Aybeg collapsed. The sultana remained immobile for some moments, as if paralysed. Then, heading for the door, she summoned several faithful slaves, who she thought would dispose of the body for her. But to her misfortune, one of Aybeg's sons, who was fifteen at the time, noticed that the bathwater flowing through the outside drain was red. He ran into the room and saw Shajar al-Durr standing half-naked near the door, still holding a bloodstained dagger. She fled through the corridors of the palace, pursued by her stepson, who alerted the guards. Just as they caught up with her, the sultana stumbled and fell, crashing her head violently against a marble slab. By the time they reached her, she was dead.

However highly romanticised, this version is of genuine historical interest inasmuch as it is in all probability a faithful reflection of what was being said in the streets of Cairo in April 1257, just after the tragedy.

However that may be, after the death of the two sovereigns, Aybeg's young son succeeded to the throne. But not for long. As the Mongol threat took shape, the commanders of the Egyptian army realised that an adolescent would be unable to lead the decisive battle now looming. In December 1259, as Hülegü's hordes began to roll across Syria, a coup d'état brought Quṭuz to power. He was a mature, energetic man who talked in terms of holy war and called for a general mobilisation against the invader, the enemy of Islam.

With hindsight, the new coup in Cairo could be said to represent a genuine patriotic upheaval. The country was immediately placed on a war footing. In July 1260 a powerful Egyptian army moved into Palestine to confront the enemy.

Quṭuz was aware that the Mongol army had lost the core of its fighters when Möngke, Supreme Khan of the Mongols, died and his brother Hülegü had to retreat with his army to join in the inevitable succession struggle. The grandson of Genghis Khan had left Syria soon after the fall of Damascus, leaving only a few thousand horsemen in the country, under the command of his lieutenant Kitbuga.

Sultan Quṭuz knew that if the invader was to be dealt a decisive blow, it was now or never. The Egyptian army thus began by assaulting the Mongol garrison at Gaza. Taken by surprise, the invaders barely resisted. The Mamluks next advanced on Acre, not unaware that the Franj of Palestine had been more reticent than those of Antioch towards the Mongols. Admittedly, some of their barons still rejoiced in the defeats suffered by Islam, but most were frightened by the brutality of the Asian conquerors. When Quṭuz proposed an alliance, their response was not wholly negative: although not prepared to take part in the fighting, they would not object to the passage of the Egyptian army through their territory, and they would not obstruct supplies. The sultan was thus able to advance towards the interior of Palestine, and even towards Damascus, without having to protect his rear.

Kitbuga was preparing to march out to meet them when a popular insurrection erupted in Damascus. The Muslims of the city, enraged by the exactions of the invaders and encouraged by the departure of Hülegü, built barricades in the streets and set fire to those churches that had been spared by the Mongols. It took Kitbuga several days to re-establish order, and this enabled Quṭuz to consolidate his positions in Galilee. The two armies met near the village of ʿAyn Jālūt ('Fountain of Goliath') on 3 September 1260. Quṭuz had had time to conceal most of his troops, leaving the battlefield to no more than a vanguard under the command of his most brilliant officer, Baybars. Kitbuga arrived in a rush and, apparently ill-informed, fell into the trap. He launched a full-scale assault. Baybars retreated, but as the Mongol gave chase he suddenly found himself surrounded by Egyptian forces more numerous than his own.

The Mongol cavalry was exterminated in a few hours. Kitbuga himself was captured and beheaded forthwith.

On the night of 8 September the Mamluk horsemen rode jubilantly into Damascus, where they were greeted as liberators.

XIV

God Grant That They Never Set Foot There Again!

Although less spectacular and displaying less military inventiveness than Ḥiṭṭīn, ʿAyn Jālūt was nevertheless one of history's most decisive battles. It enabled the Muslims not only to escape annihilation, but also to reconquer all the territory the Mongols had taken from them. The descendants of Hülegü, now settled in Persia, soon converted to Islam themselves, the better to consolidate their authority.

In the short term, the Mamluk upheaval led to a settling of accounts with all those who had supported the invader. The alarm had been sounded. Henceforth there would be no more aid and comfort to the enemy, whether Franj or Tartar.

After retaking Aleppo in October 1260 and easily repelling a counter-offensive by Hülegü, the Mamluks planned to organise a sequence of punitive raids against Bohemond of Antioch and Hethoum of Armenia, the principal allies of the Mongols. But a power struggle erupted within the Egyptian army. Baybars wanted to establish himself as a semi-independent ruler in Aleppo; fearing his lieutenant's ambitions, Quṭuz refused. He wanted no part of a rival regime in Syria. To nip the conflict in the bud, the sultan assembled his army, Baybars included, and set out to return to Egypt. When he was three days' march from Cairo, he gave his soldiers a day of rest. It was 23 October, and he decided to spend the day at his favourite sport, hare hunting, along with the chief officers of his army. He was careful to make sure that Baybars came too, for fear that he might otherwise take advantage of the sultan's absence to foment a rebellion. The small party left camp at first light. Two hours later, they stopped for a brief rest. An emir approached Quṭuz and took his hand as if to kiss it. At that moment, Baybars drew his sword and sank it into the sultan's back. The two conspirators then leapt on their mounts and rode back to camp at full gallop. They sought out the emir Aqṭāy, an elderly officer universally respected in the army, and told him: 'We have killed Quṭuz.' Aqṭāy, who did not seem particularly upset by the news, asked, 'Which of you killed him?' Baybars did not hesitate: 'I did,' he said. The old Mamluk then approached him, invited him into the sultan's tent, and bowed before him to pay him homage. Before long the entire army acclaimed the new sultan.

The ingratitude displayed towards the victor of ʿAyn Jālūt less than two months after his brilliant exploit does not speak well for the Mamluks. In extenuation of the officer-slaves' conduct, however, it should be added that most of them had long considered Baybars their real chief. Had he not been the first to strike the Ayyubid Tūrān-Shāh back in 1250, thus announcing the Mamluks' determination to assume power? Had he not played a decisive role in the victory over the Mongols? Indeed, his political perspicacity, military skill and extraordinary physical courage had earned Baybars a position of primacy among them.

Born in 1223, the new Mamluk sultan had begun life as a slave in Syria. His first master, the Ayyubid emir of Hama, had sold him because of some superstition, for he was unnerved by Baybars's appearance. The young slave was very dark, a giant of a man, with a husky voice, light blue eyes, and a large white spot in his right eye. The future sultan was purchased by a Mamluk officer who assigned him to Ayyūb's bodyguard. There his personal qualities, and above all his complete absence of scruples, rapidly brought him to the top of the hierarchy.

At the end of October 1260 Baybars rode victoriously into Cairo, where his authority was recognised without opposition. In the Syrian cities, by contrast, other Mamluk officers took advantage of the death of Quṭuz to proclaim their independence. In a lightning campaign, the sultan seized Damascus and Aleppo, thus reuniting the old Ayyubid domain under his authority. This bloody-minded and untutored officer turned out to be a great statesman, the architect of a genuine renaissance of the Arab world. Under his reign, Egypt, and to a lesser extent Syria, again became centres of great cultural and artistic brilliance. The Baybars who devoted his life to destroying any Frankish fortress capable of standing against him also proved to be a great builder, embellishing Cairo and constructing roads and bridges throughout his domain. He also re-established a postal service, run with carrier pigeons and chargers, that was even more efficient than those of Nūr al-Dīn and Saladin. His government was severe, sometimes brutal, but also enlightened, and not in the least arbitrary. From the moment of his accession to power, he took a firm attitude towards the Franj, determined to reduce their influence. But he differentiated between those of Acre, whom he wanted merely to weaken, and those of Antioch, who were guilty of having made common cause with the Mongol invaders.

Towards the end of 1261 he planned to organise a punitive expedition against the lands of Prince Bohemond and the Armenian King Hethoum. But he clashed instead with the Tartars. Although Hülegü was no longer capable of invading Syria, he still commanded sufficient forces in Persia to prevent the punishment of his allies. Baybars wisely decided to wait for a better opportunity.

It came in 1265, when Hülegü died. Baybars then took advantage of divisions among the Mongols to invade Galilee, reducing several strongholds, with the complicity of part of the local Christian population. He then turned sharply north and moved into Hethoum's territory, destroying all the cities one by one, in particular Hethoum's capital, Sis, a large part of whose population he killed, apart from carrying off more than forty thousand captives. The Armenian kingdom would never rise again. In the spring of 1268 Baybars launched a new campaign. He began by attacking the environs of Acre, seized Beaufort Castle, and then, taking his army north, arrived at the walls of Tripoli on 1 May. There he found the ruler of the city, none other than Bohemond, who was also prince of Antioch. The latter, well aware of the sultan's resentment against him, prepared for a long siege. But Baybars had other plans. Some days later he set out northward, arriving at Antioch on 14 May. The greatest of the Frankish cities, which had held out against all Muslim sovereigns for the past 170 years, now resisted for a mere four days. On the night of 18 May a breach was opened in the city walls not far from the citadel, and

Baybars's troops spread through the streets. This conquest bore little resemblance to those of Saladin. The entire population was massacred or sold into slavery, the city itself ravaged. Previously a prestigious metropolis, it was reduced to the status of a desolate village, sprinkled with ruins that time would shroud in grass.

Bohemond learned of the fall of his city from a memorable letter sent to him by Baybars, though it was actually written by the sultan's official chronicler, the Egyptian Ibn ʿAbd-al-Ẓāhir: 'To the noble and valorous knight Bohemond, prince become a mere count by dint of the seizure of Antioch.' The sarcasm did not stop there:

> When we left you in Tripoli, we headed immediately for Antioch, where we arrived on the first day of the venerated month of Ramaḍān. As soon as we arrived, your troops came out to join the battle against us, but they were vanquished, for although they supported one another, they lacked the support of God. Be glad that you have not seen your knights lying prostrate under the hooves of horses, your palaces plundered, your ladies sold in the quarters of the city, fetching a mere dinar apiece – a dinar taken, moreover, from your own hoard!

After a long description, in which no detail was spared, the sultan concluded thus:

> This letter will gladden your heart by informing you that God has granted you the boon of leaving you safe and sound and prolonging your life, for you were not in Antioch. Had you been there, you would now be dead, wounded or taken prisoner. But perhaps God has spared you only that you might submit and give proof of obedience.

As a reasonable – and now powerless – man, Bohemond answered by proposing a truce. Baybars accepted. He knew that the terrified count no longer represented any real danger, any more than Hethoum, whose kingdom had been virtually wiped off the map. As for the Franj of Palestine, they too were only too happy to obtain a respite. The sultan sent his chronicler Ibn ʿAbd-al-Ẓāhir to Acre to seal an accord with them.

> Their king sought to temporise to obtain the best possible conditions, but I was inflexible, in accordance with the directives of the sultan. Irritated, the king of the Franj said to the interpreter: 'Tell him to look behind him.' I turned around and saw the entire army of the Franj, in combat formation. The interpreter added, 'The king reminds you not to forget the existence of this multitude of soldiers.' When I did not answer, the king insisted that the interpreter ask for my response. I then asked, 'Can I be assured that my life will be spared if I say what I think?' 'Yes.' 'Well then, tell the king that there are fewer soldiers in his army than there are Frankish captives in the prisons of Cairo.' The king nearly choked, then he brought the interview to a close; but he received us a short time later and concluded the truce.

Baybars was by this time no longer concerned about the Frankish knights. He was well aware that the inevitable reaction to his seizure of Antioch would come not from them, but from their masters, the kings of the West.

Before the end of the year 1268 persistent rumours were already circulating promising the early return to the East of the king of France, at the head of a powerful army. The sultan frequently interrogated travellers and merchants on this point. During the summer of 1270 a message reached Cairo saying that Louis had disembarked on the beach at Carthage, near Tunis, with six thousand men. Without a moment's hesitation, Baybars assembled the principal Mamluk emirs to announce his intention of leading a powerful army to the far-off province of Africa to help the Muslims repel this new Frankish invasion. But a few weeks later another messenger arrived seeking the sultan. He had been sent by al-Mustanṣir, the emir of Tunis, to announce that the king of France had been found dead in his camp and that his army had departed, although a large part had been decimated by war and disease. With this danger removed, Baybars decided to launch a fresh offensive against the Franj of the Orient. In March 1271 he seized the redoubtable Ḥiṣn al-Akrād, Crac des Chevaliers, which Saladin himself had never succeeded in reducing.

During the years that followed, both the Franj and the Mongols – especially the latter, now led by Abāqā, the son and successor of

Hülegü – organised a number of incursions into Syria. But they were invariably repelled. By the time Baybars died (he was poisoned in 1277), Frankish possessions in the Orient had been whittled down to a string of coastal cities completely surrounded by the Mamluk empire. Their powerful network of fortresses had been dismantled. The reprieve they had enjoyed during the years of the Ayyubids was at an end. Their expulsion was now ineluctable.

Nevertheless, there was no hurry. In 1283 the truce conceded by Baybars was renegotiated by Qalāwūn, the new Mamluk sultan. The latter manifested no great hostility to the Franj. He stated that he was prepared to guarantee their presence and security in the Orient provided they would cease acting as the auxiliaries of the enemies of Islam on the occasion of each new invasion. The text of the treaty he proposed to the kingdom of Acre was a unique attempt on the part of this clever and enlightened administrator to 'regularise' the position of the Franj.

> If a Frankish king sets out from the West [the text reads] to attack the lands of the sultan or of his son, the regent of the kingdom and the grand masters of Acre shall be obligated to inform the sultan of their action two months before their arrival. If the said king disembarks in the Orient after these two months have elapsed, the regent of the kingdom and the grand masters of Acre will be discharged of all responsibility in the affair.
>
> If an enemy comes from among the Mongols, or elsewhere, whichever of the two parties first learns of it must alert the other. If – may God forbid! – such an enemy marches against Syria and the troops of the sultan withdraw before him, then the leaders of Acre shall have the right to enter into talks with this enemy with the aim of saving their subjects and territories.

Signed in May 1283,

> the truce covered for ten years, ten months, ten days and ten hours, all the Frankish lands of the littoral, that is, the city of Acre with all its orchards, lands, mills, vineyards and the seventy-three villages depend-

> ent upon it; the city of Haifa, with its vineyards, orchards and the seven villages attached to it . . . As for Saida, the chateau and the city, the vineyards and the suburbs belong to the Franj, as do the fifteen villages attached to it, along with the surrounding plain, its rivers, brooks, water sources, orchards and mills, its canals and the dykes that have long served to irrigate its lands.

If the enumeration was long and detailed, it was in order to avoid any subsequent quarrel. The entirety of this Frankish territory nevertheless seems derisory: a narrow tapered coastal strip bearing no resemblance to the formidable regional power the Franj once constituted. It is true that the places mentioned in the treaty did not exhaust the Frankish possessions. Tyre, which had broken away from the kingdom of Acre, concluded a separate accord with Qalāwūn. Further north, cities like Tripoli and Latakia were excluded from the truce.

So was the fortress of Marqab, held by the Order of Hospitallers, or *al-osbitar*, as the Arabs called them. These monk-knights had supported the Mongols wholeheartedly, going so far as to fight alongside them during a fresh attempted invasion in 1281. Qalāwūn therefore decided to make them pay. In the spring of 1285, Ibn ʿAbd-al-Ẓāhir tells us,

> the sultan prepared siege machinery in Damascus. He had great quantities of arrows and all varieties of arms sent from Egypt, and distributed them to the emirs. He also had iron projectiles prepared, and flame-throwing tubes the like of which existed only in the *makhazin* ('magazines') and *dār al-sinā'a* ('the sultan's arsenal'). Expert pyrotechnicians were drafted, and Marqab was surrounded by a belt of catapults, three of the 'Frankish' type and four of the 'Devil' type. By 25 May the wings of the fortress were so deeply undermined that the defenders capitulated. Qalāwūn gave them permission to leave for Tripoli alive, with their personal effects.

Once again the allies of the Mongols had been punished without the latter's being able to intervene on their behalf. Even had they wanted to react, the five weeks that the siege lasted would not have sufficed for them to organise an expedition from Persia. Nevertheless, in that year of 1285, the Tartars were more determined than ever to renew their offensive against the Muslims. Their new chief, the Il-Khān Arghūn, grandson of Hülegü, had resurrected the most cherished dream of his predecessors: to form an alliance with the Occidentals and thus to trap the Mamluk sultanate in a pincer movement. Regular contacts were established between Tabriz and Rome with a view to organising a joint expedition, or at least a concerted one. In 1289 Qalāwūn sensed that the danger was imminent, but his agents had not managed to provide him with detailed information. In particular, they were unaware that a meticulous campaign, conceived by Arghūn, had just been proposed, in writing, to the pope and the major kings of the West. One of these letters, addressed to the French sovereign, Philip IV, has been preserved. In it the Mongol chief proposes to launch the invasion of Syria during the first week of January 1291. He predicts that Damascus will fall by mid-February and that Jerusalem will be taken shortly afterwards.

Without actually guessing what was afoot, Qalāwūn was increasingly uneasy. He feared that invaders from either East or West would be able to use the Frankish cities of Syria as a beachhead to facilitate their penetration of the sultanate. But although he was now convinced that the presence of the Franj was a permanent threat to the security of the Muslim world, he refused to assimilate the people of Acre to those of the northern half of Syria, who had proven themselves openly favourable to the Mongol invader. In any event, as a man of honour, the sultan could not attack Acre, which would be under the protection of the peace treaty for another five years, so he decided to go after Tripoli. It was at the walls of that city, conquered 180 years before by the son of Saint-Gilles, that his powerful army gathered in March 1289.

Among the tens of thousands of combatants of the Muslim army was Abu'l-Fidā', a young emir of sixteen. A scion of the Ayyubid dynasty, now a vassal of the Mamluks, he would several years later become the ruler of the small city of Hama, where he would devote most of his time to reading and writing. The work of this historian, who was also a geographer and a poet, is of interest primarily for the account it affords us of the last years of the Frankish presence in the Middle East. Abu'l-Fidā' was present, sword in hand and with an attentive eye, on all the main fields of battle. 'The city of Tripoli', he observes, 'is surrounded by the sea and can be attacked by land only along the eastern side, through a narrow passage. After laying the siege, the sultan lined up a great number of catapults of all sizes opposite the city, and imposed a strict blockade.' After more than a month of fighting, the city fell to Qalāwūn on 27 April.

'The Muslim troops penetrated the city by force [adds Abu'l-Fidā', who does not seek to mask the truth]. The population fell back to the port. There, some of them escaped onto ships, but the majority of the men were massacred, the women and children captured; the Muslims amassed immense booty.' When the invaders finished their killing and rampaging, the sultan ordered the city demolished; it was razed.

> A short distance from Tripoli, in the Mediterranean Sea, there was a small island, with a church. When the city was taken, many Franj took refuge there with their families. But the Muslim troops took to the sea, swam across to the island, massacred all the men who had taken refuge there, and carried off the women and children with the booty. I myself rode out to the island on a boat after the carnage, but was unable to stay, so strong was the stench of the corpses.

The young Ayyubid, imbued with the grandeur and magnanimity of his ancestors, could not but be shocked by these futile massacres. But as he well knew, times had changed.

Curiously, the expulsion of the Franj occurred in an atmosphere reminiscent of that which had prevailed at the time of their arrival nearly two centuries earlier. The massacres in Antioch in 1268 seemed to mirror those of 1098, and in centuries to come, Arab historians would present the merciless destruction of Tripoli as a belated riposte to the destruction of the city of the Banu ʿAmmār in 1109. But it was only during the battle of Acre, the last great confrontation of the Frankish wars, that revenge became the central theme of Mamluk propaganda.

Just after his victory, Qalāwūn was harassed by his officers. It was now clear, they argued, that no Frankish city could hold out against the Mamluk army; it was therefore necessary to go on the offensive immediately, without allowing the West, alarmed as it was by the fall of Tripoli, the time to organise any new expedition to Syria. Had the time not come to put an end, once and for all, to what remained of the Frankish kingdom? But Qalāwūn refused. He had signed a truce, and he would never betray his oath. In that case, his entourage insisted, could he not ask the doctors of law to declare the treaty with Acre null and void? That procedure had been adopted by the Franj often enough in the past. The sultan refused. He reminded his emirs that under the terms of the accord signed in 1283 he had sworn not to resort to juridical consultation to break the truce. No, Qalāwūn decided, he would seize all the Frankish territories not protected by the treaty, but nothing more. He sent emissaries to Acre to reassure the last of the Frankish kings – Henry, 'sovereign of Cyprus and Jerusalem' – that he would respect his commitments. Indeed, he even decided to renew the truce for another ten years from July 1289, and he encouraged the Muslims to make use of Acre in their commercial exchanges with the West. In the coming months, the Palestinian port became the scene of intense activity. Damascene merchants flocked there by the hundreds, renting rooms in the inns near the souks and engaging in profitable transactions with the Venetian traders or the rich Templars, who had now become the principal bankers of Syria. Moreover, thousands of Arab peasants, especially from Galilee, converged on the Frankish metropolis to market their harvests. The consequent prosperity benefited all the states of the region, the Mamluks most of all. Since the channels of trade with the East had been interrupted for many years by the Mongol presence, the shortfall could be made up only through an expansion of Mediterranean trade.

The most realistic of the Frankish leaders believed that the new role of their capital as the great exchange-counter linking two worlds held out an unexpected chance of survival in a region in which they could no longer hope to play a leading role. This view, however, was not unanimous. There were those who still sought to mobilise a religious fervour in the West powerful enough to organise fresh military expeditions against the Muslims. Just after the fall of Tripoli, King Henry sent messengers to Rome asking for reinforcements. So effective were his appeals that in midsummer 1290 an impressive fleet sailed into the port of Acre, discharging thousands of fanatical Frankish fighters into the city. The inhabitants deeply mistrusted these new Occidentals, who staggered about drunkenly, looked like plunderers, and seemed to obey no commander.

Incidents began within the first few hours. Merchants from Damascus were assaulted in the street, robbed and left for dead. The authorities made some attempts to restore order, but the situation deteriorated towards the end of August. After a banquet with alcohol galore, the new arrivals fanned out through the streets. They hunted down and mercilessly slaughtered every bearded man they could find. Many Arabs perished: peaceable merchants and peasants, Christians and Muslims alike. The others fled, to spread the word about what had happened.

Qalāwūn was enraged. Was it for this that he had renewed the truce with the Franj? His emirs pressed him to take immediate action. But as a responsible statesman he could not allow himself to be carried away by anger. He despatched an embassy to Acre to ask for an explanation and above all to demand that the murderers be handed over for punishment. The Franj were divided. A minority recommended acceptance of the sultan's conditions in order to avert a new war. The others refused, going so far as to tell Qalāwūn's emissaries that the Muslim merchants were themselves responsible for the killing, one of them having tried to seduce a Frankish woman.

Qalāwūn hesitated no longer. He assembled his emirs and announced his decision to put an end once and for all to the Frankish occupation that had dragged on for so long. Preparations began immediately. Vassals were convoked from the four corners of the sultanate to take part in this final battle of the holy war.

Before the army left Cairo, Qalāwūn swore on the Koran that he would not lay down his arms until the last Franj had been expelled. The oath was especially impressive since by that time Qalāwūn was a somewhat feeble old man. Although his exact age was unknown, he seemed to be well past seventy. The impressive Mamluk army set out on 4 November 1290. The sultan fell ill the very next day. He summoned his emirs to his bedside, had them swear obedience to his son Khalīl, and asked the latter to pledge himself, just as Qalāwūn had done, to carry the campaign against the Franj through to the very end. Qalāwūn died less than a week later, venerated by his subjects as a great sovereign.

The death of the sultan postponed the final offensive against the Franj by just a few months. In March 1291 Khalīl led his army into Palestine. At the beginning of May large numbers of Syrian contingents joined him in the plain ringing Acre. Abu'l-Fidā', who was then just eighteen, took part in the battle along with his father and was even entrusted with some responsibility: he was placed in command of a formidable catapult, nicknamed 'the Victorious', so large that it had to be dismantled and transported in pieces from Ḥiṣn al-Akrād to the environs of the Frankish city.

> The carts were so heavy that the trip took us more than a month, although in normal times eight days would have sufficed. By the time we arrived, nearly all the oxen drawing the carts had died from exhaustion and exposure.
>
> The battle was joined immediately. We men of Hama were stationed, as usual, on the far right flank of the army. We were alongside the sea, and from our positions we attacked Frankish boats topped by wooden-covered turrets lined with buffalo hide, from which the enemy fired at us with bows and crossbows. We thus had to fight on two fronts, against the army of Acre opposite us and against their fleet. We suffered heavy losses when a Frankish vessel transporting a catapult began to hurl chunks of rock at our tents. But one night, there were violent winds. The vessel began to pitch back and forth, rocked so violently by the waves that the catapult broke into pieces. Another night, a group of Franj made an unexpected sortie and advanced as far as our camp. But in the darkness some of them tripped on the tent cords; one knight fell into the latrine ditches and was killed. Our troops recovered and attacked the Franj from all sides, forcing them to withdraw to the city after leaving a number of dead on the field. The next morning my

cousin al-Malik al-Muẓaffar, lord of Hama, had the heads of some dead Franj attached to the necks of the horses we had captured and presented them to the sultan.

On Friday 17 June 1291 the Muslim army, now enjoying overwhelming military superiority, finally penetrated the besieged city. King Henry and most of the notables hastily sailed off to take refuge in Cyprus. The other Franj were all captured and killed. The city was razed.

The city of Acre had been reconquered, Abu'l-Fidā' explains, at noon on the seventeenth day of the second month of Jumādā in the year of the Hegira 690. It was on precisely this day, and at this hour, that the Franj had taken Acre from Saladin in the year of the Hegira 587, capturing and then massacring all the Muslims in the city. A curious coincidence, is it not?

The coincidence is no less astonishing by the Christian calendar, for the victory of the Franj at Acre had occurred in 1191, a hundred years, almost to the day, before their ultimate defeat. 'After the conquest of Acre,' Abu'l-Fidā' continues, 'God struck fear into the hearts of those Franj still remaining on the Syrian coast. Thus did they precipitately evacuate Ṣaida, Beirut, Tyre and all the other towns. The sultan therefore had the good fortune, shared by none other, of easily conquering all those strongholds, which he immediately had dismantled.'

Indeed, in the heat of his triumph, Khalīl decided to destroy any fortress, along the entire length of the coast, that might be used by the Franj if they ever sought to return to the Orient. 'With these conquests,' Abu'l-Fidā' concludes, 'all the lands of the coast were fully returned to the Muslims, a result undreamed of. Thus were the Franj, who had once nearly conquered Damascus, Egypt and many other lands, expelled from all of Syria and the coastal zones. God grant that they never set foot there again!'

EPILOGUE

The Arab world had seemingly won a stunning victory. If the West had sought, through its successive invasions, to contain the thrust of Islam, the result was exactly the opposite. Not only were the Frankish states of the Middle East uprooted after two centuries of colonisation, but the Muslims had so completely gained the upper hand that before long, under the banner of the Ottoman Turks, they would seek to conquer Europe itself. In 1453 they took Constantinople. By 1529 their cavalry was encamped at the walls of Vienna.

Appearances are deceptive. With historical hindsight, a more contradictory observation must be made. At the time of the Crusades, the Arab world, from Spain to Iraq, was still the intellectual and material repository of the planet's most advanced civilisation. Afterwards, the centre of world history shifted decisively to the West. Is there a cause-and-effect relationship here? Can we go so far as to claim that the Crusades marked the beginning of the rise of Western Europe – which would gradually come to dominate the world – and sounded the death knell of Arab civilisation?

Although not completely false, such an assessment requires some modification. During the years prior to the Crusades, the Arabs suffered from certain 'weaknesses' that the Frankish presence exposed, perhaps aggravated, but by no means created.

The people of the Prophet had lost control of their own destiny as early as the ninth century. Their leaders were practically all foreigners. Of the multitude of personalities who parade before us during the two centuries of Frankish occupation, which ones were Arabs? The chroniclers, the *qāḍīs*, a few local petty kings (such as Ibn ʿAmmār and Ibn Munqidh) and the impotent caliphs. But the real holders of power, and even the major heroes of the struggle against the Franj – Zangī, Nūr al-Dīn, Quṭuz, Baybars, Qalāwūn – were Turks; al-Afḍal was Armenian; Shīrkūh, Saladin and al-Kāmil were Kurds. Granted, most of these men of state were 'Arabised', both culturally and emotionally. But let us not forget that in 1134 the sultan Masʿūd had to use an interpreter in his discussions with the caliph al-Mustarshid; eighty years after his clan's capture of Baghdad, the Seljuk still could not speak a word of Arabic. Even more serious, considerable numbers of warriors of the steppes, lacking any connection with Arab or Mediterranean civilisations, were regularly incorporated into the ruling military caste. Dominated, oppressed and derided, aliens in their own land, the Arabs were unable to continue to cultivate the cultural blossoms that had begun to flower in the seventh century. By the epoch of the arrival of the Franj, they were already marking time, content to live on their past glories. Although in most domains they were clearly more advanced than these new invaders, their decline had already begun.

The second 'weakness' of the Arabs, not unrelated to the first, was their inability to build stable institutions. The Franj succeeded in creating genuine state structures as soon as they arrived in the Middle East. In Jerusalem rulers generally succeeded one another without serious clashes; a council of the kingdom exercised effective control over the policy of the monarch, and the clergy had a recognised role in the workings of power. Nothing of the sort existed in the Muslim states. Every monarchy was threatened by the death of its monarch, and every transmission of power provoked civil war. Does full responsibility for this lie with the successive invasions, which constantly imperilled the very existence of these states? Perhaps the nomadic origins of the peoples who ruled this region are to blame, be they the Arabs themselves, the Turks or the Mongols? Such a complex question cannot be dealt with in this brief epilogue. But let us at least note that in the Arab world the question is still on the agenda, in scarcely altered terms, in the latter part of the twentieth century.

The absence of stable and recognised institutions had inevitable consequences for the rights of the people. At the time of the Crusades, the power of Western monarchs was governed by principles that were not easily transgressed. During one of his visits to the kingdom of Jerusalem, Usāmah remarked that 'when the knights render a judgement, it cannot be modified or annulled by the king'. Even more significant is the following testimony from Ibn Jubayr about the last days of his journey in the Middle East.

> Upon leaving Tibnīn (near Tyre), we passed through an unbroken skein of farms and villages whose lands were efficiently cultivated. The inhabitants were all Muslims, but they live in comfort with the Franj – may God preserve us from temptation! Their dwellings belong to them and all their property is unmolested. All the regions controlled by the Franj in Syria are subject to this same system: the landed domains, villages and farms have remained in the hands of the Muslims. Now, doubt invests the heart of a great number of these men when they compare their lot to that of their brothers living in Muslim territory. Indeed, the latter suffer from the injustice of their coreligionists, whereas the Franj act with equity.

Ibn Jubayr had every reason to be concerned, for along the roads of what is now southern Lebanon he had just made a discovery of vital import: although there were certain features of Franj justice that could well be called 'barbaric', as Usāmah had emphasised, their society had the advantage of being a 'distributor of rights'. The notion of the 'citizen' did not yet exist, of course, but the feudal landowners, the knights, the clergy, the university, the bourgeoisie and even the 'infidel' peasants all had well-established rights. In the Arab East, the judicial procedures were more rational, but the arbitrary power of the prince was unbounded. The development of merchant towns, like the evolution of ideas, could only be retarded as a result.

In fact, Ibn Jubayr's reaction merits even more attentive examination. Although he had the honesty to recognise positive qualities among the 'accursed enemy', he went on to indulge in pure imprecations, for he believed that the equity and sound administration of the Franj constituted a mortal danger to the Muslims. Indeed, might not the latter turn their backs on their own coreligionists – and on their religion – if they discovered well-being in Frankish society? However understandable it may be, the attitude of the renowned traveller is none the less symptomatic of a malady from which his congeners suffered: throughout the Crusades, the Arabs refused to open their own society to ideas from the West. And this, in all likelihood, was the most disastrous effect of the aggression of which they were the victims. For an invader, it makes sense to learn the language of the conquered people; for the latter, to learn the language of the conqueror seems a surrender of principle, even a betrayal. And in fact, many Franj learned Arabic, whereas the inhabitants of the country, with the exception of some Christians, remained impervious to the languages of the Occidentals.

Many such instances could be cited, for in all domains the Franj learned much in the Arab school, in Syria as in Spain and Sicily. What they learned from the Arabs was indispensable in their subsequent expansion. The heritage of Greek civilisation was transmitted to Western Europe through Arab intermediaries, both translators and continuators. In medicine, astronomy, chemistry, geography, mathematics and architecture, the Franj drew their knowledge from Arabic books, which they assimilated, imitated, and then surpassed. Many words bear testimony to this even today: *zenith, nadir, azimuth, algebra, algorithm,* or more simply, *cipher*. In the realm of industry, the Europeans first learned and then later improved upon the processes used by the Arabs in paper-making, leather-working, textiles and the distillation of alcohol and sugar – two more words borrowed from the Arabic language. Nor should we forget the extent to which European agriculture was enriched by contact with the Orient: apricots, aubergines, scallions, oranges, *pastèque* (the French name for watermelon): the list of words derived from Arabic is endless.

Although the epoch of the Crusades ignited a genuine economic and cultural revolution in Western Europe, in the Orient these holy wars led to long centuries of decadence and obscurantism. Assaulted from all quarters, the Muslim world turned in on itself. It became oversensitive, defensive, intolerant, sterile – attitudes that grew steadily worse as worldwide evolution, a process from which the Muslim world felt excluded, continued. Henceforth progress was the embodiment of 'the other'. Modernism became alien. Should cultural and religious identity be affirmed by rejecting this modernism, which the West symbolised? Or, on the contrary, should the road of modernisation be embarked upon with resolution, thus risking loss of identity? Neither Iran, nor Turkey nor the Arab world has ever succeeded in resolving this dilemma. Even today we can observe a lurching alternation between phases of forced Westernisation and phases of extremist, strongly xenophobic traditionalism.

The Arab world – simultaneously fascinated and terrified by these Franj, whom they encountered as barbarians and defeated, but who subsequently managed to dominate the earth – cannot bring itself to consider the Crusades a mere episode in the bygone past. It is often surprising to discover the extent to which the attitude of the Arabs (and of Muslims in general) towards the West is still influenced, even today, by events that supposedly ended some seven centuries ago.

Today, on the eve of the third millennium, the political and religious leaders of the Arab world constantly refer to Saladin, to the fall of Jerusalem and its recapture. In the popular mind, and in some official discourse too, Israel is regarded as a new Crusader state. Of the three divisions of the Palestine Liberation Army, one bears the name Ḥiṭṭīn and another ʿAyn Jālūt. In his days of glory, President Nasser was regularly compared to Saladin, who, like him, had united Syria and Egypt – and even Yemen! The Arabs perceived the Suez expedition of 1956 as a Crusade by the French and the English, similar to that of 1191.

It is true that there are disturbing resemblances. It is difficult not to think of President Sadat when we hear Sibṭ Ibn al-Jawzi speaking to the people of Damascus and denouncing the 'betrayal' of al-Kāmil, the ruler of Cairo, who dared to acknowledge enemy sovereignty over the holy city. It is tempting to confound past and present when we read of a struggle between Damascus and Jerusalem for control of the Golan Heights or the Bekaa Valley. It is hard not to daydream when we read Usāmah's reflections about the military superiority of the invaders.

In a Muslim world under constant attack, it is impossible to prevent the emergence of a sense of persecution, which among certain fanatics takes the form of a dangerous obsession. The Turk Mehmet Ali Agca, who tried to shoot the pope on 13 May 1981, had expressed himself in a letter in these terms: 'I have decided to kill John Paul II, supreme commander of the Crusades.' Beyond this individual act, it seems clear that the Arab East still sees the West as a natural enemy. Against that enemy, any hostile action – be it political, military or based on oil – is considered no more than legitimate vengeance. And there can be no doubt that the schism between these two worlds dates from the Crusades, deeply felt by the Arabs, even today, as an act of rape.

NOTES AND SOURCES

In two years of research on the Crusades, I have come across many works and authors who, whether through brief encounter or repeated consultation, have exerted some influence on my work. Although they all deserve to be cited, the point of view adopted in this work demands a selection. My assumption here is that the reader is seeking not an exhaustive bibliography of works about the Crusades, but references that would permit deeper study of 'the other side'.

Three sorts of work will figure in these notes. First of all, of course, are the writings of the Arab historians and chroniclers who have bequeathed us their testimony of the Frankish invasions. I shall mention these chapter by chapter, in the order in which their names appear in my account, giving the references of the original works on which I generally relied, as well as the available translations. But let me single out the excellent collection of texts edited and translated by the Italian orientalist Francesco Gabrieli and published in English under the title *Arab Historians of the Crusades* (London, 1969).

A second type of work deals with Arab and Muslim medieval history from the standpoint of relations with the West. Let me cite, in particular:

E. Ashtor, *A Social and Economic History of the Near East in the Middle Ages* (London, 1976).

P. Aziz, *La Palestine des croisés* (Geneva, 1977).

C. Cahen, *Les Peuples musulmans dans l'histoire médiévale* (Institut Français of Damascus, 1977).

M. Hodgson, *The Venture of Islam* (3 vols, Chicago, 1974).

R. Palm, *Les Etendards du Prophète* (Paris, 1981).

J. J. Saunders, *A History of Medieval Islam* (London, 1965).

J. Sauveget, *Introduction à l'histoire de l'Orient musulman* (Paris, 1961).

J. Schacht, *The Legacy of Islam* (Oxford, 1974).

E. Sivan, *L'Islam et la croisade* (Paris, 1968).

W. Montgomery Watt, *The Influence of Islam on Medieval Europe* (Edinburgh, 1972).

A third type of work concerns historical accounts of the Crusades, whether comprehensive or partial. It was obviously essential to consult them in weaving the Arab testimony, which is inevitably fragmentary, into a continuous account covering the two centuries of the Frankish invasions. I shall mention them more than once in these notes. Let me cite at the outset two classic works: René Grousset, *Histoire des croisades et du royaume franc de Jérusalem* (3 vols, Paris, 1934–6); Stephen Runciman, *A History of the Crusades* (3 vols, Cambridge, 1951–4).

PROLOGUE

Not all Arab historians agree in attributing the speech cited here to al-Ḥarawi. According to the Damascene chronicler Sibṭ Ibn al-Jawzi (see chapter XII), it was indeed the *qāḍī* who spoke these words. The historian Ibn al-Athīr (see chapter II) affirms that their author was the poet al-Abiwardi, who was apparently inspired by the lamentations of al-Ḥarawi. In any case, there can be no doubt about the essence of the matter: the quoted words reflect the message that the delegation led by the *qāḍī* sought to transmit to the caliph's court.

Ibn Jubayr (1144–1217), who set out from Valencia in Muslim Spain, made his trip to the Orient between 1182 and 1185. His observations are recorded in his book, the original text of which was republished in Arabic in Beirut in 1980. A French translation is available (Paris, 1953–6).

Ibn al-Qalānisi (1073–1160), who was born and died in Damascus, held various high-ranking administrative positions in the city. He wrote a chronicle entitled *Dhayl Tarīkh Dimashq* (Supplement to the History of Damascus), the original text of which is available only in an edition published in 1908. An abridged French edition, entitled *Damas de 1075 à 1154*, was published in 1952 by the Institut Français of Damascus and Editions Adrien-Maisonneuve of Paris.

CHAPTER I

'That year' in the quotation from Ibn al-Qalānisi is the year of the Hegira 490. Nearly all the Arab chroniclers and historians of the epoch employed the same method of exposition: they listed the events of each year, often in a rather disordered manner, before moving on to the next year.

In the twentieth century the term *Rūm* – singular: *Rūmī* – is sometimes used in certain parts of the Arab world to designate not the Greeks, but Westerners in general. This is the case especially in regions such as the northern part of the Arabian peninsula which were far more deeply affected by the Byzantine presence – up to the tenth century – than by the subsequent Frankish invasions.

The word emir – or *al-amīr* in Arabic – originally meant 'he who assumes command'. *Amīr al-muʾminīn* was the commander, or prince, of believers: the prince of the faithful. The emirs of the army were more or less the chief officers. *Amīr al-juyūsh* was the supreme commander of the armies and *amīr al-baḥr* the commander-in-chief of the fleet, a word that was borrowed by the Occidentals in the truncated form *amiral*, or 'admiral' in English.

The origins of the Seljuks are shrouded in mystery. Seljuk, the eponym of the clan, had two sons named Mikael and Israel, which suggests that the dynasty which unified the Muslim East was of Christian or Jewish origin. After their Islamicisation, the Seljuks changed some of their names. 'Israel' in particular was Turkicised, becoming 'Arslan'.

La Geste du roi Danishmend was published in 1960, both in the original Arabic and in a French translation, by the French Institute of Archaeology in Istanbul.

CHAPTER II

The principal work by Ibn al-Athīr (1160–1233), *al-Kāmil fi'l-Tarīkh* (The Perfect History) runs to thirteen volumes, and was republished by Sader of Beirut in 1979. Volumes 10, 11 and 12 deal, among many other things, with the Frankish invasions. French translations of some passages were included in the *Recueil des historiens des croisades*, published in Paris between 1881 and 1906.

On the Assassins sect, see chapter v.

Ibn Jubayr's quotation about oil comes from *Travels*, French edition, p. 268; Arabic edition, p. 209.

For more on Antioch and its environs, see Claude Cahen, *La Syrie du Nord à l'époque des croisades et la principauté franque d'Antioche* (Paris, 1940).

CHAPTER III

The Frankish chronicles of the epoch contain numerous accounts of the acts of cannibalism committed by the Frankish armies in Maʿarra in 1098, and they all agree. Until the nineteenth century, the facts of these events were included in the works of European historians, for example Michaud's *L'histoire des croisades*, published in 1817–22. (See vol. 1, pp. 357 and 577; also *Bibliographie des croisades*, pp. 48, 76, 183, 248.) In the twentieth century, however, these accounts have generally been concealed – perhaps in the interests of the West's 'civilising mission'? Grousset does not even mention them in the three volumes of his history; Runciman is content with a single allusion: the army was 'suffering from starvation . . . and cannibalism seemed the only solution' (vol. 1, p. 261).

On the Tafurs, see J. Prawer, *Histoire du royaume franc de Jérusalem* (Paris, 1975, vol. 1, p. 216).

For Usāmah Ibn Munqidh, see chapter VII.

On the origin of the name 'Crac des Chevaliers', see Paul Deschamps, *La Toponomastique en Terre sainte au temps des croisades*, in *Recueil de travaux* (Paris, 1955); also P. Hitti, *History of the Arabs* (10th edn, London, 1970, p. 638).

The Franj found the letter from the *basileus* in the tent of al-Afḍal after the battle of Ascalon in August 1099.

CHAPTER IV

On the astonishing history of Nahr al-Kalb, see Philip Hitti, *Tarīkh Lubnān* (History of Lebanon) (Beirut, 1978).

After his return to Europe, Bohemond tried to invade the Byzantine empire. Alexius asked Kilij Arslan to send troops to help him repel the attack. Defeated and captured, Bohemond was forced to sign a treaty recognising the rights of the Rūm to Antioch. Because of this humiliation, he never returned to the Middle East.

Edessa is the modern city of Urfa, in Turkey.

CHAPTER V

On the battle of Tyre and other matters concerning this city, see M. Chehab, *Tyr à l'époque des croisades* (Paris, 1975).

The Aleppan Kamāl al-Dīn Ibn al-Adim (1192–1262) devoted only the first part of his life to writing the history of his city. He broke off his chronicle in 1223, for he had become completely absorbed in his political and diplomatic activity and his many travels in Syria, Iraq and Egypt. The original text of his *History of Aleppo* was published by the Institut Français of Damascus in 1968. No French or English translation is available.

The site of the battle between Ilghazi and the army of Antioch is given different names in different sources: Sarmada, Darb Sarmada, Tel Aqibrin. The Franj called it *Ager sanguinis*, or field of blood.

On the Assassins, see M. Hodgson, *The Order of Assassins* (The Hague, 1955).

CHAPTER VI

The hospital founded in Damascus in 1154 continued to function until 1899, when it was turned into a school.

The father of Zangī, Aq Sunqur, had been governor of Aleppo until 1094. Accused of treason by Riḍwān's father, Tutush, he was beheaded. The young Zangī was then adopted by Karbūqa of Mosul, who brought him up and had him take part in all his battles.

The princess Zumurrud was the daughter of the emir Jawali, former governor of Mosul.

CHAPTER VII

The emir Usāmah Ibn Munqidh, who was born in 1095, two years before the Franj arrived in Syria, and died in 1188, one year after Jerusalem was retaken, holds a special place among Arab witnesses of the Crusades. A writer, diplomat and politician, he was personally acquainted with Nūr al-Dīn, Saladin, Muʿīn al-Dīn ʿUnar, King Fulk and many others. An ambitious intriguer and schemer, he was accused of having arranged the assassination of a Fatimid caliph and an Egyptian vizier and of having sought to overthrow his uncle the sultan and even his friend Muʿīn al-Dīn. But it is his image as an astute man of letters, a sharp observer with a keen sense of humour, that has been most durable. Usāmah's major work, his autobiography, was published in Paris in 1893. This edition contained the original Arabic text, a French version composed of a mixture of quotations and paraphrases, and a mass of observations about Usāmah, his epoch, and his relations with the Franj.

For an account of the battle of Edessa, see J.-B. Chabot, *Un épisode de l'histoire des croisades*, in *Mélanges* (Paris, 1924).

CHAPTER VIII

For more about the life and times of the son of Zangī, see N. Elisseeff, *Nur-ad-Din, un grand prince musulman de Syrie au temps des croisades* (Institut Français of Damascus, 1967).

The primary legal source of revenue for all the princes, Nūr al-Dīn included, was their share of the booty taken from the enemy: gold, silver, horses, captives sold as slaves. The chroniclers say that the price of the latter diminished significantly when there were too many of them. In some cases a man could even be exchanged for a pair of shoes!

Violent earthquakes devastated Syria at various times during the Crusades. Although the 1157 tremor was the most spectacular, not a single decade passed without some major cataclysm.

CHAPTER IX

The eastern branch of the Nile, dried up today, was called the Pelusian branch, because it ran through the ancient city of Pelusus. It flowed into the Mediterranean Sea near Sabkhat al-Bardawīl, or Baldwin Marsh.

The Ayyūb family had to leave Takrīt in 1138, shortly after Saladin's birth there, for Shīrkūh, or so the story goes, had to kill a man to avenge a woman's honour.

Originally from North Africa, the Fatimids governed Egypt from 966 to 1171. It was they who founded the city of Cairo: al-Qāhira, meaning 'the Victorious'. Their rulers claimed to be descended from Fāṭima, the daughter of the Prophet and the wife of ʿAlī, inspirer of Shiʿism.

On the vicissitudes of the astonishing battle for Egypt, see G. Schlumberger, *Campagnes du roi Amaury ler de Jérusalem en Egypte* (Paris, 1906).

CHAPTER X

The letter of the Aleppans, like most of Saladin's messages, may be found in the 'Book of the Two Gardens', by the Damascene chronicler Abū Shama (1203–67). It contains a precious compilation of a great many official documents that can be found nowhere else.

Bahā' al-Dīn Ibn Shaddād (1145–1234) entered Saladin's service shortly before the battle of Ḥiṭṭīn. He remained an adviser and confidant of the sultan until the latter's death. His biography of Saladin was recently republished, in the original Arabic with French translation, in Beirut and Paris (1981).

Saladin was not the only one to display gracious manners on the occasion of the marriage in Karak. The mother of the groom insisted on sending meticulously prepared dishes for the troops besieging the city, so that they might also participate in the festivities.

The testimony of Saladin's son about the battle of Ḥiṭṭīn is cited by Ibn al-Athīr, vol. 9, year of the Hegira 583.

An associate of Nūr al-Dīn before entering Saladin's service, ʿImād al-Dīn al-Asfahāni (1125–1201) produced many works of history and literature, in particular an invaluable anthology of poetry. His extraordinary overblown style casts some doubt on the value of his testimony about the events he experienced. His narrative *Conquête de la Syrie et de la Palestine par Saladin* was published by the Académie des Inscriptions et Belles-Lettres (Paris, 1972).

CHAPTER XI

According to the Muslim faith, God once led Muḥammad on a miraculous nocturnal journey from Mecca to al-Aqṣā mosque in Jerusalem and thence to heaven. There Muḥammad met Jesus and Moses, an encounter symbolising the continuity of the three 'religions of the book'.

For Orientals – whether Arabs, Armenians or Greeks – the beard was a symbol of virility. They were amused, and sometimes scandalised, by the clean-shaven faces of most of the Frankish knights.

Among the many Western works devoted to Saladin, we should single out that of S. Lane-Pool, published in London in 1898 under the title *Saladin and the Fall of the Kingdom of Jerusalem*. Unfortunately, this work has faded into obscurity in recent years. It was republished in Beirut in 1964.

CHAPTER XII

It seems that in 1219 al-Kāmil had a meeting with Francis of Assisi, who had come East in the vain hope of restoring peace. Al-Kāmil is said to have listened sympathetically to Francis and to have given him gifts; he then had him escorted back to the camp of the Franj. To my knowledge, no Arab source relates this event.

Sibṭ Ibn al-Jawzi (1186–1256), an orator and chronicler of Damascus, published a voluminous universal history entitled *Mirāt al-Zamān* (The Mirror of Time), only some fragments of which have been published.

On the astonishing personality of the emperor, see Benoist-Meschin, *Frédéric de Hohenstaufen ou le rêve excommunié* (Paris, 1980).

CHAPTER XIII

For a history of the Mongols, see R. Grousset, *l'Empire des steppes* (Paris, 1939). The exchange of letters between Louis IX and Ayyūb is reported by the Egyptian chronicler al-Maqrīzi (1364–1442).

Jamāl al-Dīn Ibn Wāṣil (1207–98), a diplomat and lawyer, wrote a chronicle of the Ayyubid period and the beginning of the Mamluk era. To my knowledge, his work has never been published in full, although quotations and fragmentary translations exist in Michaud and Gabrieli.

After the destruction of Alamūt, the Assassins sect survived in the most peaceable form imaginable: as the Ismāʿīlis, followers of the Agha Khan. It is sometimes forgotten that he is the direct successor of Ḥasan Ibn al-Ṣabbāḥ.

The version of the deaths of Aybeg and Shajar al-Durr reported here is that of a popular medieval epic, *Sīrat al-Malik al-Zāhir Baybars* (Beirut).

CHAPTER XIV

The Egyptian chronicler Ibn ʿAbd-al-Ẓāhir (1233–93), secretary of the sultans Baybars and Qalāwūn, suffered the misfortune of seeing his major work, 'The Life of Baybars', summarised by an ignorant nephew who left only a truncated and insipid text. The few fragments of the original work that have survived reveal Ibn ʿAbd-al-Ẓāhir's genuine talent as writer and historian.

Of all the Arab historians and chroniclers that I have cited, Abu'l-Fidāʾ (1273–1331) is the only one to have governed a state. Granted, it was a tiny one – the emirate of Hama – and the Ayyubid emir was therefore able to devote most of his time to his many literary works, among them *Mukhtaṣar Tarīkh al-Bashar*, 'Summary of the History of Humanity'. Both the original text and a French translation may be found in *Recueil des historiens des croisades*.

Although Western domination of Tripoli ended in 1289, many names of Frankish origin have persisted down to modern times, both in the city and in neighbouring regions: Anjūl (Anjou), Dueyhi (Douai), Dikiz (de Guise), Dablīz (de Blise), Shanbūr (Chambord), Shanfūr (Chamfort), Franjieh (Franque).

In conclusion, let us mention three other works:

Z. Oldenburg, *Les Croisades* (Paris, 1965), an account sensitive to the Oriental Christians.

R. Pernoud, *Les Hommes des croisades* (Paris, 1977).

J. Sauveget, *Historiens arabes* (Paris, 1946).

GLOSSARY

ʿālim (pl., *ʿulamāʾ*). A doctor of Islamic sciences, in particular legal and religious studies. The term is occasionally applied to any learned man.

atabeg. A Turkish title literally meaning 'prince-father'. Originally the *atabegs* were guardians appointed for minor princes of the Seljuk clan, but eventually they became de facto rulers.

basileus. The royal title used by ancient Greek kings; adopted by Heraclius in the year 610 and subsequently the official title of Byzantine emperors.

caliph. Anglicised form of the Arabic word *khalīfa*, literally 'successor'. The title was adopted by the first leaders of the Muslim state after the death of Muḥammad and designated the spiritual and temporal commander of the believers, or 'prince of the faithful'. By the time of the Crusades, the caliphs were mere figureheads under the domination of other leaders.

dīwān. Although the word has various meanings, the sense here is 'council' or 'court', and by extension the room in which a council or court would meet.

emir. A Turkish title designating a military commander, derived from the Arabic *amīr*, originally meaning 'one who commands', or 'prince'.

fidāʾī (pl., *fidāʾīn*, or fedayeen). Literally, 'one who sacrifices himself'. By extension, fighters who are prepared to risk their lives with abandon.

ḥammām. Public bath; also an important social institution in Arab society.

hijra. The 'emigration' of the Prophet Muḥammad from Mecca to Medina in the year 622. It marks the start of the Muslim calendar; the Anglicised form is 'Hegira'.

imām. The leader of public prayers; also the leader of a Muslim community.

jihād. Holy war against unbelievers. In Islam, *jihād* is a duty of all Muslims, although there is disagreement about the form it must take and the circumstances in which it is appropriate.

khamsīn. A hot desert wind not unlike the Italian sirocco.
Koran. Anglicised form of *Qurʾān*, the Muslim holy book.

mamlūk. Originally 'slave' (the word literally means 'owned'); subsequently, a slave trained to be a soldier and even military commander; especially applied to those of Turkish or Circassian origin, who later founded a dynasty.
muezzin. Anglicised form of the Arabic *muʾadhdhin*, the man who calls the hour of prayer, usually from atop a minaret.
mujāhid (pl., *mujāhidīn*). Fighter, or freedom fighter. The word is derived from the same root as *jihād*.
mushrikīn. Polytheists. Derived from a root meaning 'to associate', it was originally applied to people who 'associated' other gods to the One True God.

qāḍī. A judge administering religious law, which in Islam is the basis of civil law as well.

raʾīs. President or 'head'. Applied to various posts of civic responsibility.

sāḥil. Coast or coastline.
sharīf. A noble. Originally applied only to descendants of the Prophet, of the Hashemite clan.
Shiʿi. A Muslim who is a member of the religious current founded

by the supporters of ʿAlī, the fourth caliph and cousin and son-in-law of Muḥammad. Shiʿism (derived from the word *shīʿa*, 'party' or 'faction', meaning the party or faction of ʿAlī) became the major minority religious grouping of Islam. Here, in contrast to Sunni (see below).

souk. A marketplace, often consisting of dozens, even hundreds, of stalls and shops.

Sufi. A Muslim mystic, usually a member of a particular religious order with its own distinctive rites.

Sunni. A Muslim of the majority current of Islam. So-called because the Sunnis claim the authority of the *sunna*, or 'practice' of the Prophet.

ʿulamāʾ. See *ʿālim*.

vizier. Anglicised form of the Arabic *wazīr*, or 'minister'. Under the Fatimid dynasty of Egypt, the vizier was in charge of the administration of the realm, in the name of the caliph.

INDEX

The definite article al- is ignored at the start of entries. Personal names are entered in direct order, so Harūn al-Rashīd is indexed at H.

water supplies, 60, 103–4, 160, 168; none, 12–13, 155, 198; poisoned, 54, 70, 154
weapons, 42, 78, 138, 199, 249, 263; captured, 77, 97; enemy torpor, 72; Greek fire, 55; ornamental swords, 84, 177; siege, 18, 96, 131, 263, 268; *see also* archers
William Jordan (al-Cerdani), count of Cerdagne, 83

Xerigordon, fortress, 12–13

Yaghi-Siyān, ruler of Antioch, 25–7, 31–2, 35, 38; his daughter, 74
Yanbūḥ, port, 193
Yarankash, eunuch of Zangī, 144
Yemen, 180–1
Yolanda, wife of Emperor Frederick II, 236
Yūsuf al-Ayyūb, *see* Saladin
Yūsuf Batit, Greek Orthodox priest, 204

Zadar (Zara), Dalmatia, 229–30
Zangī, ʿImād al-Dīn, ruler of Aleppo, 118–19, 120–5, 143, 271; agrees to marry Zumurrud, 127, 132–3; aims to take Damascus, 126–7, 132–3; besieges Homs, 129–30, 131; captures and releases Fulk, 129, 130; finally takes Edessa, 139–42; his death, 144–5; not to be trusted, 126, 143; uses informers, 120
zoo, 236
Zumurrud, mother of Ismāʿīl, 126–7, 132–3